TSAR ALEXIS

HIS REIGN
AND
HIS RUSSIA

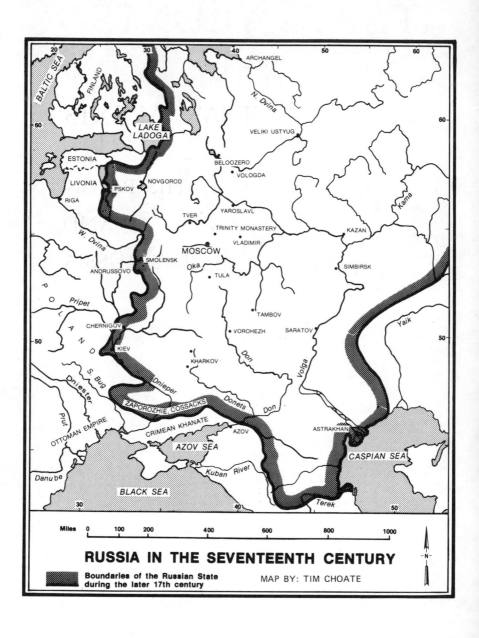

RUSSIA IN THE SEVENTEENTH CENTURY

Boundaries of the Russian State
during the later 17th century

MAP BY: TIM CHOATE

TSAR ALEXIS

HIS REIGN AND HIS RUSSIA

By Joseph T. Fuhrmann

ACADEMIC INTERNATIONAL PRESS

1981

THE RUSSIAN SERIES/Volume 34

Joseph T. Fuhrmann, *Tsar Alexis, His Reign and His Russia*

Copyright © 1981 by Academic International Press

ISBN: 0-87569-040-8

Composition by Jayne Berndsen and Jean Grabowski

Title page by King & Queen Press

Printed in the United States of America

A list of Academic International Press publications is found at the end of this volume.

ACADEMIC INTERNATIONAL PRESS
Box 1111 Gulf Breeze FL 32561

CONTENTS

FOR ESTHER AND MARY,
FOR MARIA AND CHRISTOPHER

FOREWORD

This is a biography of Tsar Alexis for people who like to read about interesting people. My objective has been to present Alexis' life in a readable way, to capture the passion, drama—even the coarseness—which so often escape scholarly studies of seventeenth-century Russia. Fortunately, the records for this period are fairly complete, even including such dialogues as I have used in these pages. Perhaps my account will not satisfy every type of reader, but I do think it clarifies the role of this gentle, resourceful tsar (who was the father of Peter the Great) in the important developments of the period. I hope the reader will finish *Tsar Alexis* with the desire to investigate more specialized studies in the "Selected Bibliography."

I am grateful to the people who assisted me in writing this book. Dr. Peter von Wahlde of Academic International Press gave me the idea for this biography and encouraged me during the difficult moments of bringing it to the public. George P. Majeska and David Miller carefully read the manuscript and made many useful suggestions for its improvement. David M. Griffiths kindly helped locate research material. Samuel H. Baron, Robert O. Crummey, John T. Alexander and Richard Hellie gave prompt and valuable advice at various times. I am also grateful to Saundra Gentile, my efficient and capable student assistant at Murray State University, who helped select the illustrations in this book and who processed them for publication, in addition to polishing the manuscript and working on the index. Above all, I thank my wife Mary for her support. She knows how much I depended on her during this project, but she may not quite know how grateful I am for her support. These and others improved the results of my labors, but they are in no way responsible if shortcomings remain.

Rendering Russian names into English always presents problems. My method may produce inconsistencies, but it is to present names in the forms most intelligible to non-Russian speaking people without sacrificing the overall Russian flavor needed in a book of this type. Thus, I chose "Alexis," which is the Greek form of the Russian name "Aleksei," because *Alexis* is how the name is spelled in English. On the other hand, it seemed to me that "Fedor," "Stefan," and "Ivan" could and should be retained in their Russian forms, "Theodore," "Stephen," and "John" being somehow a bit too English for a book about Russians. Considering the readers for whom this book is intended, such Russian terms as *pomeshchik, okol'nichii* and *voevoda* simply had to be rendered in simple, non-cumbersome English. If my equivalents do not capture all the shades of the Russian terms, surely instructors can make a few remarks to bridge the gaps for their students, or reference works may be consulted. A stronger impression may be produced in this way than if I had translated the terms with more scholarly exactitude, but in such a way as to leave general readers puzzled by my terminology and determined to learn as little of it as possible.

Russian words in the "Selected Bibliography" have been transliterated according to the Library of Congress system, but in the text I have used the modified New York Public Library system. The Russian calendar, taken from the Byzantines, was ten days behind the Gregorian calendar, used in the West, in the seventeenth century; whenever possible, dates in this book are given according to the Russian system.

I dedicate this book to my mother, wife, and children.

And now, to Tsar Alexis, his reign and his Russia.

Joseph T. Fuhrmann

Murray State University

PART ONE

THE YOUNG TSAR

Chapter One

BORN TO RULE

Michael Romanov was dying when his son Alexis hurried to his bedside on the evening of July 12, 1645. Michael had gone to matins on this, his name day, but took ill and was rushed back to his chambers. The tsar had been seriously ailing since April, when his European doctors concluded from his urine that "excess mucus" accumulating in his stomach, liver and spleen was causing "natural heat," thin blood, chills, scurvy and phlegms. Rhine wine flavored with herbs and roots was prescribed for a mild purge, the patient was ordered to avoid cold and sour drinks, to eat and drink temperately. When Michael failed to respond to this treatment, further purges were prescribed, his stomach was smeared with balsam, and powders were administered for headache.

"I am being torn to pieces inside," Michael groaned on July 12, and, expecting the end, he summoned his wife, son, the patriarch, and his closest friend, Boris Morozov. Taking leave of Eudocia and Alexis, the tsar turned to Morozov and said: "I deliver my son to you, boyar, and in tears I say: just as you served us and labored with great joy and happiness, so in the future preserve this house, estate, and its peace. In the fear of God and with every sort of wisdom see to my son's health and instruction, and just as you lived for thirteen years in unfailing patience and concern in our house and kept him as the apple of your eye, so now serve."

Michael was married to his first wife, Maria Dolgorukaya, little more than a year before her death on January 7, 1625. She bore him no children. The tsar respectfully waited a year, until 1626, before taking a new bride, Eudocia Streshneva, the daughter of a minor noble family. This marriage was blessed with two girls in two years. As much as Michael rejoiced in his daughters Irene and Pelageya, as tsar he was anxious to strengthen his dynasty with male heirs. Finally, on March 29, 1629, a relieved and smiling Eudocia presented him with their first son, Alexis.

TSAR MICHAEL. The first Romanov to rule Russia and the father of Alexis Mikhailovich.

TSARINA EUDOCIA. Tsar Michael's second wife and the mother of Alexis Mikhailovich.

Alexis grew up in the "Terem Palace," the Kremlin building which traditionally provided quarters for Muscovite rulers and their families. At the age of five, it was time for the tsarevich to receive a governor who would supervise his education and upbringing. Michael chose for this purpose the dynamic Boris Morozov, a minor aristocrat who through ability and craft had edged himself to the forefront of those influential noble landowners known as "boyars." Alexis' first text was a primer compiled especially for him by the secretary of his grandfather, Patriarch Filaret, who had ordered the work just before his death in 1633. From this volume the tsarevich learned the Russian alphabet, as well as a brief catechism and the Ten Commandments. After a year, he progressed to a *Book of the Hours,* five months later to a Psalter, and to the *Acts of the Apostles* in another three months. The boy began to write at seven.

When Alexis turned nine, he took up what was to be one of his favorite pursuits, church singing. The court choir master helped him learn the eight sets of liturgical melodies in the Eastern 'Orthodox Church known as the "Okhtoi," and in another eight months the tsarevich was thoroughly familiar with the equally complex canticles of Holy Week. In these tender years the future tsar developed that detailed mastery of church music and the Mass which so impressed observers in later years. "He had learned the order of church services down to their smallest details," the historian Klyuchevsky notes, "and in this could contend with any expert from a monastery or even a cathedral."

Alexis completed the entire Muscovite secondary studies curriculum at the age of ten. By the time Alexis was twelve, he had accumulated a library of which he often boasted in later years. The thirteen books included a lexicon, a Russian grammar published in Lithuania, and a "cosmography," a collection of maps of the world. Most of these books were gifts from Filaret, or from tutors assigned to the tsarevich from various crown chancelleries. He also received a number of German engravings from Boris Morozov, prints which succeeded in their objective to "fire the boy's imagination."

Alexis' education was pious, yet the amusements he shared with his father would have shocked most Muscovites. Michael was sluggish and unimaginative by nature, but Western entertainments so fascinated him that he staffed the Kremlin's Amusement Palace with foreigners. One of these men was baptized into the Orthodox Church as "Ivan Semenov" and entertained the tsar's household for a decade, passing his skills on to Russian pupils. On one occasion he had "five men walk on ropes, and dance and stage all the sorts of amusements that he knew; he also taught 24 men to beat drums." Alexis and his younger brother Ivan (born in

1633, when Alexis was four) took in such merriment clad in German clothes tailored on Morozov's orders.

Alexis' playthings included a German hobby horse, musical instruments, a toy toboggan and a suit of armor from the shop of the German craftsman Peter Schalt. The tsarevich's quarters were enlivened by such playthings as a gold bear enameled in azure and a stone-encrusted pigeon, though their young royal master was most proud of a silver elephant guided by an axe-wielding African whose platform also supported four warriors. Ivan's collection included a gravy boat shaped like a small horse, a sand box, a bootmaker's stand, a wine bowl, and a cup and plate.

Young Alexis and his friends often enjoyed outdoor activities. Olearius describes such an excursion, a falcon hunt Morozov organized on June 1, 1636 in celebration of Ivan's third birthday. Foreign diplomats invited to the occasion were fetched to a pleasant meadow outside Moscow on Morozov's own horses. After a merry chase, the hoods of the birds were put back on their heads and the company turned to a feast of fruit and gingerbread, vodka and meat. "The Russians celebrated the day with great merriment," Olearius recalls and, so that the foreigners "could participate in the celebration, our usual provisions were doubled."

Palace etiquette at home was more confining to the high spirits of Alexis, Ivan and their sisters. Each royal youngster had a separate apartment. The only people outside the family who saw them were servants and tutors, and a few boyars and lords of the chamber and their wives. The Russian contemporary Kotoshikhin notes that the royal women and children were surrounded by cloth screens on their way to church so that a stranger's eye would not fall on them. Similar barriers in the church made sure that the royal worshipers were seen only by the priests honored to officiate at such services. The carriages taken on pilgrimages to monasteries were covered with taffeta. During winter, the royal boys and girls with their mother and aunts used "sleighs in the shape of small huts which are draped with velvet or red cloth with mica windows and taffeta curtains on the doors at both sides." Truly, the tsar's family lived in a remote dream world—luxurious and honored, but sterile beyond measure.

The family tragedy which pursued Tsar Michael and his family reached a high point in 1639. Ivan died on January 10 of that year—poisoned so cleverly, according to gossip Kotoshikhin relays, that nearly everyone supposed that the five-year-old boy's death was natural. Eudocia lost another son, Vasily, in childbirth two months later. In a dozen years the tsarina had borne ten children, three boys and seven girls, and it now seemed unlikely that Eudocia could produce more children. (In

ADAM OLEARIUS (1599-1671). German diplomat, scholar and writer. Fluent in Russian and Arabic, he accompanied two embassies from Holstein to Moscow in the 1630s. His *Description of Travels to Muscovy and Persia and Back* was published in German in 1647. In an expanded, updated edition of 1656 it has been universally acclaimed as one of the century's most detailed and reliable works on Russia, and is often referred to in this book.

fact, she did not.) Alexis was Michael's sole surviving son, a dangerous situation for the future of the Romanov dynasty. Alexis was a healthy and intelligent boy, but what if he suffered an untimely end? This would leave Irene, Anna, and Tatyana in line for the throne. Irene, in particular, was respected at court, but a woman had never ruled over Russia, and the possibility that one of Michael's daughters would be the first was not regarded favorably in the Kremlin at this time.

For the sake of the dynasty, then, and to prevent disorders which might break out if Michael and Alexis died soon, a male alternative to Alexis had to be found. Perhaps Michael instinctively felt that his house suffered from what Klyuchevsky termed the "hereditary peculiarity" of the Romanovs: their daughters were "strong and vigorous, sometimes manly and energetic," but the boys "took after their progenitor and proved to be physically weak and short-lived."

The only way to provide Alexis with the needed heir was to find a husband for Michael's eldest daughter, Irene. Such a marriage, however, presented problems. Since even the mightiest Russian nobles were "slaves" before their tsar—and freely called themselves such (and worse) in addressing him—the idea had developed firmly over the years that no Russian was worthy of a tsarevna's hand. A spouse might be found in a foreign dynasty, of course, but this too had difficulties. In diplomatic interchanges tsars addressed foreign rulers as "brother" and "sister", but only as a polite fiction. Russians privately held that no sovereign anywhere was or possibly could be the equal of the Russian tsar. Much of this haughtiness was a product of Russia's isolation from the West. Russians had only slight contacts with other lands, few knew their languages, almost none understood or respected their customs and ways. Above all other barriers loomed religion. By the seventeenth century, the Russian royal house stood virtually alone as practitioner of the Eastern Orthodox faith; others had fallen to Catholic or Islamic conquerors or were so minor as not to merit union with the mighty Russian crown. Dynasties Russia confronted as military or commercial equals were Catholic or Lutheran. If marriage ties ever developed with them, Russian chauvinists were determined that the foreign spouse must convert and be baptized in the Russian Church by triple full immersion.

Knowing full well the problems he faced, Michael made his first inquiries in 1640 into the possibility of Irene marrying Waldemar Christian, the count of Schleswig-Holstein and son of Christian IV of Denmark by a second morganatic marriage which would prevent Waldemar from ever becoming king of Denmark. Marriage between Irene and Waldemar would improve Russia's relations with Denmark and counteract Swedish power in the Baltic—in addition to providing, in Waldemar, a male heir of royal blood should Alexis die young. Predictably, religion emerged as the main obstacle to the match. Waldemar hotly rejected the suggestion that he abandon Lutheranism for Russian Orthodoxy as the price of standing in line for the Russian throne. Seeing marriage negotiations hopelessly deadlocked on this point, a pragmatic Tsar Michael finally assured Waldemar that he himself could decide later whether or not to convert, and in the meantime a Lutheran church would be erected at Moscow for his worship. But the patriarch was so adamant in demanding Waldemar's "baptism" that the timid Michael kept his sensational concessions to Waldemar a secret, hoping, as the weak often do, that problems somehow will solve themselves if only they can be ignored.

Meanwhile, Morozov and other statesmen began to worry that marriage between Waldemar and Irene could result in Alexis being set aside in the Dane's favor. Such a development, of course, would block Morozov's career and the fortunes of his "party". Michael tried to calm these fears by "presenting" Alexis to the people in 1643. In this traditional ceremony the reigning tsar formally presented his heir to a gathering in the Kremlin, identifying the youngster as his successor and their next ruler. "Presentations" were celebrated so lavishly, and made so impressive and important that even commoners flocked from distant parts of the land to participate. Presentations traditionally occurred on New Year's Day (September 1, according to the calendar then in use in Russia) in a tsarevich's thirteenth or fourteenth year. But Alexis' presentation did nothing to reassure Morozov and his group that Alexis—and they—eventually would exercise power. With an explosive situation building in Moscow, Waldemar set out in December 1643 on an official visit to his prospective in-laws.

Enthusiastic crowds greeted the Dane at Novgorod and Pskov with gifts of bread and salt, sables and gold. Waldemar thought to refuse these offerings, until Russian officials finally persuaded him this would be an

TSAR MICHAEL'S RECEPTION OF THE HOLSTEIN EMBASSY. Ceremony at the Palace of Facets in the 1630s, according to Olearius. Sir Thomas Carlisle described such a ceremony in 1664, when Alexis sat upon the throne: the tsar is flanked by four dazzlingly attired "tall lords," eminent boyars are seated right and left as a Russian dignitary directs the movements of the foreign embassy and the ambassador himself respectfully approaches the throne. Other Russian nobles stand at the rear. In the far left corner "a gold basin and ewer, and a hand towel" stand, so that "His Tsarish Majesty could wash his hands after the Ambassadors had kissed it."

intolerable insult. Waldemar reached Moscow on January 21, 1644, and a week later, on January 28, formally was presented at the Palace of Facets in the Kremlin. Alexis set aside the animosity he felt for the intruder, and extended him a polite ceremonial greeting. Inquiring about Waldemar's health, the tsarevich extended his hand and brought him to be introduced to his royal father, the tsar. Waldemar now bowed and conveyed greetings from Christian IV, first to Michael, then to Alexis.

News was now leaking out that Waldemar had not agreed to convert to the Russian Church. The patriarch and others renewed their demands on this point; to Waldemar it seemed that earlier assurances were now being withdrawn. The small, inactive Russian press sprang to sudden life, grinding out fiery tracts affirming the Church's position. Research into past precedents was conducted frantically, compromise solutions were timidly offered—and hotly rejected by both sides. Then, on July 12, 1645, Michael Romanov died.

Russia was torn by misery and distress at the moment Michael passed away. Every social class was discontented, and each looked to the Kremlin for support. The capital was so tense that foreign diplomats reported that Alexis' ascension surely would trigger uprisings throughout the land. Even in earlier years many had murmured that Michael really had no sons, that Eudocia bore only girls and that "Alexis" was substituted for yet another daughter in 1629. Such rumors now blazed forth with renewed intensity.

Fantasy and protest reached their greatest extremes in the far north. The lands of Yaroslavl, Vladimir and Kostroma have deep woods, bleak landscape, cheerless terrain. The cold months there are incredibly severe, spring comes late and displays a brooding, melancholy quality which only partly dispels the winter gloom. The area swarmed with hermits and visionaries in the 1640s, "wild men" (and women) who patterned their lives after the most ascetic Hebrew prophets and Christian saints. One of their most remarkable leaders was Kapiton, who, as Pascal notes, mortified his flesh with fasting, chains and weights, and pressed circumcision on his male followers and Jewish dietary laws on all. When the official Church moved to arrest him for his heretical teachings, the "monasteries" and "convents" he established fled with him to still more isolated corners of the great forest. His "brothers" and "sisters" now took up social questions as well as religious issues, attacking social inequality and the crown. One of the hermits, Michael of Suzdal, called Alexis the "horn of the Antichrist."

Boris Morozov was so troubled by the situation that he rushed to have Alexis confirmed tsar. Nikita Romanov, Alexis' first cousin and the most eminent Romanov after the tsar himself, took the oath of allegiance to Alexis the day after Michael died, followed at Moscow by government officials and clerks, prominent merchants, officers and soldiers. Messengers were now hurrying throughout the realm to administer the oath in other towns. Another indication of how seriously Morozov viewed his position was repetition in 1645 of the provision in the oath made to Michael in 1613 that every citizen must report conspiracies and "evil designs" against the tsar, and deliver up guilty parties "without hesitation or delay." Europeans and Tatars were to seal this oath by their particular faiths.

Alexis' coronation was carried out so soon that many who wanted to attend could not arrive at Moscow in time. Alexis with his boyars and officials entered the Cathedral of the Assumption on September 28, 1645, in the presence of Patriarch Joseph and other high Church officials. With bells ringing and the church sounding with music, the procession made its way to a great platform where Morozov took his place at Alexis' right side. The tsar then asked consecration from the patriarch, who placed a hand on Alexis' bowed head and intoned a prayer:

> Sow in his heart Thy fear, that he be gracious to obedient subjects. Keep him in the pure faith; show him a scrupulous observer of the commandments of Thy Holy Catholic Church, that he may judge the people in righteousness and Thy saints with judgment, that he may save the children of the poor and be made an heir of Thy heavenly kingdom.

After further gestures and prayers, Joseph placed the ancient bejeweled crown of the Muscovite rulers upon Alexis' head. The patriarch then escorted Alexis to the throne, blessed him and bowed. As the solemn service droned on, censers swayed, incense billowed, candles flickered, prayers and hymns rose to the heavens. Joseph blessed Alexis a final time as the tsar and the royal party exited by the south portal.

Outside a great throng was awaiting alms. The tsar's friend Michael Rtishchev held the purse as Nikita Romanov thrice scattered coins. Alexis then entered the Church of the Archangel to venerate the tombs of earlier Muscovite rulers. After a few moments, the tsar moved through the west portico—where money again was thrown to the people—on his way back past the Cathedral of the Assumption to be greeted by his confessor, Stephen Vonifatiev. A final showering of coins returned Alexis to his chambers. But the day's festivities were not yet at an end. Further rituals awaited the new ruler at the Palace of Facets. Finally, Alexis dined in splendor with church and crown dignitaries. Some celebrated

so well they could hardly return home! As the shadows of evening fell
on Moscow, a new reign had begun.

The coronation displayed the power and grandeur of a tsar, but the
sixteen-year-old lad who sat on the throne still had to develop the qualities of a statesman. Young Alexis did not yet have a taste for power.
Three months before his coronation, it was reported that Alexis spent
his time exercising, chatting with friends at the court distillery, and in
company "with the women." No one could bother the new tsar with
petitions until after the six weeks of mourning for his father had passed.
Even then the good-natured Alexis was as devoted to pleasure as he was
bored by serious affairs.

Alexis spent most of his time after the coronation outside Moscow,
hunting and enjoying the company of friends who foreign observers said
were "attentive to their own comfort." The Swedish diplomat Kruse-
björn wrote in February 1646 that Alexis rambled about the environs
of the capital, quite unlike his father who had stayed in Moscow "as in
a cave." In later years the Greek visitor Paul of Aleppo was told that
the boyars "did not at all respect tsar Alexis [at this time] because he
was young, tender, open, of a weak constitution, and no lover of blood
and war." His mother's death on August 18, 1645, less than a month
after his father, made Alexis all the more dependent on Boris Morozov
and Irene.

Alexis had a personal matter to attend to: disposal of Waldemar.
Actually, the Dane had been demanding the right to depart for some
time, but Michael refused to admit that marriage negotiations were hopelessly stalemated. When Michael took a turn for the worst in June,
Alexis broke off his once-frequent visits to his proposed brother-in-law.
On July 17, five days after Michael passed away, Alexis received Waldemar and raised anew the question of his conversion. Waldemar refused,
reiterating his desire to leave Russia. Alexis dispatched a letter to Christian the following month, formally announcing his accession to the
throne and permitting Waldemar to return home.

Waldemar's departure ended what may have been a dangerous situation for the young tsar, for it was rumored that some court figures preferred to have Waldemar as ruler, and, that if Michael had not died at
this juncture, the marriage with Irene would have occurred and Waldemar—not Alexis—would have followed Michael on the Russian throne.
In his letter to Christian, Alexis expressed the hope that he and the
Danish ruler would enjoy good "brotherly" relations. Polite words not-
withstanding, Boris Morozov dispatched a thousand musketeers to the
far north and stationed a still larger force at Novgorod in case the Danes

launched a war to avenge themselves for their humiliation in the Waldemar affair.

Pretenders to the throne were also a problem in the early years of Alexis' reign. The most bizarre of all, Timoshka Ankudinov, made an appearance even before Michael died. A poor lad, Timoshka was bright enough to acquire a smattering of learning. As a youth he claimed to be the son of the governor of Vologda. The local archbishop was so impressed with him that he offered Timoshka his daughter's hand in marriage. But Ankudinov came to no good. He was a drunk, a gambler, and an embezzler who enjoyed pederasty, an activity "at which," Olearius dryly observes, "he was often caught." Timoshka killed his wife ("with whom he was not getting along well") and fled to Poland in 1643. He then made his way to the Ukraine where he won the protection of the Cossack leader Bogdan Khmelnitsky by claiming to be Ivan, son of Vasily Shuisky, the treacherous boyar who reigned briefly and ingloriously as tsar during the Time of Troubles. "Ivan Shuisky" appeared in Turkey in 1648 (where he had himself circumcised and adopted the Islamic faith), later progressing to Rome (and Catholicism), then to Vienna, Transylvania, Sweden, Livonia, the Brabant, Leipzig, and Wittenberg (where he became a Protestant). Ankudinov finally was arrested at Neustadt and extradited to Moscow to be executed on December 28, 1653.

Another pretender to the unsavory Shuisky name was Ivashka Vergunenok, who surfaced in Turkey in early 1646. At the same time, Ivan Luba gave out in Poland that he was the (actually non-existent) son of Marina Mniszech and the first False Dmitry. These and similar adventurers had no power, but Alexis grew anxious when he noticed that they stirred interest abroad in lands unfriendly to Russia. If disorders ever broke out within Russia, foreign powers might use such pretenders to make trouble for the tsar and his government.

Alexis always enjoyed the company of young ladies, and in February 1647, with the approach of his eighteenth year, he announced his desire to take a bride. Alexis followed the Russian royal tradition which had experts comb the land in search of the hundred most eligible noble girls. Their number was narrowed to six at Moscow, and from this group the tsar himself selected his bride. Alexis chose Euphemia, daughter of Fedor Vsevolozhsky, a minor noble. When the honor was announced to her, the girl fainted. Bothered, Alexis asked if Euphemia often fainted. "Her parents, quite naturally, had to claim that she always had been healthy," says Ellersieck, "or risk being sent to Siberia for having offered an unhealthy girl to the tsar." At length it was decided that Euphemia suffered from the "falling sickness" (epilepsy), and the unfortunate girl and her family were exiled to Siberia, where they all had time to meditate on how quickly fortunes rise and fall on this earth.

It is difficult to separate fact from fantasy in the Vsevolozhskaya affair. Some accounts claim that the mothers and sisters of the rejected girls hatched a plot to "tie up her hair so hard as to throw her into the swoon" she was expected to fall into at the excitement of being presented to the tsar. When this happened, Euphemia's rivals cried out, "she has the falling sickness!" Other versions attribute her downfall to Boris Morozov, though some evidence indicates that it was he who advised Alexis to select Euphemia in the first place. The official report would have us think that Mishka Ivanov, a peasant of Nikita Romanov, practiced sorcery and slander against Euphemia. Incredibly, the wretched Vsevolozhskys were exiled still further east, to the Kasimov district, in 1653. Euphemia never married. Some sources say that Alexis eventually recognized the wrong he did her, and granted her a large pension.

With the collapse of Alexis' initial marriage plans, three other candidates were readied by July 1647. But it was decided to terminate the search until the Swedish, Polish and Dutch ambassadors had made scheduled arrivals and departures. The tsar would then be able, in the honed words of a diplomatic report, "to turn to the marriage with greater calm and hotter joy."

The choice finally fell upon Maria Miloslavskaya, daughter of Ilya Danilovich Miloslavsky, a noble of such humble background that he was said once to have been a wine server to English merchants, while Maria gathered mushrooms to sell in the market. Ilya was brought into prominence by his uncle, Ivan Gramotin, an important crown secretary in the Foriegn Office. Miloslavsky then met Morozov, flattered him, and was accepted into his clique. Ilya presented Maria and her younger sister, Anna, to Morozov. Morozov saw an opportunity to join Maria to Alexis, and then become the tsar's brother-in-law by taking Anna for his own bride. Olearius tells us that Morozov praised the beauty of Miloslavsky's daughters so highly "that he awakened a keen desire in the young prince to see them." When the sisters came to the Kremlin to visit Alexis' sisters, the tsar indeed fell in love with Maria. Their marriage was quickly arranged. So that Miloslavsky could properly "fit out himself and his people," Alexis gave him "a large sum of money and various costly things." But Alexis' chaplain, Stephen Vonifatiev, persuaded the tsar to plan a modest wedding. Nor were the celebrations marked with the merrymaking, the excessive eating and drinking which ordinarily marked such events.

On January 16, 1648, Alexis married Maria, the woman who would live with him for the remaining twenty-one years of her life and bear the tsar five sons and eight daughters. Ten days later, Boris Morozov wedded Anna Miloslavskaya.

Fearful Muscovites speculated that sweeping innovations were now at hand. Alexis already had shortened the mourning period for deceased fathers from a year to six weeks. Many believed this to be a "western" innovation, and, with the tsar so clearly under the influence of foreigners, yet more ghastly novelties must be in the offing. "The Russian faith will be abolished," tongues clucked, "German heresies will be put in its place."

Grumbling against Morozov and his greedy friends constantly grew, as did the realization that he and the tsar were indissoluably close. As a token of special affection, Alexis' wedding presents to Morozov included a silver-plated carriage upholstered in costly furs and gold brocades. Silver bindings graced the wheels. Morozov's detractors supposedly had a chance to air their complaints during the hour before noon, when Alexis personally received petitioners. But with Morozov's creatures in every corner of the palace, the worst grievances were screened and side-tracked.

Alexis was otherwise absorbed in hunting, merrymaking, and religious pursuits. On Palm Sunday, 1648, Alexis led the annual reinactment of Christ's triumphant entry into Jerusalem, guiding on foot the patriarch's horse through the streets of Moscow. The tsar then distributed brightly colored Easter eggs to soldiers of every rank. Yet no one properly appreciated the intense dissatisfactions building throughout the land in the spring of 1648. No Russian statesman predicted that a riot would soon break in Moscow, a riot which would leave Morozov's silver-plated carriage in ruins.

Chapter Two

MOSCOW IN FLAMES

Alexis was unaware of the storm brewing in the land when he made his usual May pilgrimage to the Holy Trinity Monastery just outside Moscow in 1648. Crowds began assembling in the tsar's absence in front of the churches to discuss their grievances. The people were furious over the fact that Morozov had just intervened to have his friend Leonty Pleshcheev, chief of police, restored to office. After lengthy petitioning for an investigation into Pleshcheev's corruption and abuse of power, he was being cleared and his critics arrested and punished. "Our tsar is a fool," the people membled. "He does what Morozov and Miloslavsky tell him. They are the true masters, and the sovereign himself knows it, but he says nothing. The devil has robbed him of his wits!"

Alexis was due to return to Moscow on June 1 to celebrate another religious holiday at the Sretensky Monastery. Whenever the tsar re-entered the capital, it was the custom to greet him with bread and salt and to present him with petitions. This time a great crowd stopped Alexis' carriage, and forced him to hear their complaints against Pleshcheev.

"People of all ranks are groaning and complaining about your royal majesty," shouted the crowd, "for you pay no attention to the lowly and the defenseless. You do not stand up for us against those who oppress and destroy us. You let the rich continue their plunder."

Alexis had never been talked to in such harsh tones. Thoroughly shaken, he promised to see that justice would be done—and soon. But his first task was to understand how it came to pass that the anger and distress in his kingdom had grown so great.

The target of the crowd was one of the most complex and fascinating men of the age. Boris Morozov seemed to have no great prospects in life when he was born to a minor noble family in 1590. The lands he inherited at his father's death were peopled by a mere 151 peasant households. But the young man was blessed with ability, charm—and unlimited ambition. As he rose in the army, he was ever careful to extend his economic interests.

Morozov headed several important crown bureaus after he was made a boyar in 1634. His ability to impress and dominate people was capped by a friendship with Tsar Michael himself. Even after Morozov was asked to supervise Alexis' education his career was not limited to the capital. He was governor of Kazan in the late 1630s, and was made commander of the southern armies at Tula after the Crimean Tatars carried 6,000 Russians into slavery in a daring raid in 1644. All this time Morozov's talents as a businessman added economic power to his political influence. While serving as governor of Kazan, for example, he joined the Dutch partnership which built Russia's first modern iron manufactories at Tula, and when he left the partnership he organized his own iron works on his estates near Pavlovskoe. Only the tsar and Nikita Romanov were richer than Morozov in 1647. At the time Morozov died in 1661 he owned 9,000 households with 55,000 serfs, being exceeded in wealth only by Alexis himself. Successful as he was, however, Morozov often said that he wished he had received a good education as a young man. No Russian in these years was more open than he to the West, and Europeans praised Morozov for his sharp mind and political skill.

Morozov was the most powerful boyar in the land after Alexis became tsar in 1645. Morozov assumed personal direction over the Treasury and four other important bureaus. Sweeping away the favorites of Tsar Michael, Morozov installed his allies throughout the crown administrative structure. Boris fastened an iron grip on the Boyar Council: only junior members attended its regular meetings; Morozov dealt with senior members individually. Access to the tsar could be had only through Morozov, the man who Alexis venerated as teacher, master and friend, the one who stifled talk of Alexis' supposed "illegitimacy" and punished the rumor-mongers.

It was customary for the tsar's leading minister to line his own pockets and exercise sweeping power. People grumbled over this at the time, historians deplored it in later years. What sparked the anger against Morozov which almost cost him his life, however, was not greed, but the statesman-like reforms he sponsored during the first three years of Alexis' reign. Morozov was determined to bring state expenditure into line with revenues, and to modernize the army along western lines. But none of this could be done without alienating existing interests.

Morozov began by applying to national management the strict economies which had made his estates flourish so well. He cut the number of royal servants and court personnel, and reduced the wages of those who remained. Morozov lowered (sometimes by half) the salaries of provincial officials and musketeers, and slashed the expense accounts of diplomats abroad. Land grants increasingly replaced money payments to foreign officers in Russian service. While reducing crown expenses, Morozov worked to increase income. But taxation was already so high at the time Alexis came to the throne that it could not be raised. Indeed, many peasant households were hopelessly behind in their payments. Morozov gained some new revenues by raising tariffs. But his larger strategy was to make retail of tobacco and salt a government monopoly, and to sell them at greatly inflated prices. Some Russians considered smoking a thing of the devil, and the death penalty was imposed for it in 1634. If use of the evil weed could not be suppressed, however, should not the state at least profit from it? As for salt, its price quadrupled during 1646, making it now impossible to process adequately the cheap fish which had brought a bit of flesh into the diet of common Russians. The banks of the Volga stank with crates of rotting fish as salt in the warehouses lay unsold and running to brine.

The situation grew still worse by late 1647. Poor harvests and escalating grain prices added to popular distress. The nation's taxpayers no longer could carry their burdens, common townspeople found it increasingly hard to buy bread and fish. Moscow festered as the focal point of distress. The city buzzed with unemployed office holders and menials as well as musketeers and service nobles whose salaries had been reduced through Morozov's economies.

Morozov also alienated the large class of service nobles. These small landowners suffered because wealthy boyars and monasteries could persuade peasants to settle on their estates, where the rewards of farming were much greater. The service nobles long had demanded that the government make a genuine effort to return these fugitive peasants, and that the time limit on their recovery be extended beyond ten years—or abolished altogether. But Morozov shared the class interests and views of his fellow boyars, so he refused such petitions. In fact, it was well known that Morozov instructed his stewards to lure and even kidnap peasants from neighboring estates.

The military reforms Morozov planned also filled the smaller service nobles with anger and fear. Lacking real training, armed with bow and arrow and mounted on small, fast horses, they knew full well that a modern army armed with firearms and led by European officers would undermine their military significance. This, in turn, could spell an end to their economic privileges. The service nobles had good reason to be discontented with Morozov, as did the equally obsolete and inefficient musketeers.

If Morozov and his associates knew of popular dissatisfaction with them and their policies, Alexis himself was totally unaware that anything was amiss. Such ignorance of practical affairs made it doubly difficult for Alexis to deal with the complaints the crowd had thrown in his face as he returned to Moscow on June 1, 1648.

The mob which confronted Alexis on that day in June was pleased with his humble manner, his sincere interest in their grievances. The people took his promise to investigate and render justice at high value, and began to disperse in a fairly happy mood. Unfortunately, Pleshcheev's supporters now descended on the crowd, attacking and beating whoever they could get their hands on—as if to show that they still held power and knew how to use it. Sixteen people were arrested in the name of the tsar.

When the tsarina passed by the same spot with Morozov a half hour later, people rushed to present complaints to her. Attempts to disperse this crowd made its members so angry that they threw stones and clubs at her procession. When Maria asked Morozov why the people were agitated, he blandly assured her that hanging a few rioters for their "illegal" acts would bring it all to an end. By this time, however, Morozov's leading supporters were rushing to the Kremlin to take refuge with the tsar himself. The musketeers who guarded Alexis held the furious people back long enough to let the once powerful fugitives into the sovereign's chambers. Morozov appeared on the upper porch and in the name of the tsar ordered the people to give up their demands. The crowd chanted, "Yes, and we must have you, too!" Morozov disappeared.

The mob now turned upon Morozov's luxurious house in the Kremlin, plundered what was of value and demolished what could not be carried off. Rioters broke into his cellar to drink their fill of vodka and mead, and were soon wading in liquor to the knees. Hopelessly drunk, many were burned in the fire which moments later engulfed the entire building. A servant who tried to defend his master's property was thrown from a window and lay dead in the courtyard. Morozov's wife escaped unharmed, but she was told, "Were you not the sister of the Grand Princess, we would hack you to bits."

The rioters now separated into several groups, some to catch Pleshcheev, others to find the equally hated Peter Trakhaniotov and Nazary Chistyi—as well as their supporters and officials. Chistyi, a merchant from Yaroslavl who was a secretary of the Duma and head of the Foreign Office, happened to be in bed, nursing a fall from his horse three days before. Olearius says that when Chistyi learned a mob was on the way to his house, "he dragged himself out of bed, crept across the floor, and concealed himself under a bath broom" made of birch branches. He ordered a servant to pile packages of lard over him. When the mob burst into the room, the boy betrayed his master, not by *saying* where he was hiding—that he had been forbidden to do—but by *pointing*. The enraged people dragged Chistyi from his hiding place and beat him mercilessly.

In the words of the English translation of an anonymous Dutch eye-witness account, "the man being halfe dead, they hauled him down the stayres by the heeles, dragged him like a dog over the whole Court, and having stripped him, they flung him starck naked upon a dunghill, [and] there they put him qu[ite] to death." Chistyi's features were shattered beyond recognition. While finishing with him, the crowd shouted, "That's for the salt, you traitor!"

As night fell on Moscow, the disorders abated slightly. But not for long. The next day, June 2, on a Saturday morning, the rioters gathered before the Kremlin and persuaded the tsar's foreign bodyguards to open the gates, saying, "You are honest Germans who do us no harm. We are your friends and have no intention ever to do you any harm."

Alexis sent his popular cousin, Nikita Romanov, to tell the crowd he was disturbed by the turmoil, and to assure the people that he would right all wrongs. The people were deferential to Nikita and swore love and loyalty to the tsar. But they refused to disperse until Morozov, Pleshcheev, and Trakhaniotov were surrendered. Alexis finally agreed to hand Pleshcheev over, but the crowd was told that Morozov and Trakhaniotov already had taken flight. The people were so infuriated at the very sight of Pleshcheev that they would not wait for the executioner to do his work. Falling upon Pleshcheev, the mob clubbed him to death. Brains splattered over his face, Pleshcheev's body was dragged through the market place as the rioters yelled, "Thus will all such scoundrels and thieves be treated. God preserve His Tsarist Majesty's health for many years!" Olearius says a monk finally approached the corpse and chopped off what was left of the head, saying, "This is because he once had me cudgeled, though I was innocent."

Meanwhile, Morozov indeed tried to flee. A contemporary Swedish account tells of a stormy session between him and the tsar on Saturday morning, just before the mob arrived to take Pleshcheev. When Alexis demanded to know why Morozov had imprisoned people without his knowledge, the boyar could make no satisfactory reply. Morozov still tried to put down the uprising, however, ordering the 6,000 musketeers in Moscow to act against the rioters. But the troops made clear that they would not fight to save "the traitors." Morozov had no choice now but to leave Moscow. On his way out of the Kremlin he was recognized by a group of cartsmen and coachmen. Forced back, he managed to re-enter the Kremlin unseen, by a secret way. It was generally thought that Morozov had make good his escape, and rumors spread that he had been sighted in the streets.

At noon, on Saturday, the fires in Moscow broke out of control. Some thought that Morozov's servants started the blaze to frighten and scatter the people, but in all probability the conflagration was accidental, caused by mobs pillaging the homes of hated officials. As the flames spread wider and wider, it seemed that all Moscow might be lost. Olearius was informed that everything within the wall of that section in the center of Moscow known as the "White City" to the Neglinnaya River was consumed. The fire then "crossed the Neglinnaya bridge and entered the red-walled section of the city near the Grand Prince's largest and best tavern. As a result, the whole city, including the Kremlin, was placed in the greatest jeopardy. Not a person wanted to escape or could, since all were as drunk as could be from the vodka they had pillaged from the cellars during the fire. They knocked the bottoms out of the barrels that were too large to take out, drew the vodka into hats, caps, shoes and gloves, and got so drunk that the blackened streets were covered with them." Many were so intoxicated that they died where they lay, suffocated by the smoke and consumed by the flames.

Half of Moscow lay in ashes within a few hours. A Dutch observer reported that as many as 15,000 houses were burned and 1,700 people were killed; an anonymous Swedish source estimated that 24,000 houses were lost and that 2,000 died. "Infinite treasures and wealth in commercial goods and other property burned and perished in the fire," he continued. A half-million tons of grain worth six tons of gold went up in smoke. One merchant lost 150,000 rubles worth of property. Olearius has a bizarre tale of a monk dressed in black who dragged Pleshcheev's corpse to the flames at 11 o'clock that night, saying that only when his "accursed body" was thrown in would the fire stop. "As soon as the body began to burn, the flames began dying down before the eyes of the astounded spectators, and went out."

The mob remained in control of the capital even after the fire. Indeed, Alexis finally gave in to the rioters and had Trakhaniotov brought back from his hiding place at the Holy Trinity Monastery to Red Square, where he was beheaded on June 5 before an assembly of delighted citizens. The tsar then regaled the musketeers with food and drink for the next few days, hoping to regain their support. Ilya Miloslavsky invited artisans and merchants active in the riot to feasts at his home, while Patriarch Joseph sent his clergy about to calm tempers as best they could.

Alexis turned the Morozov clique out of power, placing authority in the hands of Miloslavsky and Nikita Romanov. He also relied upon Yakov Cherkassky, a prince who had been eclipsed by the Morozov people for the past three years. Cherkassky was extremely popular with the service nobles, who had been assembling in large numbers at Moscow since April, preparing to resist a rumored Tatar offensive from the south. Ordinarily these forces would have suppressed a popular uprising, but, like the musketeers, the service nobles hated Morozov as much as the people who took to the streets against him and his followers. When it seemed to Alexis that his changes in government personnel were bringing a measure of peace to his devastated city, he appeared at the Kremlin to assure the people again that he would right all their wrongs.

"I am very sorry," said the tsar, "now that I have learned of the excesses Pleshcheev and Trakaniotov have committed in my name, but against my will. I have people in their places who are honest and agreeable and who will mete out punishment without bribes and to everyone the same. I will keep an eye out for this myself." The salt monopoly had drawn such criticism that Morozov himself had abolished it in December, 1647, but the people cried out that the price of salt—and hence fish—were still high. Alexis promised to see that the cost of salt would be cut still further, and to abolish the remaining state monopolies.

Pleased as the mob was at these concessions, it still wanted Morozov's hide. "I have promised to give Morozov to you," Alexis said in a slow, deliberate way, responding to this demand, "and I must admit that I cannot completely justify him. But I cannot give him up and condemn him. This person is dear to me, the husband of the tsarina's sister, and it would be very burdensome for me to deliver him to death." Tears poured from Alexis' eyes as he ended his plea. "Long live the tsar!" the people shouted. But the crowd had not grown friendlier to Alexis' favorite boyar, though a compromise was finally reached. Morozov's life was spared on the condition that he be exiled from Moscow. A musketeer guard wound its way out of Moscow as the sun rose on June 12, taking Morozov to the Kirillov Monastery on the White Sea, 120 miles north.

Alexis had brought peace to Moscow, but not yet to Russia. In the next few weeks the violence experienced in the capital burst forth elsewhere in the land. Uprisings swept through eight towns in the southern steppe. The affected towns—Kursk, Voronezh, Taletsk, Chelnavsk, Chuguev, Kromy, Nonosil and Koslov—were garrison posts. The Cossacks and service nobles on duty there were furious over Morozov's penny-pinching cutbacks and plans for a future professional army. Even Narym in distant Siberia felt the tide of rebellion, while the soldiers in Tomsk actually had risen up against their commander in May, before the events in Moscow. Townsmen and sometimes peasants rioted in the far north, in Sol-Vychegodsk, Ustiug Veliky, Cherdyn and Solikamsk, when news arrived there of the disorders that had gripped the capital. The situation in these places was similar to that in Moscow: taxes were heavy and could not be collected, officials were corrupt and unpopular, grain prices were high. The relief Morozov had brought urban taxpayers by curbing trade and land ownership by individuals not inscribed on the tax rolls kept peace in the larger towns of central and north Russia. Still, the lesson was clear. Dissatisfaction   d throughout the land. Alexis had t

The your   ibly of the Land". This representativ   ople at critical moments in the past t   lief from their "Father Tsar". An A   ichael Romanov tsar in 1613. Could   now save his son?

[handwritten note: ≥ to an Ass of Re land ↑ p. 24]

Chapter Three

GOOD LAWS MAKE THE KINGDOM RIGHT

Clouds of smoke hovered lazily in the sky, burned buildings lined Moscow's streets as an important meeting took place on June 10, 1648. The riots had run their course sufficiently for wiser men to begin to plan how best to approach Alexis with reforms. Nobles from Moscow and the provinces joined with merchants and even a few foreigners in crown service to petition Alexis "to bestow his favor upon them and order an Assembly convened." Elected representatives should form this Assembly of the Land, as well as high church and state officials.

His armies in disarray, Alexis could hardly refuse this request. A revolt of slaves in Moscow at just this time further reminded everyone how dependent the tsar and his government were on the service nobles and tax-paying merchants. And so, "by order of the Sovereign Tsar and Grand Prince Alexis Mikhailovich," the petitioners gathered in the Banquet Hall of the Kremlin on June 16, together with the tsar, Patriarch Joseph, church and crown dignitaries, and the representatives of army units.

If the petitioners were politer than the rioters of two weeks past, they were no less insistent in airing their dissatisfactions. After presenting grievances "about their various affairs," they called for a new law code—a book of laws "to cover all kinds of legal cases, so that in the future all matters will be conducted and decided in accordance with that book of statutes."

"Good laws make the kingdom right!" some said. "But our laws, Sire, are confused and unjust!"

Alexis huddled with his advisers, then emerged to order a commission formed "to take charge of this matter, to draw up a book of statutes on the model of" earlier law codes. This commission would be formed under the leadership of Prince Nikita Odoevsky. It would work with elected representatives of the nobles and merchants throughout the land, "good and sensible men," Alexis solemnly intoned, "who are accustomed to such affairs of the state and of the land, so that with the help of all the elected deputies this great royal affair of the state and of the land might be confirmed and arranged." These representatives were to gather in Moscow by September 1, 1648—New Year's Day by the calendar then in use in Russia.

The "Assembly of the Land" had been summoned first by Ivan the Terrible, in 1549. It may be compared with western parliamentary bodies so long as we remember that in Russia, as in the West at that time, the Assemblies were elected only from the free and propertied classes, were convened, dismissed and reconvened according to the sovereign's will, and usually proclaimed taxes and policies already drafted by the government. Such proceedings demonstrated that the throne was taxing, declaring war and making peace, and handling crucial domestic affairs according to the "popular will" and in consultation with the "entire land." If this was window dressing, it was important enough to the government for the tsar to listen to the "advice" and complaints of the delegates, many of whom in any case were carefully selected supporters of crown policy.

The Assembly of the Land assumed a new function at the turn of the seventeenth century: election of the tsar. The dynasty founded by Prince Rurik in the ninth century became extinct with the death of Ivan the Terrible's son Fedor in 1598. An Assembly of the Land was called to choose a new ruler. Boris Godunov was so powerful that the delegates hardly had any choice, but still it is significant that the body selected to make his power "legal" was the Assembly of the Land.

When Boris Godunov died in 1605 Russia was well into those stormy dozen years which Russians remember as the "Time of Troubles." These years of famine and plague, social conflict and foreign invasion, marked the worst crisis the nation was to know before the twentieth century. The title of "Tsar" after Boris was held by inept rulers who were the prisoners (and sometimes the victims) of stronger forces behind the scenes. The throne actually stood vacant at the end, with the Poles occupying Moscow and large areas in the west. Only a rallying of "popular forces"—peasants and townspeople, churchmen and independent nobles— drove the foreigner away and began to restore order in the kingdom. The ferment of this moment was reflected in a most interesting innovation in the Assembly of the Land elected in 1612: a few free peasants were numbered among the delegates.

The Assembly's choice of a new ruler suggests that it expected to play a role of some sort in governing the nation. "Misha Romanov is still young," was the brief Prince Fedor Romanov presented on Michael's behalf. "He has not yet attained the age of reason," the old antagonist of Boris Godunov continued, "and so he will be amenable to us." This does not indicate, however, that the Assembly intended to eclipse the powers of the tsar. Nothing in the Russian tradition made such a development likely, and there is no reason to think that anyone hoped for it even in 1613. The Assembly of 1613 and another which met from 1616 to 1618 advised the throne on foreign policy and the needs of local areas. They also agreed to the levy of taxes. Important as all this was, policy-making remained in the hands of Michael's leading officials, especially the Boyar Council.

Michael Romanov's father, Filaret, finally returned from Polish captivity in 1619, and after a few days was elected patriarch. The stern, narrow-minded old man would have liked to receive the tsar's throne which had fallen to Michael six years before. In any case, Misha stood in awe of his talented, decisive father, and until Filaret's death in 1633, it was actually he who governed Russia.

Although patriarch, Filaret was totally dedicated to the traditions of Russia's autocracy, and he sought to strengthen the throne in every way. Relying upon the government bureaus (prikazy) for administration, Filaret bypassed the Boyar Council, but did bring the question of war with Poland before Assemblies of the Land which met in 1621 and 1632. Assemblies which convened in 1637, 1639, and 1642 likewise passed on diplomatic affairs. A full Assembly of the Land might have been called to approve Alexis' accession to the throne in 1645 but for the fact, as we have seen, that Morozov was in such haste to have Alexis declared ruler. Kotoshikhin says that Morozov hastily called some nobles and merchants together to "elect" Alexis "to the rulership." People were not fooled, however. This was not a true "Assembly of the *Land*," and during the next three years Alexis' enemies grumbled that one should have been convened to make him the lawful tsar. This, too, is an indication of the Assembly's growing maturity and status.

The Assembly of 1648 was similar to that of 1613. Its members were elected, not appointed, and they were elected on the basis of hotly debated issues. The deputies also were more determined than in 1613 to press the crown for concessions. As they streamed into Moscow in the summer, members of the Assembly were assigned to various tasks on, or related to, Odoevsky's commission. By the time Alexis returned to Moscow from a pilgrimage on October 3, 1648, Odoevsky and his co-workers had completed several chapters of the new code and they began to read the documents to the tsar. John Keep notes an interesting development at this time within the Assembly: it separated into two chambers, "an 'upper house' of clergy and boyars (including Odoevsky) presided over by the tsar, and a 'lower house' of elected delegates" under Prince Yury Dolgoruky. "This was a sign that the Assembly was maturing as an institution," for the division into two houses "allowed the elected deputies to express their views without being overpowered by the presence of the tsar and the boyars. Their proposals were submitted in the form of petitions to the 'upper house', and enacted into law without undue conflict or difficulty." Of the 340 members of the entire body, almost half (153) were provincial nobles, 79 were tax-paying townsmen, 40 were boyars, Moscow nobles and crown secretaries. There were also 15 musketeers, 14 churchmen, 12 Moscow merchants, and three of the most important traders in the kingdom, holders of the title *gost,* a term we are translating as "leading merchant." A good half of these 340 delegates could not read and write.

The law code was finished and formally presented to Alexis on January 29, 1649. After an official banquet with the tsar, the deputies set out for home. The document they left behind, the *Ulozhenie* (Law Code), was published in April in what was for the time a huge first edition of 1,200 copies. The twenty-five chapters and 967 articles of this volume defined Russian law until the next codification of the laws, a codification which—incredibly—did not occur until 1833.

The class which gained most from the Law Code of 1649 was the service nobility, the small landlords who held grants of land in exchange for military service to the tsar. The code ended a tradition which these nobles bitterly opposed, the right of a peasant free of debt to his lord to leave an estate the week before and after St. George's Day in November

THE ASSEMBLY OF THE LAND IN SESSION IN 1613. Miniature from the manuscript book *Selection of Michael Romanov as Tsar* (1672). The boyars are seated in a circle, lords of the chamber and men of lesser ranks stand respectfully to the side.

to take up farming for another lord. This practice worked to the advantage of the service nobles' competitors, the boyars and the great monasteries, since these larger, more productive estates could offer peasants the best security and working conditions. Boyars and monasteries sometimes went so far as to pay a peasant's debts to his lesser lord to gain the service of a new hand, for in these years labor was often more valuable than land itself. Such "raiding" often left a service noble's estate stripped of peasants and economically worthless.

The service nobles had pushed their demands in various forms throughout Michael's reign. Young Tsar Alexis also received such petitions. But so long as great boyars such as Morozov "advised" the tsar and controlled crown policy, the service nobles' demands were ignored. Those who protested and went too far in making their case could even have cause for regret later. In 1647, for example, a petty landlord complained that it was nearly impossible to petition Alexis on these matters, and even so, the tsar cared nothing for the welfare of his "loyal" serving men. The noble was arrested, tried and sentenced to death—though Alexis commuted this punishment to a stern thrashing which left its victim almost lifeless.

The service nobles won their point after the Moscow riots of 1648. Alexis now saw that the state must have the support of the service nobility, so the Law Code of 1649 bound peasants to the lands on which they were living at the time land surveys had been made between 1627 and 1631. As for runaways, chapter eleven proclaimed that peasant fugitives "are to be returned with their wives, children, and all moveable property" without any statute of limitations. Russian peasants were now *serfs.* By law they were bound to the land. In theory this did not end all peasant rights, for if the serf could not leave the land, neither could he be abused, degraded or deprived of his rights to farm the lands worked by his forebears. In reality, however, government agents took no steps to protect the serfs' theoretical "rights" before the law. Left under the absolute jurisdiction of the noble landholder, serfs could be treated any way their lords liked. Serfs were separated from the land at the whim of its owners.

The philosophical justification for serfdom was that the peasants must serve the nobles so that the nobles could serve the tsar—who in turn devoted himself to the service of God's Church and the Russian Land. Everyone served for the ultimate benefit of all. Such was the theory, and Alexis repeated it many times—to the peasants! The tsar knew, of course, that most nobles evaded their obligations, and that for all their rights and privileges they were of slight military value in wars with the West. But the Moscow riots showed that the large class of service nobles were "garrisons of order" scattered throughout a potentially rebellious land. Himself a landowner, Alexis equated landownership with the natural order of the world. His task as tsar was to defend that order, which in turn meant he had to pay new attention to the interests of small noble landholders.

The Law Code of 1649 represented a defeat for the great boyars, even though Boris Morozov had succeeded in returning to Moscow by the time it was promulgated. Impatiently viewing the situation from exile in the far north, Morozov was determined to return to the capital as soon as possible. With the tsar's permission, his old friend slipped back to his estates near Tver and Moscow, and then finally, on October 26, 1648, to the capital itself. Within five days the crafty boyar was again active in government. His arch-rival Nikita Romanov suddenly reported himself "sick" and unable to participate in government. As for Yakov Cherkassky, when he found Morozov occupying a place at Alexis' table more honorable than his own, he jumped to his feet, cursing. Cherkassky hotly resigned his offices, stormed from the Kremlin—and was amazed to see himself immediately put under house arrest. On the following day, November 1, Ilya Miloslavsky, the father-in-law of both Alexis and Morozov, replaced Cherkassky as commander of the musketeers. Miloslavsky soon took over Cherkassky's other positions as well. It was not possible for Alexis to restore Morozov to his full, former power, but Morozov was able to enjoy at least indirect revenge against his enemies.

Boris Morozov failed to prevent serfdom from being enacted into law. But the Law Code of 1649 continued his urban policies. Tax-exempt owners of town land—monasteries, clergy, nobles and merchants—surrendered their holdings to the tsar without compensation, and the property was included on tax rolls after it passed to new owners. With more property paying revenues, it was easier for urban taxpayers to meet their annual burdens.

The Law Code attached merchants and artisans to their suburbs as rigidly as it bound peasants to the estates of their lords. Town fugitives likewise were to be returned without a time limit. Actually, townspeople long had asked for these concessions, and in a display of solidarity with them the service nobles on the law commission joined their urban colleagues in petitioning the tsar for these provisions in November 1648. People who think that man naturally seeks freedom may find it strange that some Russians in the winter of 1648 demanded not less servitude for themselves, but an equal amount of it for others so that the entire group—urban tax-payers—might better fulfill its obligations to the state. But such was indeed the case here.

The new Law Code also continued Morozov's campaign against church property rights. The Church not only lost the urban lands it once held tax free, but chapter seventeen placed drastic limits on its future ability to acquire land anywhere in the kingdom. If a dying man left land to a monastery, for example, his heirs could sue to recover it. If the heirs chose not to do this, the tsar held the right to take the land in exchange for a paltry compensation—"but the estate may not be held by a monastery." Nor was the Church able to hope that the law would be poorly enforced, perhaps by officials hostile to Morozov and his anti-clericalism. Alexis appointed Yury Dolgoruky to head the Investigation Office, the bureau which under Dolgoruky's notoriously energetic—even ruthless— direction would be charged with clearing tax-exempt landowners from urban areas. The fact that Yury's wife was Morozov's aunt suggested what was indeed true, that Dolgoruky was firmly attached to the man who some five months before had left Moscow in disgrace and trembling for his life.

In short, the Law Code of 1649 bound all Russians to their residences and occupations. Serfdom looms as an important and cruel feature of the new Code. The peasants resented the loss of their traditional right to move, and in the future years anxiously hoped for its restoration.

They hoped in vain. Serfdom as defined in the Law Code was the basis for a solid alliance between Alexis and the service nobles. The tsar was the supreme ruler in Moscow, the service noble was the supreme authority on his estate. Knowing that royal absolutism was the key to their own position, the service nobles had no interest in curbing the sovereign's powers by forcing him, for example, to rule in the future together with an Assembly of the Land. Skillfully Alexis and his advisers had aligned the crown with the service nobles and the townsmen by enacting reforms in their mutual interest at the expense of the serfs, the boyars, and the Church. The Law Code supported the middle sections of Russian society against those on the bottom of the social ladder and at its top. Alexis overcame the crisis of 1648 through a coalition of crown, service nobles, and tax-paying townsmen. Peasants, boyars and church leaders were outmaneuvered and confounded.

Maria bore Alexis their first child in October, 1648, a son they named Dmitry. The celebrations naturally accompanying this event were, in fact, what provided the tsar an excuse to summon Boris Morozov back to Moscow—though in doing this Alexis was careful to distribute a generous purse of coins to the musketeers. The chronicles say little of the joy of Dmitry's parents at his birth, even less of their despair at his death little more than a year later.

Observers of the Russian scene at this time were struck by Alexis' new seriousness of purpose. The June events revealed sharp problems in the land, and it fell to Alexis as tsar to deal with them. Alexis was so shaken by the turmoil in the capital that he decided to form new detachments of "household guards" under the command of Ivan Miloslavsky, his uncle by marriage. Recalling that his Russian forces refused to fight for their tsar while foreign mercenaries held firm, Alexis hoped to recruit his new guard units abroad. Russians were selected for the honor only when it became clear that foreigners were not available.

Alexis' determination to be a strong, active ruler did not lead him to abandon hunting and the other pleasures of his earlier years. He was equally devoted to the religious rituals and pilgrimages whose beauty inspired him from early years. Sometimes it fell to Alexis to act as the religious leader of his people. For example, a large fire broke out in Moscow on the night of October 4, 1650 and, as thousands of houses burned, the tsar appeared before the suffering people and had prayers for their deliverance offered in the churches. None of this prevented Alexis from playing a close, personal part in state affairs. Thus it fell to him in late October to judge the ringleaders of the Pskov riots, disorders directed against wealthy boyars and their "German friends" of that city. The tsar was inclined to be harsh with these men, but finally forgave them because Morozov begged amnesty on their behalf. Neither Morozov nor anyone else, however, exercised the same influence over Alexis as before the terrible summer of 1648.

Chapter Four

MOSCOW THE THIRD ROME

Russians in Alexis' time were convinced there was only one true faith under the heavens, and only one emperor who ruled by the hand of God. The Christian message was first preached in the Roman Empire, of course, and with the conversion of Emperor Constantine Rome became the first Christian kingdom. When Rome fell into heresy and betrayed the true faith, the center of Christianity migrated to Constantinople. The "New Rome" spread the gospel far and wide, even to Russia, and held the Christian faith pure and undefiled for more than a thousand years. Then, alas! the Greeks proved unworthy of the trust God had granted them. The Greeks agreed to reunification of the Church on terms the Pope dictated at the Council of Florence in 1439. Did the Byzantines simply hope to gain military aid from the West and save their land from the infidel Turk? If so, God showed his opinion of the maneuver in plain terms: Constantinople fell to Islam's hordes in 1453. In this way Moscow became the new center of the true faith, the "Third Rome."

The Third Rome doctrine took shape soon after the fall of Constantinople. Zosima, leader of the Russian Church, hailed Ivan the Great as the "new Constantine" of the "new city of Constantine, Moscow," as early as the year in which Columbus discovered the New World. Filofei, the learned monk of Pskov, further elaborated the Third Rome idea in the next decade. "My greetings to you, who have been elected by the Most High," was Filofei's salutation to Ivan. Reminding his prince that Rome fell through heresy, and that the "hatchets of the sons of Hagar" had despoiled the churches of Constantinople, Filofei declared:

> Of all kingdoms in the world, the Holy Apostolic Church shines in thy royal domain more brightly than the sun. Take note, most religious and gracious Tsar, that all kingdoms of the Orthodox Christian Faith have been merged into thy kingdom. In all that lies under heaven, thou alone are a Christian tsar. So take note, most religious and gracious Tsar, that all Christian kingdoms have been merged into thine alone, for *two Romes have fallen, but the third still stands and a fourth there shall never be.* Thy Christian kingdom will be replaced by no other.

The Third Rome could not have been ruled by a truer Christian than Tsar Alexis. Passion for the faith penetrated his entire life; it was the key to so many of his thoughts and actions. Contemporaries unanimously testify to Alexis' zeal for the Church, but the most useful information on this comes from a visit made to Moscow by Patriarch Macarius of Antioch from 1654 to 1656. The patriarch's son, Deacon Paul, left an extensive description of the religious life of Alexis and his people.

Paul and Alexis were both members of the Eastern Orthodox Church, but when the Greek came to Moscow he felt he had stepped into an entirely different world. Paul would have been surprised to hear that scholars in Sweden and Estonia then were debating the question, "Are the Russians Christians?" Macarius and his party never doubted it for a moment. Paul was amazed at how dedicated Alexis was to church services, though they went on for hours, and often all night, even in the coldest weather. Paul was shocked to see the tsar humble himself before

sacred icons, the poor, the loathsomely diseased, and above all to the
patriarch, the visible successor of Christ, the leader of His Church. It
seemed to Paul that Moscow contained thousands of churches, that
their bells were constantly sounding, that Russians of every class "sur-
pass even the saints in the number of their prayers." As the hours of a
typical winter mass dragged on, water and wine froze in their vessels and
the patriarch intoned a long, inspiring sermon. "God grant him modera-
tion!" Paul exclaims. "His heart did not ache for the emperor nor for
the tender infants."

Nor did the court complain over such ordeals. "Their emperor and
empress are the leaders of the nation in religious observances," the deacon notes of Alexis and Maria. "How, then, should the courtiers be
otherwise than devout?" Indeed it was so, as we see from but one typical example.

On Saturday evening, December 22, 1655, the Greeks were asked to
rise for a vigil service. The celebration began with lesser vespers, and at
the eighth hour the tsar himself arrived. The cold of the iron pavement
was "enough to kill us," and Paul admits he attempted to escape, but
was checked by "the emperor standing before the south door, and the
empress before the north door," so that patience became a necessity. His
greatest surprise, however, was to see the "boys and little children" of
important crown officials "standing bareheaded and motionless, without betraying the smallest gesture of impatience." At the end of the
service the patriarchs blessed Alexis and his wife. When they left the
church, the sun was already up. The Greeks were "nearly dead with the
fatigue of standing from the ninth hour of the night to the sixteenth."
No wonder this "perpetual standing" in their churches gave Muscovites
a foot disorder "which attacks all ranks from the emperor to the beggar
and is incurable." After this experience Paul could not stand for three
days, and his feet returned to normal only after two months. About an
hour after the Greeks left the cathedral that morning, the bells tolled
once more, "and we returned to it again, though we were perishing and
dying with fatigue, want of sleep and cold."

The weather was more compassionate during the warmer months,
but Alexis' religious devotions were as rigorous as in the hardest days of
winter. And they showed as clearly his Christian humility. On Palm
Sunday, for example, a solemn procession with icons and crosses brought
the tsar and his boyars from the Cathedral of the Assumption to Red
Square. When the patriarch arrived, palms and willow branches were
handed out. After a service at the place where royal proclamations were
read to the people, the patriarch was seated on a white steed, ready for

the dramatic re-enactment of Christ's triumphant entry into Jerusalem. Writing just before the Revolution of 1905, R. Nisbet Bain was justified in remarking that "no Russian in modern times had ever seen "a religious ceremony such as this." Alexis handed his sceptre to an attendant and then led the patriarch's horse back to the cathedral as musketeers lining the streets spread their cloaks before the procession.

Alexis and his people thought continually of God even during the summer, after the rigors of Lent and Easter had passed. Paul of Aleppo reports that in this season, when the nights are short, "they ring for vespers before nightfall," after 3 p.m., and for matins at 4 a.m. Before summer Sundays and festivals, the bells rang nearly all night. This greatly upset the Greeks, for at the sound of the bells "the very earth trembled from midnight to daybreak."

Patriarch Macarius first asked permission to return home on December 22, 1655—during the Mass described earlier in this chapter—but Alexis was so pleased to have this distinguished visitor in Moscow that he prevailed upon him to stay for a time. When the Greeks finally left Moscow during Lent of 1656 the Russians dismissed them with presents and affection. Paul admitted that he and his companions had waited so long for this moment that they could hardly believe "that our departure was a reality, so great was our joy." They were delighted "to escape from the sleepless vigils" of Easter, "the overwhelming fatigue, and the restless standing up during the week of the Passion." Yet Paul confesses that he was also strangely sad at leaving Moscow, and "I afterwards wished we had stayed." What a people!, he concludes. "Without doubt the Creator has granted this nation to be his peculiar people, for all their actions are according to the spirit, and not to the flesh; and they are all of this disposition." The Greeks had not taken a bath in the two years they stayed in Russia.

Russians believed that Moscow was the Third Rome, but they admitted the grave faults of the people of Muscovy. Filofei himself expressed

CHRIST'S ENTRY INTO JERUSALEM. Re-enacted in Russia during Alexis' time on Palm Sunday. The procession made its way from St. Basil's Cathedral (far left upper corner) across Red Square to *lobnoe mesto* (lower left), the small, circular platform from which proclamations and edicts were read to the people, to hear a few words from the tsar. The procession then passed through the Gate of the Savior to the Cathedral of the Assumption in the Kremlin. Musketeers are shown prostrating themselves at each side. Note the tree hung with fruit on a wagon, boys on the platform singing hymns while toward the rear the tsar leads a white forse bearing the patriarch.

concern for the condition of the Russian Church. He begged the tsar not to interfere with monastery lands and church courts, he protested vices among the Russians ranging from sodomy to simony, he deplored the incorrect manner in which his people made the sign of the cross. Peculiarities in the way Russians celebrated the liturgy had increased by the time Alexis became tsar, and these "mistakes" isolated Russia from the rest of the Eastern Church. Russians crossed themselves with two fingers symbolizing the dual nature of Christ rather than with three fingers representing the Trinity; the name of Jesus was incorrectly rendered "Esus"; the liturgy was graced by seven, not five offertory loaves; one loaf rather than several rested on the altar; church processions turned northward rather than southward to circle the building; minor differences had wandered into the creed and even into the Lord's Prayer; double instead of triple alleluias were sung. Preaching was not only a thing of the past, but to shorten the Mass still further the bizarre practice had arisen of priests and their assistants reciting several portions of the liturgy simultaneously. As alert Russians came more into contact with other Eastern Orthodox Churches, it became more difficult to ignore these shortcomings, or to deny that the Church of the "Third Rome" was not in need of serious improvement.

Popular morals had fallen into sad disarray by Alexis' time. European visitors to Russia were amazed at the public drunkenness they saw, the sexual looseness, the generally coarse tone of life. Olearius noted that monks and priests as well as lay people of every class drank enormous quantities of vodka, and then sprawled drunkenly on streets and town squares. The people quarrelled constantly, he says, and even old people and little children had ready on their tongue such words as "dog," "son of a bitch," and worse. Olearius warned not to expect good manners even from among the upper classes. "After a meal, they do not refrain, in the presence and hearing of all, from releasing what nature produces fore and aft. Since they eat a great deal of garlic and onion, it is rather trying to be in their company. Perhaps against their will, these good people fart and belch noisily—and indeed they did [so] intermittently during the secret audiences with us." Russians even abused smoking. Olearius observed that poor people exchanged a kopeck for tobacco as eagerly as for bread. They lost much work time smoking it, and "many houses went up in smoke because of carelessness with the flame and sparks."

Alexis was concerned about the condition of the Russian Church and of Russian society. His education, intelligence and hospitality to Eastern Orthodox clergy visiting Moscow made him especially receptive to the idea of church reform. Alexis was helped toward this by his close friend, Fedor Rtishchev, a young boyar and statesman who was perhaps the most popular Russian of his time. Rtishchev would have felt at home in the West as a junior colleague of Erasmus or Sir Thomas More. Worldly success comes easily to such men, though they care more for other things. Their gentle spirits radiate a mellow charisma which move and elevate people, even crass opportunists unlikely to imitate them in any way. The purity of character and motives of such idealists leads them to think that mankind is generally good. The evil in man they explain through poor religion and bad education—and the solution to this evil is held to lie in reform of the Church and the cultivation of "sweet learning". Though not of the same creative stature, Rtishchev was a Humanist in the manner of Erasmus and More, for he likewise believed that the ultimate purpose of Christianity was to elevate man in this life, to make him daily more like Christ.

The European Humanists were concerned that their generation master Latin and Greek, read new and more accurate translations of scripture and church literature, and integrate the finest pagan thought into the Christian tradition. Rtishchev shared many of these goals, though his intellectual surrounding was not as advanced as Western Europe at the end of the fifteenth century. Russia had no universities in the middle of the seventeenth century. Most Russian priests could not even attend the few poor seminaries which existed at that time. If a handful of Muscovites made an effort to acquire a semblance of higher learning, most saw no need of "foreign knowledge." Even those who demanded the reform of popular morals often saw no need for "learning," a thing tainted with foreign "heresy" and hence likely to sow confusion in the Third Rome. Moreover, educated Greeks who appeared in Moscow in these years hardly inspired confidence that what they had to offer would make ignorant people better Christians. "Greek" was a byword in Russia for one who is shifty, greedy, unprincipled. "Judas sold Christ once," it was often said, and "the Greeks sell Him to us a thousand times!"

Russians who did hope to draw upon Greek learning were grateful for the fact that the Ukraine in recent times had begun to feel the influence of Greek letters. The Ukraine was under Polish rule, but its people were linked ethnically to the Slavs who populated Muscovy. Faced with Catholic competition, the Ukrainian Orthodox Church was forced to produce a more educated, articulate clergy. Peter Mogila, the talented, energetic metropolitan of Kiev, formed his celebrated Academy in 1632. This was a true center of higher learning, and the Ukrainian priests who mastered its curriculum were brought into the mainstream of the Eastern Orthodox Church. Ukrainian scholars could then bring their learning to Moscow. A few appeared in Moscow towards the end of Michael's riegn to educate Russians, to make new Slavic translations of church literature, and to correct "errors" which over the years had slipped into older Russian liturgical texts.

Fedor Rtishchev was anxious to establish an academy in Moscow patterned after Mogila's Academy. For this purpose, in 1649 he took over the Church of St. Andrew at the abandoned Monastery of the Lord's Transfiguration on the bank of the Moscow River, near Sparrow Hills. Two dozen Ukrainian monks eventually made their way here. Rtishchev wanted the learned brothers to translate new texts into Russian, to teach philosophy and grammar, rhetoric and logic. The chambers of the cloister rang into the night with friendly discussions between Rtishchev and the masters, while by day he encouraged officials to accompany him to St. Andrew's to learn Greek and other esoteric subjects. And, Rtishchev was close to Tsar Alexis. Day after day, for hours on end, he regaled the eager young tsar with his visions of the future. Alexis helped Rtishchev organize the academy. Personal inquiries from the tsar brought Damascene Ptitsky, Arsenius Satanovsky, and Epiphanius Slavinetsky from the Ukraine to Moscow in 1649 and 1650. By that time Muscovite monks and priests were flocking to the cloister at St. Andrew, creating what Klyuchevsky called a "fraternity of scholars, a free academy of learning."

Tsar Alexis was closely attached to other reformers as well, notably a band of sturdy, remarkable clergy known as the "Zealots of Piety." These men had spoken out as early as the mid-1630s against the condition of the Church and society of the Third Rome. They were delighted that one of their number, Joseph, was elected patriarch in 1642, and that three years later the equally devout Alexis became tsar.

Over the next several years Alexis did much to help the Zealots in their work. The ban against smoking issued under Michael was reaffirmed in the new Law Code of 1649. Offenders were to be whipped and their nostrils slit–even the death penalty could be inflicted for use of tobacco. The tsar also took action against public profanity. "Certain secretly appointed people were sent to mix with the crowd on the street and in the markets," says Olearius, and with the help of the musketeers and the executioners assigned to them "were to seize swearers and punish them on the spot by beating." Alexis and the Zealots likewise struck out against music and the popular festivals which so fascinated the common people. Instruments often were seized by the wagonload in Moscow and burned. Avvakum, the famous defender of the old faith, relates an amusing incident about a troup of comedians with two dancing bears who came to his village. The rugged Avvakum attacked this party single-handed! He dispersed the actors, broke their drums and masks on a field outside the village, and clubbed one of the bears senseless. The bear revived, "and the other I let go into the open country."

Alexis and the Zealots attempted to combat drunkeness throughout Russia. During Michael's reign tavernkeepers encouraged their customers to drink as much as they could, for if a year's profits did not equal those of the previous year, the tavernkeeper had to make up the difference from his own pocket. The Zealots in 1651 persuaded Alexis to begin to abolish this accounting system. Some taverns were closed, others were to sell vodka only in quantities large enough, it was hoped, to make strong drink less available to the lower class people who abused it the most.

The efforts of the Zealots had mixed results. Some observers claimed that fewer drunks ran naked and screaming through the street. Popular musicals and shows generally were driven from the cities and towns, but the war against profanity, smoking and heavy drinking failed terribly. Yet the Zealots did not give up. If anything, their failure to reform society made them struggle all the more to purify the Church. Meanwhile, an amazing religious revival also was sweeping through Russia. During the first years of Alexis' reign peasants in remote areas formed holy communities, while in other places Vernadsky notes that simple women guarded their churches, driving away drunks and urging the better-behaved parishoners who remained to think earnestly upon the beauty and mystery of the Mass.

The tsar's confessor and leader of the Zealots, Stefan Vonifatiev, searched out fiery evangelists in every corner of the realm—brave priests and deacons ready to reintroduce the church sermon as a means of calling the people to God. The most celebrated revivalist of the day was the passionate Ivan Neronov. Born into a peasant family in the Vologodsky district in 1591, Ivan was mystical and pious from his earliest years. Neronov denounced the drunken, immoral priest of his village so harshly that Ivan was forced to flee in the night. For a time he was at the Trinity Monastery near Moscow and befriended the scholar Dionysius. But Neronov's restless, combative nature did not let him settle down to the correction of church books. As a priest in northern Russia, he was often beaten for attacking bear shows and other popular entertainments. After one such occasion Neronov was punished by public flogging, then imprisoned for forty days before the order came from the capital to set him free.

Neronov met Vonifatiev and Rtishchev on a visit to Moscow in 1649. They insisted he stay in the city, where in a short time Neronov became a fantastically popular preacher. The crowds were so large when he held forth in the Cathedral of Our Lady of Kazan that people spilled into the streets and packed the square before the church. Brave souls precariously perched at windows and at other odd scraps of space. The thunder of Neronov's voice blended with shouts and groans from the congregation until, at last, he too broke into tears.

The religious passion of these days is seen also in the dramatic Easter celebration of 1652. Foreigners living in Russia for more than a half century told the Swedish diplomat de Rodes that "they had not seen the Russians observe their fast so strictly as in that year." Some enthusiasts, "who perhaps wanted to be taken for saints," died of starvation, while opposite extremists emerged from Easter week so emaciated that, in a fit of passion they took the last rites and ate themselves to death.

The devout mood of the capital was heightened still further by the discovery and veneration of the relics of certain Russian saints in early 1652. The solemn reburial of Patriarchs Job and Hermogen in Moscow and of St. Sabba the Miracle-worker at nearby Zvenigorod greatly stirred the emotions of the faithful. Reports flooded into Moscow at this time that miracles suddenly were occuring at the tomb of Metropolitan Philip at the Solovetsky Monastery, on the bleak shores of the White Sea. Such healings were positive proof that Philip was a saint, and Alexis dispatched Nikon, metropolitan of Novgorod and his close friend, to fetch Philip's body back to Moscow.

Nikon returned to the capital on July 6, 1652. As he approached the city Moscow lay spread out before him shimmering in the sunlight, bells ringing from the onion-domed churches which guarded every street. The tsar, church dignitaries, and crown officials stood in magnificent robes with the common people outside the city to greet him. Waxlights flickered, banners waved and icons were held high to mark this solemn moment.

Moscow had just been swept by a great fire which destroyed a third of the city and caused widespread suffering and death. This surely encouraged the popular passion for St. Philip which was to come. His relics were on public display for three days, reverenced and kissed by the faithful. Paul of Aleppo was later told that "St. Philip performed a number of miracles—opening the eyes of the blind, raising the sick from their chairs and couches, and curing demoniacs—before they carried him to the Cathedral of the Assumption on July 9 and placed him in a silver-gilt shrine . . . where he still works many miracles." Moscow was at that moment in what Baron aptly calls "a state of religious exaltation."

While the people were dazzled by miracles at St. Philip's shrine, Alexis and his advisers confronted the thorny issue of selecting a new leader of the Church. Patriarch Joseph had died on April 15, and Alexis was only waiting for Nikon's return to ask him to become patriarch. Events were to show this choice to be one of the most fateful decisions of Alexis' entire reign.

Chapter Five

A SPECIAL FRIEND

Alexis was seventeen when he met Nikon in 1646, and Nikon was forty-one. Life had been extremely hard for this peasant boy, born Nikita Minov in the bleak, snow-bound region of Nizhnyi Novgorod. His mother died while Nikita was an infant, and to escape the cruelty of his step-mother he entered a monastery at the age of twelve. His father per-suaded him to return to the world, and to marry. Nikita was a bright student, and by the time he was twenty had acquired more than enough education to be ordained a priest. Minov was such a successful preacher that after two years a group of Moscow merchants brought him to their parish, where he served successfully for a decade.

Tragedy now fell upon Nikita's house. When his three sons died sud-denly and almost at the same time, Nikita and his wife took this as a sign that they should abandon the world and spend the remainder of their lives in devotion and prayer. She entered a convent at Moscow in 1634, he was tonsured as Brother Nikon at the tiny Anzer Monastery on the harsh, frozen shore of the White Sea. Nikon now plunged into intensive study, acquiring the remarkable knowledge of scripture, church history, doctrine, and law which guided his career in later years. He also devoured the lives of the hermits and saints, as if to penetrate the secret of their faith so that he might pattern his life after theirs. Nikon's devo-tions were incredible, even by Russian standards. He did a thousand genuflections daily, and prayed and fasted with such severity that he had visions. Nikon accused his fellow monks of insufficient zeal and, after a quarrel, left Anzer for the Kozheozersky Monastery in 1641. The brothers here were so taken with Nikon that against his will they elected him abbot in 1643. Located in Novgorod province fifty miles from the nearest inhabited spot, the monastery grew and prospered under Nikon's leadership.

Nikon's fame now spread even to the capital, where Vonifatiev vigilantly awaited news of every man who might be useful in renewing the spiritual life of the nation. During a visit to Moscow on monastery business in 1646 Nikon met Vonifatiev, who then presented him to the tsar. Contemporaries often speak of Nikon's imposing six-foot, six-inch frame, of the tragic intensity which beamed from his eyes and stern brow. Little wonder that Alexis and his confessor immediately fell under the sway of Nikon's physical presence and magnetic personality. Alexis had Nikon appointed abbot of the New Monastery of the Savior so that he might remain in Moscow. Sometimes Alexis visited the monastery. Every Friday morning Nikon celebrated morning Mass for the tsar at the Kremlin, after which Alexis engaged his "special friend," as he soon came to call Nikon, in intense, far-ranging discussions. In these talks Nikon expressed social and political—as well as religious—concerns, and Alexis ordered him to make it his duty to intercede on behalf of widows and orphans, to defend the poor who were oppressed by the mighty, even to release prisoners from the jails as he saw fit. Now all could see that Nikon was a rising star. Petitions poured into his monastery, people detained him on the road to hear their requests. In 1648 Alexis made Nikon metropolitan of Novgorod, the second highest position in the Russian Church. When Nikon returned to the capital to winter with the tsar, many asked if it were not simply a question of time until he would become patriarch.

The following year, 1649, was enormously significant in shaping the future relationship between Alexis and Nikon. In Novgorod Nikon immediately showed himself to be a brilliant leader of the Church. He used the new learning to correct local church books. Nikon also implemented the program of the Zealots by introducing sermons into the Mass and rejecting illiterate or unqualified candidates for the priesthood. He even imprisoned and excommunicated offending clergy. At Novgorod Nikon also grew "attached to ecclesiastical splendor and magnificance," which Billington thinks compensated Nikon "for the bleakness of the region and the asceticism of his personal life." Moreover, Nikon persuaded the tsar to grant his bishopric certain privileges.

In particular, the Novgorod monasteries were exempted from the jurisdiction of the Department of Monastery Lands, the crown office

NIKON, THE MOST TALENTED PATRIARCH IN THE HISTORY OF THE RUSSIAN CHURCH. His determination to elevate the powers of the patriarchate reminds one of such popes as Gregory VII and Innocent III. Like them, he was called ambitious. Yet this ambition was not a personal greed for honor and power, but rather a conviction that his office deserved the highest respect. Nikon is depicted here in everyday dress.

created in 1649 to oversee church estates. Nikon even made clear to Alexis that, although he signed the new Law Code, he disapproved of the manner in which it curbed the traditional rights of the Church.

Alexis in 1649 began to develop a broader view of the role the Russian Church should play in the rulership of the kingdom and in the Eastern Orthodox world. It is paradoxical, perhaps, but in the very years Alexis deprived the Church of *economic* privileges, he elevated its *political* status. This resulted from a dramatic visit of Patriarch Paisios of Jerusalem who arrived in Moscow on January 27, 1649. Like so many other dignitaries from the Orthodox East in these years, Paisios had journeyed to Moscow for "alms," for the generous financial support Alexis granted fellow Christians suffering the Turkish yoke. Paisios tactfully lectured Alexis on the responsibilities which were coming to fall upon him and his Church. Russia was the home of the only Orthodox Church independent of Moslem or Catholic power. Should not Russia help liberate the less fortunate Christians of the East? The Ukraine was then in rebellion against Poland. In fact, on his way north in December, Paisios chanced to be in Kiev to witness the triumphal entry of the rebel leader Bogdan Khmelnitsky into the city. If Khmelnitsky finally proved unable to free the Ukraine on his own, would not Alexis have the obligation to help? Paisios called upon Alexis to be a "new Moses," to "assume the high throne of the great Emperor Constantine" and to "liberate pious Orthodox Christians from unclean hands, from wild beasts—and shine like a sun among the stars."

Alexis knew the power of Poland and Turkey too well to give Paisios hasty promises. Yet he did begin to meditate on the future role that he, his state, and his Church might play in the Orthodox world. This may explain another crucial innovation in November, 1651. From that time Patriarch Joseph joined his signature with that of Alexis on state documents, as if to emphasize that in Holy Russia the tsar and patriarch somehow jointly ruled the land. What lay behind this innovation, destined in time to bear such stormy consequences? Joseph was hardly responsible for the departure. Unassertive by nature, he was dying in these months and everyone knew it. Do we already see Nikon's iron march to power? The metropolitan of Novgorod certainly believed, as Alexis did, in the moral unity of church and state. Great as Nikon's influence was with the tsar, it rose still higher when Nikon subdued the Novgorod riots of 1650 peacefully and without aid from Moscow. In 1651 Nikon again journeyed to Moscow to winter with the tsar.

The transfer of the relics of St. Philip from the Solovetsky Monastery to Moscow in 1652 had the effect of humbling Alexis still further before the Church. Metropolitan Philip was nothing less than a martyr to the tyranny of the crown. Daring to speak out against the brutal policies of Ivan the Terrible, he was murdered at Ivan's orders in 1569 and buried at the White Sea, far from the tsar's evil view. The miracles suddenly worked at his tomb showed that Philip was not merely a martyr, but a saint. Nikon suggested to Alexis that Philip be brought to Moscow at the time the remains of Job and Hermogen were being laid in the Cathedral of the Assumption. The tsar did not reply immediately to this suggestion. At a church synod in Moscow on March 20, 1652, however, Alexis announced his decision. He told Patriarch Joseph, Nikon and the other assembled churchmen that Philip had appeared to him recently in dreams, saying: "It is long that I lie away from the tombs of my fellow metropolitans; send for me and bring me to them."

"And so," Alexis concluded, "I have long wanted to bring the relics of St. Philip to Moscow, and to place them in the Cathedral of the Assumption."

Nikon was dispatched to the Solovetsky Monastery with a curious letter from the tsar to be read at Philip's tomb just before it was opened. Addressing the saint as if he were still alive, Alexis begged him to come to Moscow "to absolve the transgressions of my great-grandfather, Tsar Ivan." The letter continued: "Yes, it is I, Tsar Alexis, who wish to see thee and prostrate myself before thy saintly remains." In this way Alexis hoped that Philip would forgive the dead tsar and bless his own reign.

While Nikon was gone from Moscow, Patriarch Joseph died. Many of the Zealots petitioned the tsar and his consort to make Stefan Vonifatiev the new patriarch. Not considering himself qualified for the office, Stefan recommended Nikon—who was also Alexis' choice. Alexis wrote Nikon in May 1652, praising him and begging him to become the new leader of the Church, "so that there may be elected to the patriarchate a man known to God." Alexis declared that "without you we shall not undertake anything at all," and in his own hand he signed this message, "God's servant, Alexis, Tsar of all Russia."

Nikon finally returned to the capital on July 6, 1652. In later years Avvakum recalled that when Nikon arrived "he played the fox with us, and it was bowings and scrapings and 'Good morrow to you!' for he knew he was to be patriarch and wished to remove all obstacles thereto."

Whatever Nikon's motives were in these days, when a church synod formally offered Nikon the patriarchate on July 23 all were surprised to see him boycott the meeting and refuse the office. Following Russian custom, the synod then drew lots bearing the names of Nikon and two abbots. The honor fell to Antony, one of Nikon's teachers. Because of age and to please the tsar, Antony declined the patriarchate. Alexis reiterated his desire that Nikon be chosen, and the synod sent word to Nikon that it had picked him a second time. But Nikon, who learned that Antony had been properly selected, refused the office even more firmly than before. He begged to be left in peace as metropolitan of Novgorod. More delegations were sent to Nikon—all returned emptyhanded. Alexis finally sent a group of high officials of church and crown to bring Nikon to the Cathedral of the Assumption—by force, if necessary.

Were these refusals a ploy on Nikon's part? Did he think he would be begged to accept the patriarchate, and that in the process his final authority would be greatly strengthened? Perhaps. Yet it is doubtful that Nikon was motivated solely by greed for power. If we consider Nikon's entire life, it seems that at this moment he felt he could not be *burdened* with leadership of the Church unless he also had power to bring about the changes he felt had to occur. Foreseeing opposition to his policies, Nikon had to have the undivided loyalty of the tsar and boyars, as well as church leaders. Thus, at the cathedral, Nikon once more refused the patriarchate.

"I am not of sufficient capacity to be primate," he pleaded.

Then came a dramatic sight. The tsar and everyone in the church fell to the pavement before Nikon, and in tears again begged him to accept the office. Astonished at Alexis' humility, Nikon raised the tsar to his feet and joined everyone in sobbing openly. A moment passed. "Then I remembered," Nikon later reflected, "that the heart of the king is in the hand of God, and I feared any longer to refuse."

Nikon reminded his people that, although Russia was a Christian land, "yet in practice we follow neither the canons of the Apostles and church Fathers, nor the laws of the Holy emperors." If you want me to be your patriarch, Nikon continued, "give me your word and take a vow in this holy apostolic cathedral church, before our Lord and Savior, Jesus Christ, and before the holy gospel and before the most holy Mother of God and before His holy angels and all the saints, to keep Christ's evangelical dogmas and the rules of the holy apostles and of the holy fathers, and the laws of the pious emperors intact."

Nikon's closing words were of the greatest significance: "If you also promise sincerely to obey us, as your superior and pastor and most esteemed father, *in all that I shall make known to you* of God's dogmas and of the laws, for the sake of this, for your desire and your petition, I cannot refuse this great pontificate."

Alexis, tears streaming from his eyes, joined the others in begging Nikon to become patriarch. The assembled company accepted all of

Nikon's terms, and sealed their agreement on the Holy Gospels before the tomb of St. Philip. Two days later, on July 25, Metropolitan Cornelius, a Zealot who had joined Avvakum in petitioning Alexis to make Stefan Vonifatiev patriarch, consecrated Nikon to the office. The new patriarch then made the traditional procession around the walls of Moscow on a horse, the bridle of which was held by Alexis himself. A banquet in the palace and the exchange of presents between the tsar and the patriarch ended the ceremony.

No one in Moscow knew that beneath the pomp and ceremony of these days the patriarch and the tsar had reached an important—and unprecedented—secret agreement. In later years, when Nikon had fallen from power and suffered countless tribulations, he reminded Alexis that in deep confidence they had reached an understanding that Nikon would serve as patriarch for three years. This would give Nikon the opportunity to test the loyalty of the tsar and his court. Alexis would then decide whether or not to support Nikon as patriarch for another term.

For the moment, however, Alexis had no doubts. "You are my special friend," the tsar told Nikon. "In you I have found someone to lead the church and advise me in governing the land." Nikon gravely nodded agreement at these words—and moved to shake the foundations of the Third Rome.

Chapter Six

ALEXIS AND THE WEST

While Nikon was leading a religious procession in Moscow in September 1652 he noticed that some of the people lining his way were not bowing and making the sign of the cross in response to his blessing. When told these people were foreigners, the new patriarch grew angry. "It is not right that the unworthy foreigners thus should receive a blessing not intended for them," Nikon exclaimed. The patriarch was determined that foreigners never again would blend into crowds with Russians. An order was issued "to all the foreigners to divest themselves of Russian clothes forthwith, and," according to Olearius, "to dress, in the future, in the garb of their own country."

Though hostility to the foreigner in Russia was reaching a high point by this time, Alexis had been confronted by swelling xenophobia since the beginning of his reign. Russian churchmen brooded over the likelihood that western customs and faiths were contaminating their people. Russian merchants complained about their difficulties in competing with foreign traders, and submitted eight petitions between 1627 and 1648 calling upon Michael and Alexis to limit foreigners' commercial activity to wholesale trade at border towns. Patriarch Joseph often grumbled to Alexis that foreigners built churches and chapels in the capital, wore Russian clothing, lived next to Russians, and hired them as servants. Joseph recommended that foreign officers, craftsmen and merchants be permitted to live only in Russian border towns, not in the interior.

Alexis sympathized with the love for church and country connected with these complaints, but he was unwilling to accept the demands themselves. Alexis knew that Russia needed more foreign officers to command and train Russian troops if Russia were ever to become as powerful as the West. As for European craftsmen and imports, the tsar took a very personal interest in obtaining them for his country. Instructions penned in the tsar's own hand called upon agents going abroad to buy military goods, to recruit foreign specialists for work in Russia.

Friendly as he was to the West, Alexis soon came into sharp conflict with the English. The Russian government had long regretted that Ivan the Terrible had granted English merchants—the first to reach Archangel by sea—duty-free trade rights in Russia. The Dutch and traders of other nationalities soon proved more competitive than the English, but they had to pay customs fees. Still, Alexis hoped for good relations with England, and in 1645 Ambassador Gerasim Dokhturov was sent to inform Whitehall that Alexis was the new tsar. Civil war then had broken out between Charles I and the merchants of London, whose distant colleagues operated in Muscovy. Parliament offered to receive Dokhturov's credentials, but he refused to present them to anyone but the king. Alexis was furious over Dokhturov's reports on the English situation: "And now Parliament instead of the king governs London and the entire English and Scotch land; counselors (dumnye liudi) are elected from every class. . . . And the king has begun to do everything according to Parliament's will." Alexis openly supported his brother monarch by letting Charles' agents buy grain at low prices as his contest with Parliament resumed in the coming months.

News came to Moscow in the summer of 1649 that Charles I had been executed that January. Alexis issued a stormy edict on June 1 against "you English" who "have done a great wickedness by killing your sovereign, King Charles." For this "evil deed," the tsar concluded, "you cannot be suffered to remain in the realm of Muscovy." English merchants lost their duty-free trade privileges and might operate only at Archangel.

Russian hostility to foreigners also appeared in the new Law Code of 1649. Churchmen long had opposed letting Russian servants work for foreigners who were "un-baptized," that is, who had not joined the Orthodox Church. These households did not observe Russian fasts, and even if they denied meat to their domestics on those days, the odor of cooking meat would ruin the Russians' fast! Churchmen petitioned Michael in 1628 to prohibit foreigners from hiring Russians for house service so that "Christian souls would not be defiled and would not die without confession." Thus, not surprisingly, the Law Code Alexis proclaimed in 1649 forbade Russians to serve un-baptized foreigners as domestics. The code also made clear that the government did not intend to let more un-baptized foreigners settle in Moscow, specifying that in the future such people may not buy or mortgage houses and house lots from Russians," while Russians caught participating in such transactions "will be in great disgrace before the Sovereign." What of churches in the homes of foreigners? "Tear down such churches!" the code proclaimed. "Henceforth there will be no churches in foreigners' houses" within Moscow. Non-Orthodox places of worship "must be out of town, beyond Zemlyagorod, in distant places away from God's churches."

The situation in 1652 was even more difficult for foreigners in Russia than during the earlier years of Alexis' reign. Nationalists moved to apply laws which earlier had lain on the books unenforced. A church synod in March 1652 spelled out punishments both for Russian domestics and the "unbaptized pagans" they were caught serving. First offenders were beaten with sticks. Whipping came for a second offense. A third transgression brought a stiffer lashing, after which both ears were cut off and the guilty person was exiled to Siberia. "This is now strictly carried out," Johann de Rodes reported to the Swedish government from Moscow that month. According to Rodes, some ten or twenty musketeers went about Moscow, unexpectedly descending upon the homes of foreigners, punishing guilty servants and masters. When several foreigners of long residence in Moscow offered to observe Russian fasts if only they might keep Russian servants, they were sharply advised to convert.

The Lesley case was reaching its sensational high point at this very moment. Alexander Lesley was an elderly Scotch general who had been in Russian service for more than two decades. He often went to Holland, Germany and Sweden to buy military supplies and to recruit mercenaries and artisans. Enjoying the confidence of both Michael and Alexis, Lesley may have been singled out for this very reason. Lesley's wife—"an intelligent and conscientious housekeeper"—was accused by her servants of beating them, giving them dog meat on fast days, keeping them from church with difficult work and, "what was most reprehensible of all," clucks Olearius, to have tossed an icon into a glowing oven, "where it was consumed." Her husband and Lieutenant William Thompson were charged with firing at a cross atop a Russian church.

The Lesleys, their children and servants were dragged to Moscow for an inquest. The lady admitted she worked the servants strictly, but the couple denied all other charges. Some servants backed the Lesleys' case even under threat of torture, but the general and his wife were able to stay in Russia only by agreeing to join the Russian Church. De Rodes reported in March 1652 that other unbaptized foreigners were threatened with the loss of their estates unless they followed the Lesleys' example, and that most foreign officers at this point wanted to flee Russia. Meanwhile, Stefan Vonifatiev promised Alexis that if given a free hand, by New Year's Day (September 1, according to the Russian calendar) he would bring almost all unbaptized foreigners in Russian service into the true church.

Alexis suffered great pressures in early 1652 to take sweeping action against unbaptized foreigners. Patriarch Joseph tried to persuade the tsar that unconverted foreigners should give up their estates, and not be given new ones in the future. Olearius observes that after Joseph "lit the fire" on this issue the boyars at court "who had long wished to lay their greedy hands on the well-run estates of the foreigners, assiduously heaped wood on it. Every day they urged His Tsarist Majesty to carry out the just petition of the Patriarch."

But Alexis resisted these pressures. He knew that confiscation of the lands of non-Orthodox foreigners would drive invaluable soldiers, craftsmen and other skilled people from Russia and leave no hope of recruiting similar people in the future. Alexis did not want this to happen, not even if it meant disregarding the advice of Nikon and his other favorites. The chance for a compromise of sorts came when Lesley agreed to be baptized.

According to Olearius, his family stayed at a monastery for six weeks taking instruction "in the articles of faith, and especially in the ceremonies, of the Russian church." They were then immersed in water, taking the baptismal names Avraam and Evdokaya (Abraham and Eudocia). Miloslavsky and his wife stood as Godparents to the Lesleys, gave them elegant Russian clothes and sponsored their Orthodox remarriage in their home. Alexis showed his pleasure at their conversion by granting the new Russians a present of 3,000 rubles. Alexis was thus hoping to show nationalists that persuasion and reward could gain converts, while demonstrating to non-baptized foreigners the advantages of conversion. But few foreigners followed the example of the Lesleys, probably no more than a dozen. The Russian calendar year seemed to be ending by late August in defeat for the Church. Foreigners remained in Moscow, they still held land and received salaries, and they sometimes even ignored the restrictions of the Law Code of 1649.

A dramatic change in the fortunes of the nationalist party came with the Russian New Year. As we have seen, Nikon secured a decree in September 1652 preventing non-baptized foreigners from wearing Russian clothes. And this was not a mere paper edict. Olearius tells of the consternation the order caused in the foreign camp. Some foreigners could not get tailors to make them new clothes right away, yet their standing at court demanded they be there without interruption. Many appeared in clothes which had laid molding in trunks since the Livonian War seventy or more years before. "These clothes occasioned no little laughter, not only because of the antiquated and diverse styles but also because the garments were too big for some and too small for others."

A still greater victory for xenophobia came a few days later, on October 4, 1652. Alexis decreed that all non-baptized foreigners were to vacate their houses in Moscow and move a half mile east of the city wall to an area reserved to them alone. This spot on the Yauza River came to be known as the "Foreign Quarter," the *Nemetskaya sloboda*. In retrospect, this microcosm of the West in Muscovy clearly fostered—not retarded—Western influence in Russia. But at the time everyone thought that the Russian nationalists had won a great victory. Foreigners now dressed in a distinctive way, and most were removed from "unnecessary" contact with Russians. For a time foreigners were even forced to hire Poles and Mongols as domestics.

Braced by his victory over the foreigners, Nikon now turned his attention to a more explosive issue—reform of the Church.

Chapter Seven

NIKON SHAKES THE THIRD ROME

Nikon was angered at how crown officials had treated the Church in the early years of Alexis' reign. Nikon joined Patriarch Joseph and other church leaders in signing the Law Code of 1649, but privately they were furious that the clergy was being stripped of property rights enjoyed in the past. As metropolitan of Novgorod, Nikon persuaded the tsar to exempt monastery lands of the area from government control. The Zealots of Piety and other churchmen applauded Nikon's obvious ability to defend church interests against crown authority.

As patriarch, Nikon launched a broader offensive to loosen the crown's hold over the Church. Nikon failed to have the Monastery Office closed, but many of its powers were abolished. The Office came to exercise jurisdiction only in civil suits between peasants living on monastery estates. The monasteries themselves regulated their holdings, as was the case before 1649. Nikon even persuaded Alexis to renew the charter Michael had granted his father (Patriarch Filaret) in 1625—a charter which had lapsed with Filaret's death—making the patriarch supreme over church lands. This increased Nikon's revenues, and made the Church virtually independent of the state. These power moves were capped by a quiet maneuver on Nikon's part to establish the argument that the Church is superior to the state: the patriarch introduced into Russian church records a new translation of the "Donation of Constantine."

The Donation of Constantine remains one of the most celebrated forgeries of all time. The document tells us that the Roman Emperor Constantine was stricken with leprosy while persecuting the Christians. No one could cure him. As death approached it was suggested that Sylvester, the Bishop of Rome, could heal him—if he would. The Pope had mercy on the emperor, came out of hiding and restored his health. A grateful Constantine not only adopted the Christian faith but, planning in any case to establish a "New Rome" (Constantinople) and move to the East, "donated" his Western lands to Sylvester and his successor bishops. Constantine is made to admit in a discussion with Sylvester that the "imperial power" is but "earthly," while the papal throne "shall be gloriously exalted above our empire and earthly throne." The relevance of this to Russia, of course, came from the conviction that Moscow as the "Third Rome" inherited all the historic rights of the "First Rome," the western Church.

It was to take Nikon several years to demonstrate the explosive implications of the "Donation" for his church and the Muscovite state. For the moment, however, he moved so cautiously as to trigger no controversy. Although the Renaissance scholar Lorenzo Valla had exposed the document as a forgery in 1439, in abridged form it was included in the records of the Russian church council of 1551. Whereas Patriarch Joseph omitted it from the Russian code of canon law known as the *Pilot Book* printed in 1650, Nikon placed the full text in his edition of 1653.

The Zealots of Piety were pleased over Nikon's efforts to make the Church more independent of the crown. They had been distressed to see the Church lose privileges in the early years of Alexis' reign, and were glad to see them restored—and even broadened—so quickly. The Zealots also hoped that Nikon would continue on a national scale the efforts he had made in Novgorod to reform popular morals. Indeed, Alexis was persuaded to take a new measure to reduce popular drunkenness by decreeing that after September 1, 1652 each village would have only one liquor store. Sales were limited to a bottle per customer, nothing was to be consumed at the shop, and no sales were permitted on Sunday or during important fasts.

Nikon "ordered the destruction of any tavern musicians' instruments seen in the streets" in the summer of 1653. Olearius further relates that the patriarch then "banned instrumental music altogether, and ordered the seizure of musical instruments in the houses." On one occasion, five wagon loads of instruments "were sent across the Moscow River and burned there." Foreigners managed to retain their instruments, nonetheless, as did such important Russians as Nikita Romanov. But other Russians felt the pinch of Nikon's puritanical campaign. A foreign diplomat in January 1653 reported that, though the tsar was still hunting bear, wolf and fox outside Moscow, upon Nikon's urging "he ordered the taming or death of all the wild bears and wolves kept in cages for the local hunters."

Nikon and the Zealots parted company on the matter of bringing the Russian Church into line with international Eastern Orthodox practice. Nikon knew the Russian Church was about to come into increasing contact with its neighbors. Muscovites no longer could ignore the "mistakes" in their liturgy and church books, or claim that the Third Rome was in the right and that others should change to meet Russian standards. Nikon was urging that Russia go to war with Poland to regain the Ukraine and Belorussia. If Russia were victorious, eventually this would bring the Church in these areas under the jurisdiction of the patriarch of Moscow. The Ukrainian and Belorussian Churches already had been "reformed" along Greek lines, a fact which gave further strength to the argument that the Russian Church must abandon the national peculiarities which its Mass and liturgy had developed over the years. In his more daring moments Nikon dreamed that Russia would be recognized universally as the center of Eastern Christianity, and that the four great patriarchs of the East—Constantinople, Jerusalem, Antioch and Alexandria—would appear on Russian soil to concelebrate Mass with their colleague from Moscow. Alexis' own visions of greatness among emperors and kings made him all the more disposed to support Nikon's program for church reform.

The Zealots of Piety, on the other hand, were suspicious of "Greek things," even when they came by way of the Ukraine. "The saints of old were greater than we," they often observed. "How could their practices be wrong?" "Byzantium fell to the Turks because of the sins of the people," it was further claimed. "How, then, could Greek ways be superior to ours?"

The Zealots were bitterly suspicious of Fedor Rtishchev's "love of learning," and they brooded anxiously over Patriarch Paisios' visit to Moscow in 1649. Stefan Vonifatiev and his friends rejected the visions of greatness some entertained for the Third Rome beyond the lands of Muscovy, and when Paisios left for home in June the Zealots saw that he was accompanied by Arseny Sukhanov. This Russian monk was educated in Greek letters, but he heatedly denied the Greek contention that theirs was the best way, and that the Russian Church should modify itself to that standard. Arseny was ordered to tour the Balkans and the Christian East from Egypt to Georgia, observing Christian practices and collecting Greek texts for a more careful examination in Moscow.

Arseny returned to Moscow in June 1653 with, as Vernadsky (our authority on this entire matter) says, "a vast and immensely valuable collection of Greek manuscripts which he deposited in the Moscow Printing Office Library, as well as a number of modern Greek church books printed in Venice." Arseny had sad tales to tell of Greek intolerance towards the smallest deviations from their practices. For his part, Arseny had defended—with skill and good sense—practices peculiar to Russia as products of ancient custom fully harmonious with the spirit of Christ's church. The conclusion Arseny drew from his travels was that Russian tradition should stand its ground as inferior to that of no other land.

Clever as his arguments were, Arseny could see plainly that the Moscow he had returned to was in the hands of Nikon's Greek and pro-Greek Slavic scholars. Among their most distinguished representatives was Arsenios, a Greek scholar who arrived with Paisios in 1649 and remained in Moscow to help revise Russian church books to bring them into conformity with Byzantine originals. Arsenios had some difficult moments when his Russian hosts learned that not only had he studied philosophy and medicine in Italy, but had been baptized there into the Roman Catholic Church! Still more damaging was the revelation that Arsenios later had converted to Islam, and had served the Turks in Moldavia and Wallachia. All this confirmed the darkest suspicions of Russian conservatives that Greek learning was tainted by non-Orthodox influences, and strengthened their argument that the Third Rome had nothing good to "learn" from the outside world. But Nikon decided to trust the thoroughly apologetic Arsenios, and fetched him from a prison cell at the Solovetsky Monastery to the Printing Office in Moscow. Arsenios worked there with Slavinctsky and others at correcting Slavic translations of Greek church literature. Their work became all the more urgent in 1652, when war loomed with Poland for the Ukraine and Belorussia.

The implications of scholarship for even simple Russians became clear in early 1653. The new psalter ready for publication reduced to four the number of genuflections in the prayer of Ephraem of Syria during Lent, and specified that three fingers must be used to make the sign of the cross. When Nikon's orders to print this manuscript reached the Moscow Printing Office, Ivan Nasedka, its editor, and two associates, resigned in protest. Nevertheless, the new psalter was published on February 11, 1653, in time for Lent.

Nikon issued a pastoral letter commanding his flock to observe four genuflections during Ephraem's prayer and to make the sign of the cross with three fingers; the twelve traditional prostrations to the knee would become half bows to the waist. Seeing the consternation these changes caused the Zealots, Nikon tried to reconcile them by promoting close associates of Cornelius and Neronov to high church office. But the Zealots were not to be bought off with such trifles. Like many Russians, they were firmly attached to every detail of the old Mass as the true and beautiful manifestation of Christ's presence among the people of Russia. To change the Mass would be to abandon what was right for something else. If those outside the Third Rome celebrated the liturgy differently, was it not clear that they were the ones who should change—not those who held to the way of the saints?

Avvakum tells us in moving terms what Nikon's February decree meant to him and his friends. The cold and gloom of the Russian winter break in that month, the days grow brighter and the spirits of the people are raised. But not for Avvakum, not that year. "We met together and took counsel" after receiving Nikon's order, he later recalled. "It was as if winter was of a mind to come; our hearts froze, our limbs trembled." Neronov, the leader of the dissenters at that time, retired to a monastery where he spent a week immersed in prayer. Then a voice spoke from an icon of the Savior: "The hour of tribulation has come; it behooves you to suffer and be strong." So it was to be.

Neronov huddled with Avvakum, Bishop Paul of Kolomna, Archpriest Daniel of Kostroma and "all the brothers" at Moscow who were ready to resist Nikon's innovations. Avvakum and Daniel drafted an answer to the reforms demanded in Nikon's letter, a counterstatement which was submitted to the patriarch himself.

Nikon would not withdraw his reforms, nor would he tolerate those who spoke out against the innovations. Quite the contrary, Nikon broadened the controversy by striking out at his critics. Daniel was arrested. So that he could be subjected to monastic discipline, he was shorn as a monk. Avvakum tells us that Nikon tore off Daniel's cassock and "insulting him the while, had him taken to the Miracle Monastery and put in the bakehouse." Daniel eventually ended up in Astrakhan where, if we are to believe Avvakum, he was cast into a dungeon with a crown of thorns on his head to die. When Neronov protested Daniel's imprisonment, he too was jailed.

Avvakum was the next to feel Nikon's wrath. Musketeers arrested Avvakum while he was celebrating vespers, and imprisoned him in the patriarch's residence for three days with nothing to eat or drink. ("No one came to me but mice and black beetles, and the crickets chirped, and of fleas there was an abundance.") Avvakum was dragged about, beaten, spat upon and cursed—but nothing shook his will to resist. Then came the passion of Archpriest Longin of Murom. In the very presence of Alexis and Maria, the archpriest was sheared and stripped. "But Longin was consumed with the zeal of God's fire," writes Avvakum, "and he defied Nikon and spat ... straight into his eyes." For his courage Longin was chained and beaten again with whips and brooms.

Nikon's enemies had been thoroughly routed by the end of the summer of 1653. Neronov was dispatched to Kola, a lonely fortress on the Arctic Ocean, while Avvakum suffered the first of his Siberian exiles, trekking on carts, boats and sleighs with his family (and a child born on the way) 2,000 miles to Tobolsk. Daniel and others were rotting—almost literally—in various monastery prisons. Efforts of the gentle Stefan Vonifatiev to mediate between the dissenting parties failed miserably. As for the "Zealots of Piety," their unity and dreams were gone forever. Nikon was, for the moment, supremely triumphant and ready for a new challenge—war with Poland.

Chapter Eight

ALEXIS GOES TO WAR

A spirit of rebellion was gathering strength in the Ukraine and Belorussia at the time Alexis became tsar in 1645. These fertile borderlands of the medieval Russian state had fallen to the Poles and Lithuanians just after the Mongols conquered the Russian heartland in the middle of the thirteenth century. The rise of Moscow in following years made the Mongol domination of Russia increasingly shaky. The once insignificant city "gathered" neighboring principalities, accumulating economic strength as well as military victories and political and diplomatic experience. By the early sixteenth century Russian statesmen were coming to feel that the new Muscovite state soon would be ready to challenge Poland's position in Belorussia and the Ukraine.

Poland had devoted considerable attention to strengthening its position in south Russia by this time. Important nobles in the Ukraine had married into Polish households and converted to the Catholic Church. But the lower nobility, the szlachta, were anxious to lead the people in a struggle for independence. The peasants, torn with hatred for their Polish landlords, seemed particularly likely to rise up, especially as it became clear that the pro-Catholic Uniate Church would not succeed in winning them from the Orthodox faith.

The Cossacks could also be counted upon to aid in the struggle against Poland. These rough, freedom-seeking fugitives had made their way from Polish and Russian estates to the wild frontier which knew no king, to the place where a man could enroll in a military community and lead a hearty life hunting, fishing, and tending livestock. In the area south of the Ukraine they were known as "Zaporozhie" Cossacks, that is, Cossacks "beyond the cataracts" (za porozh'e) of the Dnieper River. Their unbelievably daring raids against the Turks, the Crimean Tatars and the Poles thrilled the Ukrainians and Belorussians and kept their lands in turmoil.

The Ukraine found its leader in the *hetman* (commander) of the Zaporozhie Cossacks, Bogdan Khmelnitsky. This gallent, spirited, and

BOGDAN KHMELNITSKY. Leader of the Zaporozhie Cossacks. Oil portrait by an unknown artist.

often unscrupulous man was born on an estate which his father had received as reward for service to the Polish king. Bogdan likewise fought for Poland against the Turks. Returning from two years of captivity in Constantinople, he probably intended to follow his father in cooperating with Poland. Disillusionment began when authorities ignored Bogdan's case against a neighboring (Polish) landowner who stole Bogdan's property and flogged his son to death. Final rupture with the Poles came when Bogdan was imprisoned by Polish enemies of Wladyslaw IV. Thirsting for vengeance, Khmelnitsky fled to the Zaporozhie Cossacks on the lower reaches of the Dnieper River. The Cossack Assembly elected him hetmen on April 19, 1648, based upon a promise to lead them on a campaign against the Poles. The Ukraine blazed with the spirit of freedom as peasants and townsmen rushed to arms.

Khmelnitsky's first victories over the Poles were so brilliant that at one point he seemed to have shattered Poland's power forever. But Poland recovered under its brilliant king, John Casimir, and it became increasingly apparent that the Ukrainians and Cossacks alone did not have the power to drive the Poles away. Khmelnitsky shifted between approaches to the Crimean Tatars and the tsar, with occasional discussions for a compromise peace with the king of Poland. By 1653 it was clear that Poland eventually would re-establish control over the Ukraine. The only question was whether Moscow could permit this to happen.

Russia had steered clear of conflict with Poland in these years. Khmelnitsky asked for help from Moscow, proposing that the tsar become overlord of the Ukraine. But Poland was a formidable power, and Alexis could not lightly undertake hostilities. Nevertheless, the tsar brought Khmelnitsky's proposals before a council of church and state leaders as early as February, 1651. Carefully estimating Russia's resources, the council sent Bogdan good wishes—but refused to act. "I send to them with all my heart," he lamented, "but they only play with me."

Timid souls at Moscow hoped that somehow the Cossacks, Ukrainians and Belorussians might achieve success on their own. Such hopes were fading by 1653. Meanwhile, advocates of Muscovite intervention were heartened greatly by Nikon's election to the patriarchate. Patriarch Joseph had favored intervention, but his was a timid, uninfluential voice. Nikon was seen as a stronger personality, and his program to use Ukrainian scholars and reform the Russian Church along Greek lines made clear the importance of unifying Moscow and Kiev. Cossack diplomats worked through him and Morozov to bend the tsar and other influential statesmen towards their cause.

Alexis decided to accept the Ukraine as a protectorate early in 1653, but, knowing this would mean war with Poland, his government moved slowly and with caution. Khmelnitsky was not informed that Moscow would move in his favor until summer. In the fall, an Assembly of the Land was called, "as was proper," to approve the move. The Assembly voted on October 1, 1653 to take the Cossack armies "with the lands and towns" of Little Russia (as the Ukraine was often called) under the protection of Tsar Alexis. In his official address to the troops the tsar reminded his men that "every good and perfect gift comes from above, from the Father of Lights, and greater love hath no man than that he lay down his life for his friend." The tsar was cheered by generals and soldiers, boyars and commoners as all were blessed by the patriarch. By the time Alexis dismissed the troops, he was completely in tears.

Alexis was disappointed at Khmelnitsky's failure to accompany his emissaries to Moscow to swear allegiance to the tsar. Bogdan secretly hoped somehow to gain independence for the Ukraine and Belorussia, and part of this game was not to appear before Alexis in the manner of a humble subject. But, for the moment, none of this prevented good relations between the two men. When the news came in January, 1654, that Khmelnitsky had sworn an oath of allegiance to the tsar, Alexis was so pleased that he gave his coat and hat to the messenger who brought the tidings, Artamon Sergeevich Matveev, a commander of musketeers and a man who eventually would become one of the tsar's closest friends.

A Cossack delegation came to Moscow in early 1654 to negotiate a joint war plan. Hot and lengthy arguments finally produced an agreement that the bulk of the Russian armies would strike Lithuania while a smaller force hurried to the Ukraine on a campaign against the Poles. Khmelnitsky agreed to muster 20,000 Cossacks in support of Alexis' campaign to seize Belorussia from Poland. The Cossacks on the Don River agreed to harass the Crimean Tatars to prevent them from invading the Ukraine as allies of Poland.

Alexis decided to accompany his soldiers into Lithuania, a striking departure from the Kremlin-bound war habits of most Russian tsars. The tsar spent the spring of 1654 reviewing his armies near Moscow. To speed the departure of the troops, he decided to observe Whitsuntide early and to hurry his customary pilgrimages to the Holy Trinity and St. Sabbina Monasteries.

An army division under Alexis Trubetskoi left Moscow for the Ukraine on April 26, 1654. The advance guard bound for Lithuania departed from the capital under Odoevsky's command on May 15. Alexis, Maria and Nikon said farewell to the troops on both occasions from a gallery linking the palace to the Cathedral of the Annunciation. The patriarch sprinkled the troops with holy water as another division set forth on May 16.

The time now came for Alexis to leave for the front. His personal army assembled before the Kremlin, on Red Square, on the bright, clear morning of May 18, 1654. Alexis joined his soldiers as Nikon blessed and sprinkled them, then the regiments departed in solemn, ceremonial fashion. To heighten the grandeur of the event, the tsar and his men marched through town gates flanked by stepped platforms draped in red cloth. Priests stood on the steps, crosses in hand, sprinkling the warriors with holy water and calling down God's blessings for their work on the battlefield. Alexis led the procession, followed closely by his men.

The tsar led the main army to Smolensk, important for its magnificent fortress and because the city gave access to the lower Dnieper and trade routes to the west. It had been a great blow to Russian merchants when they lost this city to the Poles during the Time of Troubles in 1611. Smolensk was defended by a large Polish garrison, but Alexis was determined to take it, an attitude which is all the more striking since some of the tsar's advisers worried over defeat and took advantage of Alexis' open character to badger him with their dissatisfactions. Alexis told Trubetskoi in a letter of May 31, 1654 that the people with him were "not of one spirit," that they often complained and found fault. Alexis was encouraged by initial victories, however, as well as the great outpouring of sympathy he received from the Orthodox population of the areas through which he moved. On July 5, 1654 Alexis pitched his tent less than two miles from the main objective, Smolensk.

Besieging the area and receiving necessary supplies, Alexis ordered a night attack on Smolensk on August 16, 1654. Polish sources admit that 7,000 of their number were killed and 15,000 wounded during this siege. Alexis described his losses in letters from the front to his sisters at home. "Our troops quite bravely attacked a tower and came to a wall [of the city]. And great was the battle. And for our sins the Poles rolled powder under the tower, and many of our troops fled from the wall and others were burned from the powder. More than two hundred Livonians were killed, and three hundred of our troops were killed, and a thousand were wounded." Smolensk finally fell to the Russians on September 23, 1654.

Alexis' victory at Smolensk did not conceal the frustration he was feeling as a military leader. Life was simpler for Alexis at the Kremlin, sheltered as he was there by officials, hunting, and religious pursuits. Leadership at the front brought new problems and demanded different judgements. For example, the tsar's foreign officers complained to him that Russian troops customarily tortured their prisoners, and he was warned that if he did not take action about this soon, the enemy would begin to reciprocate. Alexis promised to do something, but his measures had little effect. The tsar's soldiers also pillaged the churches of Mogilev. In the Smolensk area they plundered the Russian population, raping women and killing their husbands. Alexis ordered the offenders executed, and deprived the nobles who brought them to the front of their property for permitting their serfs to act in such a way. The tsar was enough of a disciplinarian for foreign diplomats to report that he was "tyrannizing" his soldiers at the front. Before the capture of Smolensk Alexis had the Scotch officer Butler hung on an iron hook for not fighting satisfactorily. He lingered there three days before dying.

Chapter Nine

NIKON SHAKES THE FOUNDATION

With Alexis and the troops about to take the field, Nikon ignited a campaign at home to reform the Church. Seeing that his loudest enemies were routed and exiled by March 1654, Nikon called a meeting of 34 church leaders to hear a defense of his policies. The men assembled in the tsar's palace, before Alexis himself.

Nikon sternly reminded his listeners that the council at Constantinople which elevated Moscow to patriarchate status in 1598 also had decreed that practices peculiar to the Russian Church eventually should be eliminated in favor of Greek tradition. Nikon was a complex man, many motives stood behind the various episodes of his career—and at this moment one motive stands out quite clearly. Nikon was unable to tolerate the "errors" which were his responsibility to correct. Much as Nikon pressed Alexis to restore rights unjustly taken from the Russian Church, the patriarch felt the Russian Church would not be fully worthy of its rights until it adhered to the principles which guided Christians throughout the East. At first glance it seems that Nikon craved "power," but the patriarchate as such had no meaning for him. He took the office only when it carried agreements which could make it meaningful, which would give the patriarch the power to cast out human error and bring men to God. Idealism was deeply rooted in the spirit of this heroic, uncompromising man. His opponents caught occasional direct glimpses of this idealism, but not knowing Nikon as well as they supposed, they marked it down to momentary lapses in the life of a man steeled to never-ending combat. They did not see Nikon's idealism as the guiding force of his entire life.

The Moscow church meeting of March 1654 shows how little Nikon cared to work through consensus. It was in no sense a policy-making session. Nikon solicited no support for reforms already initiated, nor did he discuss innovations planned for the future. The church leaders were to sign a statement supporting further correction of Russian Church books according to Greek manuscripts and "by the old Slavic [parchment] books." Nikon did not have his way easily on this point. Archbishop Simeon of Tobolsk, and Alexis' confessor, Stefan Vonifatiev, flatly refused to sign. Bishop Paul of Kolomna agreed, but under a protest which eventually brought him exile and death. To strengthen his hand still further, Nikon wrote Paisios, the patriarch of Constantinople, asking his advice on how to reconcile differences between their churches.

Alexis left Moscow for the front in May, 1654. As the crowds cheered his departure, Nikon already planned his next move—an attack on the "devilish" new icons which recently had appeared in Russia.

The icon has occupied a unique place in the spiritual life of Russian Christianity. To simple, illiterate, but deeply religious people the icon showed Christ, the saints, scenes from the Bible and church history. The icon served as a window into heaven. Russian history is rich with icons which won battles, mastered plagues, healed the sick and the blind. Visitors were amazed at their sumptuous covers of silver and gold adorned with pearls and precious stones. Foreigners sometimes complained that icons were "inartistically rendered" because of their dark colors, their abstract, elongated figures. Such grumbling did nothing to decrease the passion Russians felt for their holy icons.

Alexis led all others in his devotion to icons, and often intervened to see that miracle-working images were cared for and housed in churches built especially for them. In 1647, for example, he sent elaborate instructions to the governor of the Cheremis region to have a newly found wonder-working icon brought to Moscow "with great honors; have it accompanied by priests and deacons with holy images, candles, censers, and the ringing of bells; and you yourself, with all the people of the city and district, go with the wonder-working icon out of the city [of Tsarev-Kokshaisk] as far as you think fit."

The Russian Church was concerned that its icon painters be true Christians, men who were, in the words of the 1551 Council, not prone to "drink, rob, or murder," but rather were "meek, humble, pious," ever ready to take apprentices to be instructed in "piety and purity" and the statutes of the Church. The icon painter was not to express individualism and personal taste in his art, but was "to represent fittingly the bodily image of our Lord God and Savior Jesus Christ and the Most Pure Mother of God and the heavenly Hosts and all the saints" according to "accepted image, likeness and model, following the works of old painters and drawing from good models." If an apprentice failed to lead a Christian life, the Council declared, if he proved "addicted to drink, to impurity, to scandal," or "if God does not open the secret" to him of painting well, the pupil "will be forbidden to continue painting icons." "Not all men can be icon painters; God has granted men various handicrafts, and men can turn to these for their nourishment and subsistence, without painting icons and putting God's likeness to shame and discredit."

The Zealots and other Russians were appalled to see Western elements creep into icon painting from the workshops of Novgorod and Pskov. These "Frankish" icons displayed new subjects and contained innovative composition, color scheme and treatment of detail. Worst of all, they treated their figures in a realistic rather than an abstract manner. Avvakum put the matter eloquently when he lamented that the icon painters who now worked "in unseemly fashion" paint Jesus "with a puffy face, red lips, curly hair, thick hands and arms, swollen fingers, fat thighs," "paunchy and fat like a German," while the image "of the Annunciation of Our Blessed Lady" depicts her "pregnant, with her belly hanging over her knees," as if "in the wink of an eye Christ is to be found all grown in the womb!" But it was unfair—even absurd—for Avvakum to blame all this on Nikon, "that fierce dog" and "fiend" who supposedly wanted "lifelike painting" in the "Frankish or German manner." Nikon had no objection to Western secular art in Russia; indeed, on one occasion he posed for a Dutchman to do his portrait. But Nikon was determined to hold to traditional norms in rendering icons. He would have joined his arch-enemy Avvakum in the lament, "Alas! poor Russia, Alas! Whatever did you want with German manners and ways?"

In the summer of 1654 Nikon struck out at icon painting done under Western influence. He sent secret agents throughout Moscow to search out "Frankish" icons from the homes of rich and poor alike. When these icons were brought to him Nikon gouged out the eyes of the figures, and then had musketeers display the defaced images around the city. He also published an edict in the name of the tsar stating that anyone who painted such icons in the future would be punished harshly.

The people of Moscow were stunned by Nikon's attack. Even those who did not favor the new trends venerated icons in general, and many murmured against Nikon, calling him a sinner, an iconoclast, an abuser of God's holy images. Events of the following days persuaded Muscovites that God was angry with them, as well as with Nikon, for the sins of the patriarch. A plague fell on Moscow in July, and on the afternoon of August 12 there was an eclipse of the sun. Crowds gathered to debate the meaning of these events. Paul of Aleppo, who happened to be in the capital at this time, tells us the people began to say that "All this is through the wrath of God, for our patriarch's contempt of our holy icons!" The people called Nikon a "son of a bitch"—and worse. With Alexis gone and few troops in Moscow, attempts were made against Nikon's life. Nikon was frightened, and, when he had to travel about, his guards had their weapons at the ready.

People from areas not affected by the plague at first were permitted to leave Moscow. But soon the entire city was afflicted, and then only boyars managed to depart. When news of the plague reached the tsar, he was naturally concerned about his family, especially his long-desired son and heir Alexis, born on February 5, 1654, little more than five months before the plague struck. Tsar Alexis ordered Nikon to remove his family from Moscow to a safe place. The patriarch set out for the Trinity monastery with the pregnant Tsarina Maria, the infant Tsarevich Alexis, the tsar's daughters Eudocia and Martha, his sisters Irene, Anna and Tatyana.

Michael Pronsky was left in charge of Moscow after Nikon's departure. He reported that after September 1 "the infection spread with such violence that all the six musketeer regiments were exterminated; all the churches except the cathedral had lost their priests, so that there was no longer any one in town to bury the dead; they put them under the ground in the houses where they died." Paul of Aleppo says the shortage of priests made last rites and proper burials impossible, forcing the city authorities to dig "large pits into which they threw the bodies indiscriminately, without ceremony." Paul claims the Moscow register showed that "480,000 souls had died of the plague" by September, and "most of the streets and houses were cleared of their inhabitants." The dogs and pigs of Moscow devoured corpses, the animals growing so wild that at one point no one dared walk the streets alone. Paul and his half-starved companions desperately feared falling victim to the plague. "Our only consolation or relief," he said, "was the absence of all that shouting and howling over the dead so much used by women of our country, who have learned it from the Arabs."

The plague totally discredited Nikon before the people of Moscow. Many thought that the patriarch's attack on Frankish icons was what brought God's punishment upon the city. As the pest raged on, it seemed as if Nikon had turned coward and fled. The subsequent measures Nikon took to combat the sickness were paltry and sanctimonious: he sent two miracle-working icons to Moscow along with a letter urging the people to save themselves through devotion and prayer. It jolted many to see the patriarch's best measures lavished upon protection of his royal master's property. For example, a patriarchal letter commanded the boyars "to paste over the doors and windows" of the storehouses containing Alexis' clothes and fabrics "so that no air should pass into them." The entrance gates of the palace were to be closed "so that no person whatever" should enter its rooms.

Pronsky combated the plague as best he could. The suffering Muscovites were his greatest obstacle. The people were exhausted by sickness and death, harassed by measures to combat disease, infuriated by the departure of Nikon and his co-workers. Riots swept through Moscow as the people demanded a vengeance which in Nikon's absence could not be had. Unable and unwilling to break the violence with force, Pronsky let it run its course. He then turned to the "eminent people," to merchants and the more responsible artisans, to restore the best order which could be had under the circumstances. On September 11 the plague claimed its noblest victim, Pronsky himself.

Nikon felt for his people but, as usual, his outward behavior failed to communicate his inner feelings. Nikon left Moscow only because the tsar had ordered him to leave, and Alexis took this step through fear for his family and because the patriarch was the alternate head of state. Nikon had to keep the wheels of state moving in the tsar's absence and in the midst of a desperate war, and if he could not do this at the capital, he had to relocate elsewhere. With the royal family comfortable and secure at the Trinity monastery, Nikon set out alone to spend the Feast of the Nativity "in the mountains and forests," dwelling, as Paul of Aleppo says, "in a tent, under the rain and snow, with no other companion but his fire." But the plague soon reached the Trinity cloister, and the royal family hurried on to the Kalyazin monastery.

Nikon set up temporary headquarters at Kalyazin during the summer of 1654, and began issuing orders in the name of Tsarevich Alexis to combat the plague. Thieves and robber bands were also a problem by this time. Nikon's first instinct was to deal gently with these people. He offered these criminals safe conduct to public places, where they could claim total amnesty for future good behavior. When no one accepted this lenient treatment, Nikon—typically—took the harshest measure possible. Not only were robbers executed, priests were to refuse them confession and communion before death. Nikon apparently thought the threat of losing eternal life would deter brigandage, a measure which likewise failed to decrease crime. But in later years, when Nikon himself stood in the dock, the Eastern patriarchs condemned this "uncanonical" edict.

The enemies of Nikon's church reforms used the plague to raise a clamor against the patriarch. "Is it not clear," they asked, "that the plague is a sign of God's disfavor?" "Should not Russia return to the old, true way?" The patriarch issued a stream of statements from Kalyazin denouncing this talk, retorting that the plague was God's punishment for the crown's interference with the Church following the Law Code of 1649. Alexis had suspended those articles of the code, but Nikon held that they should have been repealed altogether. This argument, of course, occurred privately, between tsar and patriarch. Publically Nikon reiterated the old idea that God visits plague upon man as a punishment for his sins. Nikon claimed the pestilence took the lives of those who ignored "good counsels," dissidents who "have perished and caused others to perish." Nikon warned the faithful not to be seduced lest they too fall victim to death. By late August the plague was inching its way towards Kalyazin, and Nikon planned to take the royal family as far north as Novgorod.

Then the plague, so mysterious in its movements and ways, suddenly subsided. In a little more than two months it had carried off a third of Russia's population, sweeping nearly 500 miles beyond Moscow, killing ten thousand families in Kolomna alone. But a journey to Novgorod no longer seemed necessary by October, and Alexis even decided it was safe to rejoin his family and the patriarch. Alexis ordered Nikon to meet him at Vyazma. The tsar set out from Smolensk on October 5, 1654 and on the twenty-first clasped his family for the first time in five months. Alexis in later years credited God's grace and the prayers of the patriarch for the survival of his family and the young heir, Alexis Alexeevich.

Alexis at this juncture rewarded Nikon in a fateful way: the tsar elevated the patriarch to temporary co-rulership over the entire kingdom. Tsar Michael had acted similarly in 1619 in granting his father, Patriarch Filaret, the exalted title "Grand Sovereign" (veliky gosudar). Until the older man's death in 1633, the two sovereigns usually both signed important acts of state. As if thinking of this precedent, Alexis also made his patriarch "Grand Sovereign."

Although Alexis was filled with love and gratitude towards Nikon, he was also motivated in this by a practical consideration. Alexis expected to be absent from Moscow in coming months, continuing on campaign with his armies against Poland and Lithuania. He wanted someone in the capital in whom he had total confidence to exercise power in his absence. The orderly nature of Alexis' mind demanded that this man, Nikon, bear a title indicating his position. Nikon protested this honor, and relented only when Alexis would have it no other way. Nikon's opposition also may have been softened by his understanding with the tsar that the patriarch's secular powers were only temporary and would be exercised in the name of the tsarevich while Tsar Alexis was absent at war. Nikon believed that the power of the patriarch over the Church was indeed supreme; he later argued that the ecclesiastical realm was superior to that of the state. But Nikon never supposed he would or should become a permanent secular leader.

Alexis settled down to spend the winter with his family at Vyazma. Reports of the Swedish observer de Rodes imply that the tsar wanted Nikon to return to Moscow, but the patriarch refused to go. Nikon claimed that the stars were unfavorable to such a trip. He also feared popular anger, for many felt that by his flight with the royal family he had ignored the tasks a spiritual leader should perform for his flock.

For his part, Alexis bombarded the Muscovites with moral statements from Vyazma. The tsar was peeved about the sad way the people had conducted themselves in the face of the plague. On January 15, 1655 the tsar wrote Ivan Morozov in Moscow: "We have learned that in Moscow during the plague time, husbands took monastic vows apart from their wives, and wives the veil apart from their husbands, but many [such monks still] live in their homes with wives, and many of those shorn carry on trade in the commercial rows [of the city, and that] drunkenness and thievery have increased. You should investigate whether or not this is true, and write to us quickly by a special messenger."

Four days later Alexis wrote Yakov Cherkassky saying, among other things, that soon he hoped to return at least briefly to Moscow to perform his customary religious observances, comfort the boyars and people in their distress, see his family, and return to the battlefield. Letters of the same month to his new favorite, Artamon Matveev, show Alexis' continuing preoccupation with man's sinful, fallen condition, and his hope that God eventually would bring health and salvation to Russia.

Finally, by February 10, 1655, the plague in Moscow had subsided enough to allow Alexis to set out for the city. Nikon quietly slipped into Moscow the same month to be on hand a few days later to greet Alexis and the royal family. The people were so thrilled to see Alexis that they forgot the tragedies which recently had engulfed them.

Nikon had now to regain control over events by acting in a bold manner. He made his move that month on the Sunday of Orthodoxy— the first Sunday of Lent—while celebrating mass at the Cathedral of the

Assumption. Addressing Alexis and two distinguished visitors, Patriarch Macarius of Antioch and Metropolitan Gabriel of Serbia, Nikon sermonized that Russians must join other Orthodox people in making the sign of the cross with three fingers. He had been firmly supported on this already by Macarius and Gabriel. Nikon then turned his attention to "Frankish" icons, an issue which he now infused with both political and religious significance. "Frankish" icons by now were widespread throughout Moscow, they adorned the homes of every class. Nikon focused his attack, however, upon boyars who owned the tainted images, boyars who resented the power Nikon wielded through the tsar. Nikon hoped to curb these nobles by humiliating them on this issue.

Nikon's agents had seized a large number of "Frankish" icons in recent days, and they were brought to the patriarch immediately following mass. Nikon condemned those who painted in the new style and, raising each icon, loudly announced the house from which it had been taken and threw each to the floor with such force that its wood panels shattered in every direction. Macarius gravely nodded agreement to Nikon's command that fragments of the ungodly images be burned.

The congregation was now in a total uproar, for Nikon's performance renewed old suspicions that he was an iconoclast. The people in the cathedral shouted out against his actions and moved to attack him. Only Tsar Alexis kept his head, and it was he who brought the issue to a peaceful end. Watching Nikon's rage, he came to him and calmly said: "No, Father, do not have them burned; let them be buried in the ground." Knowing this would be done, the people returned, shaken, to their homes.

Nikon's thirst for combat was not satisfied by his grand moment in the cathedral. He knew that many boyars who had campaigned with Alexis had looted organs from Catholic churches and brought them to their mansions. Nikon thought these musical instruments were "profane" and had them confiscated. The outraged nobles tried to present their grievances at a meeting of the Boyar Council, only to find that Alexis and the Council supported Nikon and denounced each offender by name. As a matter of fact, the Council itself had little control of events by this time—March 1655. Everyone knew that Nikon settled issues by "advising" Alexis, after which the Council mouthed their decisions. No one who valued his position dared object. Nikon exercised an equal control over a church synod called before Macarius and Gabriel in March 1655 to approve the use of three fingers in making the sign of the cross, as well as of the missal which had been translated from the Greek and published two years before.

Alexis had rested in the Kremlin for less then a month at this juncture, but was anxious to return to the front. His trust in Nikon complete, the tsar left for Smolensk on March 11, 1655. Thirteen days later, Alexis broke camp for a drive still further west. Victory seemed within his grasp, and Alexis moved to claim it.

Chapter Ten

THE END FOR POLAND?

Alexis was brought back to the front by renewed disorders in his own army. When Russian soldiers in the Smolensk area went on a rampage of murder and rape in February 1655, the tsar again resorted to harsh methods to bring the situation under control: culprits who were caught were hanged, the nobles who brought them into battle lost their lands. Alexis' letters in the spring of 1655 bristle with concern about deserters and recruits faking illness to escape duty. "Punishment without measure will be visited upon those who do this," Alexis thundered, "but whoever serves us till the end will see what royal favor will be granted him."

Such promises and threats restored enough discipline for Alexis to press for significant victories against the Polish king, John Casimir, in the spring of 1655. Threatening as this was for Poland, absolute disaster loomed when Charles X of Sweden fielded a daring surprise attack from the north in the summer.

At the age of thirty-two Charles often had wondered whether he would ever have the opportunity to find a place among the great conquerors of history. The Thirty Years War had ended at the very moment he was sent as generalissimo of the Swedish armies in Germany in 1648. Peace negotiations at Nuremberg had sharpened Charles' diplomatic skills, but the disappointed soldier had no flair for the other arts of peaceful statesmanship, and he hardly pretended otherwise.

Charles hoped to follow his eccentric younger cousin, Queen Christina, on the throne. Christina dressed as a man and refused to marry. In a decade of active rule, Christina bestowed half the crown lands upon favorites, some of whom were actually stranger than she. A late attraction to Catholicism brought Christina such unpopularity that even she no longer could ignore it. The queen abdicated in Charles' favor in 1654, converted, became a nun, and finally was buried in Rome. For his part, the new king spent a year touring his sturdy and progressive, if sparsely populated kingdom, healing discord and rallying resources for a reign which he already had made clear would be renowned for conquest.

Charles planned to add Poland's Baltic lands to those held by Sweden, then to turn on Denmark in a final struggle for the northern seas. Declaring war on Poland, Charles slipped away from Sweden in July,1655, with 50,000 crack troops and fifty fine warships. While Alexis took Minsk and Vilno that month, Charles occupied the parts of Livonia still in Polish hands. Warsaw fell to the Swedes without a struggle in early August, and Alexis received the surrender of Lvov on October 20. With the once mighty Polish kingdom in collapse, Alexis was greeted as a conquering hero in Moscow on December 10, 1655.

Alexis had gained an impressive victory in Poland—and a dangerous new enemy in Charles X. Though Russia profited from Sweden's blows against Poland, it was hardly a solace to Moscow to see Sweden consolidate its spoils. This would give Muscovy a western neighbor spanning the Baltic with greater power than Poland had ever been able to command. It now seemed that Russia and Sweden might come to blows, in which case it was to Moscow's advantage to revive Poland as an ally. As Alexis pondered these difficult issues, someone appeared who dared drive Russia still closer to war with Sweden—an impulsive border commander named Afanasy Lavrentevich Ordin-Nashchokin—who had in-credibly—launched his own war against Charles X.

Afanasy Ordin-Nashchokin was from a noble Pskov family which had fallen into poverty and lost its ancient boyar title. Afanasy's grandfather briefly rallied the family's fortunes. Known as Denis "the Warrior," Platonov notes that he had acquired several estates, and, at the time of Ivan the Terrible, led his fellow Pskov landlords in campaigns against Lithuania. Afanasy's father was undistinguished, however, and in 1622, at the age of seventeen, his son began what at first promised to be nothing more than a typical military career among the service nobility of Pskov.

Afanasy's education was excellent by Russian standards, however, including German and Latin, mathematics and rhetoric. His knowledge of the Pskov region prompted Moscow to send Ordin-Nashchokin to negotiate a border dispute with the Swedes in 1642. The young diplomat then was dispatched to Moldavia to conclude peace with Vasily "the Wolf," a talented, aggressive ruler who sponsored innovations similar to those of the most active reformer tsars. Nashchokin returned a critic of his government's Moldavian policy. This hindered his career, though the influential boyar statesman Fedor Sheremetev drew upon Nashchokin's advice concerning the Thirty Years War and the situation in Poland and Lithuania. O'Brien's study of Afansy's early correspondence shows that as Ordin-Nashchokin's relations with Sheremetev gradually grew warmer,

Sheremetev forwarded Nashchokin's reports to Tsar Michael and assured their obscure author that he was "known to the tsar." Nashchokin returned to Pskov to find the peasants and townspeople of the region suffering from heavy taxes and economic distress. Afanasy tried unsuccessfully to calm popular dissatisfactions, but when a large rebellion flared up at Pskov in 1650 he fled the popular anger by retreating to Moscow. Nashchokin returned to military service when war was declared on Poland in 1654.

The turning point in Nashchokin's life, the episode which brought him to the attention of the tsar, came at Dunaburg in 1655. Nashchokin repeatedly attacked this Polish stronghold, but suffered heavy casualties and was forced to fall back. Afanasy was beside himself with rage when the Swedes took the city in July. Though Russia then still maintained an uneasy peace with Sweden, Nashchokin took it upon himself to attack Dunaburg, charging that the Swedes had insulted the tsar and stolen his lands. Alexis was pleased with this wild guardian of his interests. Nashchokin was too honest for us to think that his sole motive was to curry official favor, though Ellersieck is certainly justified in observing of the episode that "the way to the tsar's heart lay through a fierce and partisan defense of his pretensions." Nashchokin's influence with the tsar began at precisely this moment.

Nashchokin argued that Russia's foreign policy should be directed towards gaining ports on the Baltic. The Baltic is a gloomy, brooding sea swept by strong westerly winds which produce short, irregular waves strong enough to frighten even seasoned sailors. The Baltic shores adjacent to Russia are ice-bound five months per year, but this still offers a navigation season longer than that provided by the White Sea route—the only water route to the West under Russian control at this time. The Baltic is a major trade artery, a sea whose thousand-mile span washes 5,000 miles of coast line. Ordin-Nashchokin and other Russians grew restive when it became apparent that now, in 1655, the entire eastern Baltic lay in Swedish hands.

Nashchokin never tired of observing that for Russia to carve a "window" on the Baltic it must reach a friendly understanding with Poland. Afanasy Lavrentevich even hoped that, with the childless John Casimir's dynasty facing extinction at his death, the Polish nobles eventually would elect Alexis or a close relative to the Polish throne. To balance Sweden's newly-won power and to win its own place on the Baltic, Nashchokin insisted that Russia must reach an accommodation with Poland.

Reconciliation with Poland became all the more pressing in late 1655, as developments began to turn in favor of John Casimir and his people. A short time before, when Cracow fell to Charles in September, the Polish cause had seemed so helpless that John had fled to Silesia. In October the Swedes laid siege to the fortified monastery of Czestochowa, defended by Prior Kordecki and a heroic (if fatalistic) garrison of soldiers and monks. The seventy-day siege which followed showed the Polish people and the world that Swedish armies could be successfully resisted. Monk and soldier were succeeding where king and noble had failed. A flaming new spirit of resistance spread from Czestochowa's battered walls to engulf the entire land, a spirit which amazed all who saw it. John Casimir finally returned in December, 1655 to lead the army which Stephen Czarniecki had raised on the king's behalf.

Diplomatic developments also worked to Poland's benefit. Frightened by the sudden disbalance of power in Eastern Europe, Vienna moved to form an international coalition against Charles X. Poland also benefited from Moscow's growing fear of Swedish power. Russian diplomats arranged a ccase fire with Poland at Polotsk at the end of April 1656. Alexis joined his representatives there in May and took part in various diplomatic discussions, though Prince Odoevsky continued as the chief Russian negotiator. The Swedes retreated to the Baltic, where it was now their turn to make a valiant stand. Poland had, for the moment, been saved.

At this juncture Alexis made a serious mistake. He moved towards war with Sweden before a workable understanding was reached with Poland. The tsar joined other Russians in supposing that the Muscovite armies were primarily responsible for Poland's defeat—and this in turn made them think that Russia was mightier than Sweden. Nikon's voice swelled the chorus calling for war against Charles X. The hot religious passion of the patriarch was as compelling in its own way as the cold logic of Nashchokin and the diplomats. Alexis declared war on Sweden on May 17, 1656. He set out with Yakov Cherkassky's large army for a second invasion of Livonia on July 26, this time to confront the legions of Charles X.

Alexis' main objective was to capture Riga, a picturesque Baltic port founded by Bremen merchants five centuries earlier and taken from Poland by Sweden in 1621. Riga's busy docks and bustling marketplace were joined by narrow streets lined with high storehouses and spacious graneries. The citadel and churches displayed a somber Germanic character, and Alexis was eager to see the city and add it to his domain.

The tsar's army laid siege to Riga in August, 1656. After two months Alexis could see that the heavy casualties he sustained were in vain, for he simply could not take the city. Russian forces from eastern Livonia to Ingria and Karelia were blessed with better fortune, however, a fact which strengthened Moscow's position in a new round of discussions beginning on August 12, 1656, which aimed at settling territorial disputes with Poland and bringing Warsaw into an alliance with Russia against Sweden. Alexis was to surrender Lithuania, but he retained Vilno and Belorussia.

By the time a tentative alliance was reached in September 1656, Russian diplomats had grown sufficiently bold to demand that Alexis eventually succeed John Casimir on the Polish throne. The point first had been formally raised after the fall of Lvov in 1655, when the Russian peace mission there suggested that Alexis be recognized as the king-elect of Poland. The proposal was pressed again in September 1656, and the Polish emissaries accepted it—along with a truce—pending ratification of both by the Sejm, the Polish Diet. Meanwhile, both powers were to continue their separate campaigns against Sweden. The war Russia began to recover Smolensk and the Ukraine now seemed about to end with the union of Russia and Poland!

Indeed, the Russian armies' stunning victories in Poland caused others to look hopefully to Tsar Alexis in 1656. Christians in Moldavia, and in Georgia in the Caucasus were coming to view Russia as the rising star of the east, the possible instrument of their own liberation. Nikon eagerly played intermediary to persuade Alexis to conclude a secret agreement with Moldavia to oust the Turks and—as in the case of Khmelnitsky and the Cossacks—to take that land under Muscovite protection so that "there may be one fold and one shepherd." Destiny beckoned to Alexis during 1656 as it had to no earlier Russian tsar, and it beckoned from more than one direction.

Even the tsar's improvised camp reflected the confidence he felt at this time. When the Danish ambassador, Kaas, was conducted to Alexis' tent on September 10, 1656 he saw Alexis seated in a magnificent chair, Miloslavsky standing to his right, Morozov to his left. A week later, a Danish embassy supped in the tsar's presence, after which Alexis received Kaas in another room where a goblet of wine from the tsar's own hand was raised in a toast to the king of Denmark and his future friendship with Moscow. Alexis radiated the easy self-assurance of a man who saw victory within his grasp.

Russian armies had registered important victories by the fall of 1656, and Russian diplomats had gained numerous concessions. Alexis did not realize how much of this would be undone in the following decade. But he did know that in his absence from Moscow Patriarch Nikon had unleashed mighty controversies which were weakening the state. Alexis now was forced to turn his attention to this threat. The time had come to return to the Kremlin and yet another host of pressing problems.

PART TWO

THE LIFE OF A TSAR

Chapter Eleven

DAYS IN THE LIFE OF A TSAR

Alexis began his day early, rising about four o'clock with the aid of the nobles so favored as to attend him in his bedchamber. Unlike his French contemporary Louis XIV, Alexis did this with no great ceremony. Indeed, according to his English physician Collins, the tsar slept in his shirt and pants, without sheets. He and the tsarina maintained separate apartments, and on Sundays and special church holidays they abstained from marital relations. At other times Alexis might join his spouse in her bed, or she in his. On the morning following such a night Alexis and his wife cleansed themselves with water. "Until they have done this," says Kotoshikhin, "they do not enter a church or kiss the cross, for this is considered lewd and sinful, and is denied not just to the tsar and tsarina, but to the common people as well."

The tsars and their families dwelt in the Kremlin building known as the "Terem" Palace—the *Teremnyi dvorets,* which had been rebuilt in 1635-1636. When Michael was elected to the throne, however, the entire Kremlin was in such shambles that he was forced to live elsewhere in Moscow at the hospitality of boyars and merchants while the money was being raised to repair his quarters. The wood foundations and walls of the Terem Palace remained, but three new upper stories—there were five in all—were done in brick and stone. (The tsar was afraid of fire, it was said, and wanted his loved ones to be safe.) The apartments within remained dark and gloomy, for the rooms are small and the ceilings low. Yet the polychrome figures dancing against the gold of the ceilings and walls lent the Terem Palace a strange life and vitality, and the royal family spent many happy hours together there. Alexis and his brother Ivan lived in the "loft," the highest story of the palace. Here they frolicked and grew, totally oblivious to the worldly cares which were to ensnare them all too soon. They loved the patter of rain falling on the roof, the flickering pale light of snowy winter days, the sounds of Moscow's life rising from below.

When Alexis became tsar he chose the fourth floor of the Terem Palace as the place where he would live and work. The five rooms were completely renovated and refurnished. After a brief morning grooming in his bedroom—which was the fourth room from the stairway—Alexis went into the fifth room, his private chapel, for matins. There he heard readings appropriate to the particular day, kissed and venerated icons of the day's saints and was sprinkled with holy water fetched from monasteries dedicated to their memories. Alexis now sent greetings to his wife and expressed concern for her health. Most of Moscow was now stirring to life as the royal couple proceeded to another chapel for further prayers and a brief mass.

The Royal Court of the Kremlin was buzzing by now with the chatter of officials who had assembled near the "red staircase" which led from the courtyard to the tsar's apartments on the fourth floor. At a given signal the more favored dignitaries lumbered up the stairs to the antechamber, leaving their junior colleagues at the bottom of the stairs to be summoned later as needed.

The tsar generally received people in the second room of his suite, the Room of the Cross, which was also where the Boyar Council met. More highly regarded statesmen might pass into the Golden Room, the third chamber directly adjacent to the bedroom. People of all ranks greeted the tsar and took their leave with a full bow to the ground, and when talking to him did not look directly into his face.

Alexis' officials generally spent two hours delivering morning reports, answering questions and, if the sovereign seemed in a properly receptive mood, entering requests for choice assignments and personal favors. Only the tsar was seated at this time, flanked by secretaries and such favorites as Morozov, Miloslavsky, and those who followed them in succession as the years passed. When an official finished his report he stepped back "from his majesty's presence" to join the various groups standing by the walls, to return to the antechamber for a seat, or to descend to the courtyard for a breath of fresh air.

The morning session lasted until nine o'clock, at which time Alexis and his company retired for yet another morning mass. Important church holidays were celebrated in a Kremlin church, but on ordinary days the tsar used a convenient palace chapel. Alexis transacted crown business during mass, for every moment of his day was so infused by religion that to him it did not seem disrespectful to mix political and religious affairs. After mass the tsar returned to his palace for another hour of consultations. Then it was noon and time for lunch.

Olearius tells us that Alexis' meals were not announced "with trumpets as in other courts," but by a servant running to the kitchen and

cellar and calling out at the top of his voice, "The Sovereign's dinner!"
An army of butlers, carvers, servers and cupbearers then sprang into
action, trays were presented to the official in charge of the royal table
for scrutiny. A royal meal was surrounded by tight security. The tsar's
food was watched from kitchen to table by trusted officials, his beverages were tasted several times by the very server who poured them into
the royal goblet. Fifty or more dishes usually were brought to the dining
hall, but Alexis cared little for such fancy fare. He merely picked at the
elegant dishes and, if they met with his approval, had them sent to the
tables of his friends, "the foreigners as well as the Russians," says
Olearius, "and especially to [his] doctors, physicians and healers." Alexis
himself nibbled cabbage and plain berries, or took a pickled mushroom
or a cucumber with bread and salt. All this was washed down by a small
amount of wine and beer or water with oil of cinnamon, the "aroma
imperiale" at the Kremlin, according to Dr. Collins.

Ordinarily Alexis dined alone. Occasionally he invited the patriarch
or other favorites to join him, though of course they sat at separate
tables. During festivals, however, Alexis dined in public, and it then required many tables to accommodate his numerous guests. On such occasions seventy dishes were presented to the tsar, who dined well and was
a good and genial host. Wine flowed from pitchers held by his own
hand, toasts and good wishes were offered to all, and no one left without a sense of good cheer, perhaps even a gift.

Alexis compensated for eating well on such festive occasions by
rigorous fasting during Lent, Shrove-tide week, the six weeks before
Christmas, and two other weeks—a grand total of sixteen weeks a year.
At these times Alexis accepted but a single meal each Wednesday, Saturday and Sunday, a serving consisting merely of small amounts of milk,
eggs, plain berries, cabbage, legumes, dry fruits and vegetables. Meat
was excluded altogether during fast weeks, and Alexis permitted himself fish but twice a week. His beverages were confined to water, beer,
and mead.

The tsar followed dinner with a three-hour nap. The later part of the
afternoon Alexis passed with his family, in favorite pastimes, or in never-
ending consultations with master craftsmen and architects concerning
the appearance of the Kremlin. Alexis' receptivity to Western culture
set him at odds with his surroundings, particularly the Kremlin. The
walls, gates, churches and buildings of this architectural ensemble vibrate
with a strange, barbaric genius which is quite impressive to most foreign
observers. But Alexis was not entirely happy with the old Russia, especially after his Polish campaign. The tsar's sojourns in Vilno and Polotsk
let him see foreign life for long periods of time. Ironically, Alexis used

TSAR MICHAEL DINING IN PUBLIC

these very campaigns to seek out Polish prisoners who could renovate the Kremlin along the lines of the civilization with which Russia then was locked in combat!

Wallpaper—which the Russians called "golden skins"—appeared in the Kremlin's palaces and secular buildings at this time. Russian benches and straight-back chairs which satisfied even such a passionate "Westernizer" as Boris Godunov were eclipsed by Polish and German pieces with lattices and elaborate rococo carvings. Traditional Russian tables were set aside in favor of imported tables with decorative paintings and finished in highly polished black lacquer. Alexis was especially proud of a table measuring 77 by 28 inches he acquired in 1675, a table which sported elegant figures and a double-headed eagle with crown. Benches and tables still comprised most of the Kremlin's furnishings in these years, the tables being covered with green or scarlet cloth, or with gold rugs, on special days. Chairs and notably armchairs were considered special items, and were reserved solely for Alexis and his immediate family, or for the patriarch on his ceremonial visits. Alexis was fond of his elegant German armchairs. Mirrors were not yet common in the Kremlin. A few hung on the walls, but most were small glasses used by the royal family for dressing and primping in their bedrooms. Alexis slept in a massive carved four-post bed curtained with brocaded silk.

The tsar found the Kremlin's gardens and orchards a welcome contrast to the gloomy splendor of its buildings. His father also had delighted in these grounds. We know of a fine day in 1635 when the royal gardener Nikita Rodionov presented apples and pears to Tsar Michael and his son, Tsarevich Alexis. Other accounts tell of royal blood being poured into a pit in one of the "upper" Kremlin gardens after Michael's doctors put him to a bleeding in 1643. Alexis issued orders in 1657 to plant here several types of roses he had admired growing in the gardens of the Pharmaceutical Bureau, "without losing any time." Sometimes the tsars established new gardens for their sons. Michael had a garden spaded for Alexis near the Terem Palace in 1635, while Alexis in 1664 organized a new garden in the same area for Alexis Alexeevich, a garden where grills and gratings sparkled proudly with bright red paint.

Alexis loved birds, and they were displayed tastefully in the Kremlin gardens. Canaries and nightingales twittered merrily from their cages as parrots looked on in a more somber mood. Alexis was most pleased by female quail; we read of him placing several of these birds in silk cages in a garden room of the Kremlin in 1667. Quail usually were kept in special stone hutches two or three stories high in various places about the Kremlin. Alexis also hunted with birds. From olden times falconry was popular with tsars, and Ivan the Terrible had organized a special bureau in 1550 to supervise the court falconers. But Alexis had a greater passion for falconry than his forebears, and he often went to Sokolniki to relax. (Sokol'nik means "falconer" in Russian, and Sokolniki is now a station of the Moscow subway.) Early in his reign Alexis had a timbered house called "Prokovka" built elsewhere near Moscow to house some of his birds. The tsar loved to come here, and once was depressed over the refusal of two falcons to eat. A foreign surgeon's assistant had the bright idea of offering the sicklings a dish of chopped bird meat which, to Alexis' delight, they quickly gobbled down. The tsar rewarded the ingenious man with twenty-five rubles, two fine sables and permission to stay home when his regiment went on campaign in 1658.

Alexis' passion for hunting with birds is demonstrated most vividly by a new "Falconry Manual" he ordered published in 1656. Parts of this handbook seem to have been written by the tsar himself. The introduction proclaims that Alexis was issuing the manual "for the honor and increase of his royal, beautiful and glorious sport of falconry." "Beautiful to look at and exhilirating is the high flight of the falcon, beautiful also the flight and attack of the merlin." And when is the best time to view this spectacle? "For the true sportsman there may be no question about season and time!" "It is always time, and the weather is always fine to take the field," for the art of falconry keeps away "all sorrow and spleen." A final postscript in Alexis' own hand offers this reflection: "These maxims are for your souls and bodies; but never forget about truth and justice, and charitable love and military exercise; there is one time for work, and another for enjoyment."

Alexis also hunted with hawks or chased larger game in the mounted company of his friends. When Nikon became patriarch he persuaded the tsar to order, as a foreign diplomat noted, "the taming or death of all the wild bears and wolves kept in cages for the local hunters." Alexis was devoted to strict moral codes, but not to the point of denying himself the pleasures he withheld from others. The tsar was still observed hunting bear, wolf and fox outside Moscow in January 1653. In the winter Alexis also relished professional fighting matches where the contestants, armed only with spears and staves, faced wild bears in deep pits in a struggle to the death.

The tsar spent many late afternoons in the Amusement Palace of the Kremlin. The atmosphere here was more sedate after the Zealots persuaded Alexis in 1648 to ban "pagan instruments" and popular songs, many of which were almost unbelievably coarse. But in other respects the tsar quietly refused to sacrifice his pleasures to religious enthusiasm. While Nikon and the Zealots were closing animal shows throughout

Russia, trainers with bear-and-goat acts knew full well that the tsar had a purse awaiting them at his Amusement Palace. Alexis also appreciated wrestling matches, juggling and acrobatic demonstrations. When the tsar was in a more serious mood, jewelers, arms-makers and metalsmiths were summoned to display their finest work. Or Alexis indulged in a round of cards, backgammon, draughts or, above all, chess. Collins tells us that Alexis also kept at the palace a company of elderly men, some 120 years old, "with whom he delights to converse and to hear what passed in his ancestors' time." Alexis was attached to these men and, as they died, the tsar often attended their funerals and ordered them buried at important monasteries.

The tsar's thirst for entertainment brought to his chambers people more bizarre than old men who recalled bygone years and distant lands. Soothsayers and tale-spinners, jesters and fools in bright hues of red, yellow and green peeking from fox-skin caps with pointed flaps—many was the time such people flooded into the Amusement Palace to brighten a gloomy day and raise flagging spirits. Alexis' collection of dwarfs was even larger than the sixteen who had so charmed his father. The royal dwarfs lived in fine quarters and cared for the court parrots. Bain recounts the petition of the dwarf Ivashka, who during the plague of 1659 remained in the Kremlin in charge "of four parrots and one old one," which he fed for twenty weeks on almond cakes, and "kept alive and well." "And as regards my patience and the feeding of thy sovereign birds," the dwarf addressed his royal master, "is it not all known even unto the oven-heater Alexander Boshkov, who visited me every day and examined thy sovereign birds?" Ivashka received the twenty rubles he requested for these services.

"Holy men" flocked to Moscow from every part of the land, "poverty-stricken pilgrims" who came to Alexis to share with him their hymns, revelations and pious teachings. "Fools for Christ" also lived in the Kremlin. Some were feeble-minded individuals whose infirmities were taken as a sign of holy blessing whereas others possessed normal faculties and merely behaved "foolishly" as a rejection of worldly vanity. One of the boldest of these men was Cyprian, commonly called "the man of God," who, according to Paul of Aleppo, "perpetually goes about the streets entirely naked, and is much revered by the people, even beyond bounds, as an eminent saint." Alexis often dined with these holy ones, and supported them with lavish charity.

After a happy afternoon of entertainment, companionship and sport, Alexis sat down for the evening meal. The tsar and his court then appeared at vespers where, as earlier in the day, affairs of state were transacted during the service. Foreign observers marvelled at Alexis' endurance, for he never seemed to blink at the fact that the evening liturgy usually ran late and sometimes lasted all night! The pious tsar of Holy Russia accepted this as an obligation which repetition had made pleasant, and he apparently gave it no thought. Alexis never complained about standing in church four, five and six hours at a time. On a normal day he prostrated himself to the ground a hundred times, a thousand or fifteen hundred on fast days. The tsar loved midnight prayers and what Collins called "the old vigils of the Church." Alexis also prided himself on his excellent mastery of church song and liturgy, canons and practices.

Even when vespers were finished Alexis' day might not have reached its end. His physician, Dr. Samuel Collins, mixes fact and rumor in his account of Muscovy, but he may be accurate in telling us that the tsar often visited the desks of his officials in the small hours of the morning to see which decrees were being issued and which petitions were being denied. Frequently Alexis ended his day in a final session with his chaplain. Avvakum notes in his *Life* that "in the middle of the night" Alexis came to Stefan Vonifatiev "for his blessing," and in this way interrupted a conversation between the two priests.

Chapter Twelve

DAYS IN THE LIFE OF A TSARINA

Women played an active role in the public affairs of early Russia. No one shines more brightly in the chronicles than Olga, the tenth-century princess who ruled following the death of Igor. Olga put down the uprising which took her foolish husband's life, then turned her formidable talents to reorganizing tax collections and the administration of her domains. While cultivating excellent relations with Germany and Rome, she appeared at Constantinople to negotiate sweeping commercial and military agreements, and to be baptized by the emperor and patriarch. When Vladimir considered conversion in 988, his nobles reminded him that "if the Greek faith were evil, it would not have been adopted by your grandmother, Olga, who was wiser than all other men." For the next two centuries Kievan women owned and managed property, sent representatives on trade missions abroad, settled quarrels among warring princes and acted in political roles. Upperclass Kievan women were often well educated at a time when kings and nobles in the West were content to remain illiterate. The contrast is strikingly illustrated by Anna, a daughter of Yaroslav the Wise, who was given in marriage to Henry I of France in the eleventh century. The king marked crown documents with an "X" while his wife serenely signed herself "Anna Regina" in Slavic characters.

Most Russian women lost their freedom after the Mongol conquest of the thirteenth century. The idea grew that the women of princes were special creatures who would be defiled by the glance of lesser souls, or fall prey to the "evil eye," to witchcraft or sorcery. Since the highest feminine virtues in any case were obviously chastity and prayer, it was supposed that among royal women all this could be practiced best in complete isolation from ordinary company in what became in effect a religious prison—the Terem Palace.

The women of the Kremlin in Alexis' time were rigidly isolated and attended only by specially selected servants and noble ladies. The young girls had lads brought in as playmates, but they were withdrawn as soon as they ceased to be mere boys. Meyerberg, the Austrian ambassador to Russia in 1663, remarked that for all the male grandees and court attendants, few actually could boast of seeing the tsarina or a daughter or sister of the tsar. Indeed, the Kremlin physicians scarcely had contact with them. When a doctor was summoned to attend a royal female, the shades of the windows were tightly drawn and he took her pulse through a piece of gauze so as not to touch her bare flesh!

Isolated as they were, the tsar's women usually possessed ignorant minds and trivial spirits. The world hardly knew they existed and their being was of no consequence to it. For the older females one part of the day passed in the same round of stale games, another among the monotonous clacking of the looms or in the fantastically complex embroidering of fine cloth with gold thread in which they were perpetually involved. The tsar's daughters saw him only on special occasions; even contact with their brothers faded as time went on. The terem area of the Kremlin would ring sometimes with merry laughter provoked by juicy gossip, news of some indiscretion on the part of a servant girl, or, still better, a noble lady-in-waiting.

The royal ladies and young boys attended crown ceremonies but in ways strictly dictated by Muscovite tradition. They witnessed diplomatic receptions, coronations, presentations of the tsarevich, elections of church prelates and meetings of the Assemblies of the Land from a hidden vestibule along the west wall of the Palace of Facets directly facing the sovereign's throne. In Alexis' time the grilled viewing screen was upholstered in red cotton and taffeta, the side windows being draped for privacy in red cloth from England and Armenia. The beady eyes of St. Evfimy of Suzdal sparkled at the royal family from an icon fixed in the right corner of the gallery.

The tsarina, her children and other royal ladies were not generally seen even at mass. They usually attended church in the early morning or late evening, and the only other laymen present were boyars and lords of the chamber. Even at that, the women and boys were hustled along partitioned corridors to areas of the church concealed by silk hangings. "When they go on pilgrimage to the monasteries," says Kotoshikhin, "their carriages are also closed with silk curtains." For winter travel, he continues, "little cabins lined with red velvet or cloth are fitted on sleighs; the doors on each side have mica shutters and silk curtains. In summer they drive in coach-like vehicles, also screened with cloth, and entered by steps." But at least travel was a welcome break in their grinding routine, and it brought the female members of the dynasty (and Alexis' sons) into contact with the tsar himself. Nor were all the trips religious pilgrimages. In late May, for example, Alexis took his wife, children and sisters on a vacation to Obrazovsky, three miles outside of Moscow, where specially constructed tents and much fun awaited the happy party.

One cannot escape the conclusion, however, that life for the royal ladies was boringly difficult. Kotoshikhin speaks of Alexis' sisters and daughters "spending their days in prayer and fasting," so that despite "princely pleasures" they "bathe their faces in tears." Marriage would have been an escape from this luxuriously dreary existence, but it too was denied the female members of the royal family. As we saw in the first chapter, even the most aristocratic Russians were mere slaves in comparison with their royal master, the tsar. Marriage of the royal women to them would have been degrading and totally unacceptable. As for wedlock to princes abroad, as Kotoshikhin observed, "these are not of the same faith, and Russians must not change their faith or let it be put to scorn; also, they do not know the language or the politics of other realms, and this would bring shame upon them."

A few exceptions to this aloofness did occur. Boris Godunov married his daughter Xenia to Prince John of Denmark, but the groom died immediately after coming to Russia in 1602. In the next decade Vasily Shuisky and the first False Dmitry wedded Polish ladies, hardly favorable precedents considering the careers of these two tsars. The most promising start in a new direction came in 1640 when Tsar Michael began efforts to marry his daughter Irene into the Danish ruling house.

But Waldemar's arrogance, as well as religious differences and political intrigue, made this a hopeless project from the start. The excitement of those months remained with Irene merely as a poignant reminder of what might have been.

Irene often begged Alexis to permit her to take the veil, but he loved her too much to give her up. Paul of Aleppo was told that the tsar paid Irene "great respect, and listens to her prudent counsels," gave her numerous banquets and had special cathedral services celebrated in her honor. And so, for this "reading, philosophical, learned, and sensible lady," as for the others, the years grew into decades and the twilight of life.

Tsarinas traditionally attended church privately or in the early morning and at night, as did the other distaff members of the royal family. Maria was conservative in her attachment to the old Russian ways, but Paul of Aleppo tells us that Nikon insisted that she depart from tradition by making "a particular place for herself" in the cathedrals in the view of everyone.

We have an account of one such appearance. On a sharp, frosty Sunday morning in December 1655 Maria descended from the palace and entered the Cathedral of the Annunciation. Many were eager to catch a glimpse of the tsarina, and the musketeers struggled in the courtyard to keep them back. The wives of the leading court nobles preceded Maria in the same order as their husbands walked before Alexis, "every two dressed in a different way, but most of them in dark or violet-colored velvets, having on their heads, above the kalpak, a small white veil hanging loose; above it a kind of lappet of sables or costly black fox slit in two, to the shape of their heads, and mantles on their backs." Maria's mother leaned on her right arm, her sister flanked her on the left. After her came her ladies-in-waiting and lesser attendants, the married ones wearing a large white veil, the maids a briefer headdress of fine sables.

The choir chanted a polychronion in her honor while Maria performed her devotions and took a place by her chair, after which her veil was lowered at the right so that the congregation might glimpse at least this much of her beautiful face. Maria's parents and uncle had now approached to stand at the right, while her maids had gathered to her left, on the north side of the cathedral near the door. At this point a curtain was lowered from the central pillar to the wall, so that the women were enclosed on every side and protected from the gaze of the congregation. Patriarch Nikon now approached Maria, blessed and sprinkled her and resumed his place, after which the tsar made his grand entrance into the church. Following the sermon of the day, Nikon gave communion to the

TSARINA MARIA MILOSLAVSKAYA

royal couple, the court dignitaries, the priests and monks. Nikon and
Macarius then unrobed in the sanctuary, and returned in their monastic
capes to bless the tsarina again. At the end, the tsar, the patriarchs and
the entire congregation filed through the entryway of the church. After
the doors were closed, Nikon returned and attended Maria as she "paid
her reverence to the icons one by one, to the relics of the saints, and to

the casket containing the tunic of Our Lord. Then they conducted her out, and she departed."

Maria's greatest responsibilities were within the Kremlin, where, as in any home, she directed her family's domestic affairs. In addition to nagging and punishing a great army of servants, the tsarina had to supervise the wardrobe of her husband, her children and all the royal ladies, including Alexis' sisters and aunts. It also fell to Maria to oversee the sewing projects of the tsar's women, as well as those of the servants, who stitched away at more mundane but equally necessary clothwares. Maria often obtained dowries and approved suitors and husbands for various ladies of her family and the court. She was constantly drawn into squabbles over precedence among the royal ladies and their retinues, and she directed charitable activities that were extensive and demanded skillful management.

The income necessary to support most of her charitable concerns came from artisan shops and landed estates which belonged to the tsarina. Maria took interest in some of these establishments. In fact, this was an age in which the lady entrepreneur was beginning to make a true appearance in Russia. We know of several women who, when widowed, assumed direction of the enterprises they inherited. Some of these women were foreigners, for example, Anna Akema, who, after the death of her husband Filimon, married Werner Müller. Anna became an iron manufacturer in her own right by surviving these two men. Maria, the wife of John of Sweden, not only took over his post, paper mill and other interests when he died in 1668, but tried (unsuccessfully) to expand into glass manufacturing as well. Daria Digby burned ash and charcoal north of Moscow in the early years of Alexis' reign, and at the end of the century Maria Löfken and the wife of Vladimir Voronin continued their deceased husbands' manufacturing activities. The most interesting of these businesswomen to us, however, was the tsarina's sister, Anna. When her husband Boris Morozov died in 1661 Anna took over his estates and ironworks and managed them until her own death in 1668, when her brother-in-law, Tsar Alexis, took part of the properties of the childless couple in escheat.

Maria was constantly alert to the interests of her father, Ilya, that ambitious individual whom Collins praised as an "able" man with "a vast memory," a "goodly" physique, with "limbs and muscles like Hercules, a bold man of vast parts," but driven by a character "covetous, unjust, and immoral." From the moment his daughters married Alexis and Morozov, Miloslavsky adopted a fine style of life. "He was given a house in the Kremlin, near his Tsarist Majesty's residence," but he had it "torn down forthwith and a magnificent palace built from the ground up." True to the fashions of the period, Miloslavsky adorned this residence with western furniture, painted ceilings, wall portraits and scenes.

After the fall of Morozov in 1648, Ilya Miloslavsky became the leading "assistant" to the tsar. Among his important posts were leadership of the bureau which supervised foreign officers in Russian service, also the Grand Treasury, and the Pharmaceutical Office. The bribes and embezzlements for which Ilya became notorious helped build a fortune which soon branched out to include landed estates, and the production and sale of iron, potash, hemp, and other goods. Miloslavsky attended Alexis on public occasions and sometimes represented him on diplomatic missions abroad. But Alexis never loved his father-in-law, and on the following occasion showed his feelings towards Ilya in a most dramatic way.

The Boyar Council was discussing the terrible defeat of Prince Khovansky in Lithuania in 1660, and the loss of almost his entire army of 20,000 men. The sovereign asked advice on what to do next, but was taken aback to hear Miloslavsky declare—with no military experience— (though Alexis himself had honored him with the title "generalissimo") that if he were favored with an army, he would return to Moscow with the king of Poland in chains. "How dare you boast of your military skill, you hireling, you worn-out little man!" Alexis raged. "When have you gone out with the regiments? What victories have you won over the enemy?" The tsar leaped out of his seat, boxed Miloslavsky's ears, yanked his beard and, kicking him across the floor, personally threw him out and slammed the door.

Alexis reached the end of his patience with Miloslavsky when it was rumored in 1662 that in the last eight years he had counterfeited 120,000 rubles in copper coins. Alexis turned completely against Ilya Danilovich now, but Maria secured his continued favor with her royal husband. Ironically, according to Muscovite protocol, Ilya no longer was able to address Maria as "daughter." Yet without her he would have fallen overnight.

Ilya was sexually active until his late years, so much so that a perplexed tsar begged him either to marry or stay away from court. Age finally settled this problem, as it does so many others. Ilya suffered a stroke which so disabled him that he could recognize no one without the person being identified. The old scoundrel died in 1668. Collins dryly notes that he would have done the Russian state still greater damage "had not that great statesman Nashchokin succeeded and supplied his place in many offices."

Maria was called upon by people other than her kin to exercise influence upon their behalf. The *Domostroy,* the Russian manual on how to order home life so that families might be contented and prosper, instructs a wife when asked about a person to answer: "I know nothing and have heard nothing; I do not inquire about things that do not concern me; nor do I sit in judgment over the wives of princes, boyars, or my neighbors." Maria Miloslavskaya certainly did not conduct herself in such a passive manner. It was commonly known that this wise and compassionate woman took an interest in the world around her, that she shared her opinions with the tsar, and that, to a degree, he was guided by them. Petitions were presented to her as well as to him, and it must be significant that in 1652, when Avvakum and other Zealots moved to make Stefan Vonifatiev rather than Nikon patriarch, their statement was addressed to both Alexis and Maria.

Pious and traditional, Maria remained fundamentally attached to the old Russia. Those who knew the tsarina found her to be charming and compassionate, though she had a vindictive side to her character which could visit harsh punishment upon those who crossed her path. Like Alexis, she possessed strong common sense which expressed itself best and most clearly in the successful management of their economic enterprises. As she understood devotion, she was devoted to her husband, her family, her church and her people—in that order. She married Alexis at the age of twenty-two and lived with him twenty-one years. They had five sons and eight daughters—thirteen children in all, and she died a week after the strain of the last. Maria was then forty-three years old. Observers agreed with Collins that she was still a "tolerable beauty."

Chapter Thirteen

A POPULAR AND PIOUS TSAR

Much of Alexis' time was devoted to the celebration of festivals. These ceremonies demonstrated the unity between the tsar and his people. Alexis enjoyed them hugely and carried out his role with great care. He particularly relished New Year's Day, when twenty thousand people gathered on the Kremlin square to celebrate the festival with their tsar. According to Olearius, the proceedings began as the patriarch and 400 priests streamed from the Cathedral of the Assumption, banners and icons lifted high, the ancient holy books held open. Alexis and his court entered the square from the other side. The tsar, head bare, greeted the patriarch with a kiss on the mouth, after which Alexis pressed to his lips a large cross encrusted with diamonds and other precious stones. The patriarch blessed his sovereign and the people, wishing happiness to all during the coming year. To this the people shouted in reply, "Amen!"

Palm Sunday was another important festival. The tsars traditionally celebrated this day by leading the patriarch seated upon a white horse across Red Square into the Kremlin, symbolically reenacting Christ's triumphal entry into Jerusalem and the humility of earthly powers before Him. Alexis performed his role with great devotion—and collected five rubles from the patriarch after the ceremony was finished and the crowds had gone! Alexis observed Easter by handing out intricately painted Easter eggs to the boyars and his court, army officers of all ranks and the merchants. Foreign traders were not so honored, however. In fact, on this occasion it was they who brought presents to Alexis—or risked his displeasure.

In fact, Alexis took constant care to demonstrate his importance to foreigners, to impress them with the power and magnificence of the Russian tsar. Diplomatic receptions were held in the Granovitaya Palata, the "Palace of Facets", so named because the grey stones of its facade are faceted like pomegranates and sparkle in the sunlight. Marco Ruffo began the Palace of Facets in 1487, but it was finished by Pietro Solario in 1495. The Italian architects consciously simulated the walls of the Castello in Ferrara and the Pitti Palace of Florence, but in its lavishly frescoed walls and splayed windows of rich, brilliant mica, the Palace of Facets is unmistakably Russian. The vaulted chamber is seventy-seven by seventy feet, and its high polychromed ceiling makes a tremendous impression on visitors.

The tsar and his court within were no less striking. In an age which thought of the "Sun King" as residing in the palace of Louis XIV of France, Sir Thomas Carlisle, the British ambassador to Moscow in 1664, made the following observation after entering this hall for a reception by the tsar. "And here it was we were like those who coming suddenly out of the dark are dazzled with the brightness of the sun: the splendor of their jewels seeming to contend for priority with those of the day, so that we were lost as it were in this confusion of glory. The Tsar like a sparkling sun (to speak in the Russian dialect) dazzled forth most sumptuous rays, being most magnificently placed upon his throne with his sceptre in his hand and his crown on his head. His throne was of massy

silver gilt, wrought curiously on the top with several works and pyramids, and being seven or eight steps higher than the floor it rendered
the person of the Prince transcendently majestic. His crown (which he
wore upon a cap lined with black sables) was covered quite over with
precious stones; it terminated towards the top in the form of a pyramid,
with a golden cross on the spire. The sceptre glistened also all over with
jewels."

Several years earlier Alexis had commissioned a Danish craftsman to
adorn his carriage with gold valued at 2,500 rubles. Even the horses used
in the tsar's processions were adorned richly. Lieseck, secretary to an
embassy from the Holy Roman Emperor in 1675, noted that one part of
a royal Russian procession particularly amazed the members of his
party. "In front rode an equerry followed by men leading sixty-two
magnificent horses whose harnesses and clothes were resplendent with
gold and silver."

Russians consistently impressed foreign diplomats with the splendor
of Alexis' court. The dispatches and memoirs of these European observers marvel over the attire of Kremlin officials, as well as the jewels and
pearls which graced their garments and the sable and black fox caps
which covered their heads. Costly rugs covered the floors while elegantly
painted Biblical scenes looked down from the ceilings. Carlisle described
the "four tall lords" who stood below the tsar, each with a battle-axe on
his shoulder, each from time to time "with a profound gravity" casting
his eyes upon his sovereign, as if "inviting us to an admiration of his
grandeur." These attendants were clad from head to foot "in white vests
of ermine, and having great chains of gold, and their caps of that large
sort which they use in the ceremonies, but whereas others were of black
fox, these were of ermine, as well as their vests; their very boots also
were covered with the same." As for the two-hundred boyars present,
they "were as so many beams of the sun," all clothed "with vests of
cloth of gold, cloth of silver set with jewels, all placed in order upon
benches covered with tapestry about the wall." The tsar's leading merchants were provided "rich robes to appear at such ceremonies" so that
they too added to the luster of the scene.

The tsar himself, of course, was the most elegantly attired person,
and the throne upon which he perched became increasingly magnificent
and costly. The tsar's crown sparkled with diamonds, and Olearius observed of Alexis' father that his golden sceptre seemed so heavy that
"he transferred it now and then from one hand to the other." Foreigners were so impressed by all this that many did not mind the fact that
alongside the throne "stood a gold basin and ewer, and a hand towel,

TSAR ALEXIS' THRONE

so that His Tsarist Majesty could wash his hands after the ambassadors had kissed it." Or perhaps some visitors comforted themselves with the realization that even this kissing of the tsar's hand was denied Turks, Tatars, Persians, and other non-Christians. Members of a Danish embassy in 1659, however, privately grumbled over their experience with Kremlin etiquette. The high point of their reception came at the moment when, with Miloslavsky and Morozov looking on from the tsar's right and left, the Danes were given the supreme honor of kissing Alexis' "dicke und fette hand."

As well as "thick and fat," Alexis' hand may not have been perfectly clean. Russians saw no reason to trouble themselves with baths in an age when filth and grime abounded. As for Alexis' weight, despite a sparse diet and considerable physical activity, he was from early years "inclined to fat" (Collins) and, just as a tree adds rings with age, so did his belly grow. But at least this Romanov looked like a true tsar. In an age when few men were so large, Alexis stood a full six feet, as if to promise a son as gigantic as Peter the Great. Nature also favored Alexis with a large frame—all of which gave him a majestic bearing. But contemporaries also were struck by the tsar's friendly appearance. We so often read of his "clear eyes" radiating kindness and sympathy for others; we are often told that his gentle features put at ease those who first approached him with dread. Alexis had a fair complexion, plump rosy cheeks, chestnut hair and a full beard. When the tsar was angered, however, people noticed a low forehead and stern countenance. This, too, befitted an absolute monarch.

Alexis often left Moscow for pilgrimages. He and the leading figures at court journeyed each year to the Trinity monastery on Trinity Sunday and St. Michael's Day (September 25). According to Olearius, the tsar and his party travelled the last half league to the cloister on foot. While the visitors were at the monastery "the abbot must furnish, without charge, provisions for the Grand Prince and his company, and feed for the horses." While here, Alexis mixed duty with pleasure. "Since the locality is extremely pretty and well stocked with game, the Grand Prince usually goes hunting there for amusement." Alexis also visited the Monastery of the Savior outside Moscow, a cloister which was greatly expanded and patronized by his father Michael so that a daily mass would be said for the souls of the Romanovs buried in the crypts under the main church. The tombs, which numbered six in Alexis' time, were covered with embroidered velvet palls, the edges of which were decorated in pearls. "At the head of each tomb is an icon," says Paul of Aleppo, "and also a candlestick with a light always burning."

Alexis' most beloved monastery was dedicated to St. Sabba the Younger, built at Zvenigorod, forty versts northwest of Moscow, to resemble the Trinity monastery. Macarius and his party were amazed at the humility and generosity the tsar displayed at the cloister when he took them there in 1656. The tsar shared the ordinary fare of the brothers, his nobles seated at a separate table to his right. But Alexis paid most attention to "the poor, the blind, and the lame" of the monastery, who sat at a table directly in front of him and received food and drink from the tsar's own hand. The meal was brief by Alexis' standards (lasting a mere two hours) since meat was not served. After a devotion and the eucharist, Alexis poured a goblet of wine for each member of the company, bidding each to take his cup and drink, referring individually and by name to each father and elder down "even to the meanest of the monks and the cooks."

The tsar lamented the deaths which had occurred at St. Sabba during the recent plague, saying: "Satan envied me the greatness of my happiness; whereas formerly there were more than 300 monks in my convent, he has destroyed most of them, and there are now left only 170." At one point Alexis took Patriarch Macarius to the infirmary to visit brothers who were paralytic and diseased, "so that he [the patriarch] might bless them and pray over them." Paul admits that some of the Greeks could not remain in the room "for the disagreeable, putrid smell" and the terrible appearance of its inhabitants. But the tsar and the patriarch visited each in turn, and Alexis "kissed the patients' head, mouth, and hands, from the first to the last." Alexis and Macarius finally went to a special cell which contained a monk who had been run over by sleigh and was continually praying that death would come and end his suffering. The tsar tried to console him while the patriarch, weeping, recited several prayers over him. Alexis was pleased by the humility of his distinguished Greek visitor, and before leaving this cell the patriarch approached the afflicted monk "to kiss his head, his mouth, and his hands, as he had done to the others."

When the tsar made ready to leave St. Sabba, the monks awaited him near the gate. Alexis distributed money from his own hands to everyone, "to the priests six dinars, to the deacons four, and to the lowest of the monks three." Macarius blessed the tsar three times, whereupon the brothers conducted their guests to the carriages. From here Alexis continued his pilgrimage, travelling fifteen versts and resting that night at another monastery.

Petitions were not presented to the tsar while he travelled. One Muscovite who did not respect this rule paid dearly for his failure in June 1667. The man was a Belorussian captain who for three years had not received his wages from Peter Saltykov, governor of Belorussia and director of the Department of Smolensk Affairs in Moscow. The captain approached the royal carriage, hoping to bring his case before the tsar, but Alexis thought the man might be an assassin. Using the pointed staff so cruelly wielded by Ivan the Terrible against his own son, Alexis tried to push the man away—but accidently struck him in the heart and killed him. When Alexis' companions searched the captain for weapons, they found nothing more than a wooden spoon and a petition for his salary. The tsar then smote his breast and cried out, "I have killed an innocent man, but Peter Saltykov—God forgive him—is guilty of his blood!" Alexis sent for Saltykov, rebuked him and turned him out of office. The

Smolensk Department was placed under the Foreign Office with orders for its director, Ordin-Nashchokin, to investigate the "misdemeanors" of Peter Saltykov. Alexis was so stung by the death of the captain that, according to Collins, "this action was but whispered, and that too with much peril of a man's tongue."

On the other hand, Alexis was so receptive to petitions while in Moscow that people felt quite free to bring their problems to him. Foreign officers wanting to leave Russian service often approached Alexis on his name day, as he was entering church. New Year's celebrations ended with petitions thrown to the sovereign "with tumultuous shouts" after which, according to Olearius, the documents were "collected and taken to the Tsar's chamber." Leaving the city or returning from a journey, travelling to a cathedral or departing for the hunt—on these and similar occasions people thronged his way, crying out to him and holding their petitions high. Alexis had these papers carefully gathered and read to him in his apartment, at which point some were accepted, other rejected. Petitions even were brought to his apartment at the Terem Palace where, according to Voyce, "the center window of the Golden Room, known as the Petitioners' window, had a device for raising and lowering a small box between the room and the ground. Into this box the poor and the wronged might place their petitions and complaints addressed directly to the tsar."

Petitioners hurried the next day to a special bureau to learn the disposition of their cases. "Those petitions marked refused are given back to their owners" says Paul of Aleppo, with a warning "not to present any more such petitions." But happy were those who received favorable action, especially when this forced crown officials to pay sums of money to settle their complaints. Sometimes Alexis himself handed the money over as a way of sharing the joy of those who benefited from his favor.

Alexis felt particular compassion for prisoners. He often went to the jails to bring them comfort and gifts; sometimes he even released an inmate who aroused special sympathy. Before mass on Easter eve Alexis brought each inhabitant of one Moscow prison an Easter egg and a sheepskin coat with the glad tidings, "Be joyful, for Christ Who has died for your sins has risen!" On Christmas morning four hours before dawn Alexis hurried to a prison and to a hospital for poor soldiers to distribute alms and holiday cheer. According to Ellersieck's sources, Alexis "observed the anniversary of his father's death [in July 1651] by paying the debts of all Russian commoners who were in prison for debts of six rubles or less." Two hours later he left Moscow again. A tsar such as Alexis was constantly on the move.

Chapter Fourteen

WHEELS OF STATE

The Russian tsar was an absolute ruler responsible to no parliament, checked by no law, judged by no mortal. He wielded his power "by the Grace of God" so that a strong sword would ever be ready to defend the Orthodox Faith and the Russian Land. He was supreme lawmaker and the highest judge of the realm. The tsar was physically like any other man, but his person was surrounded with an aura of such holy majesty that one fell to the ground before him so as not to gaze directly upon his face.

Powerful as western monarchs were in the years of Machiavelli and Hobbes, contemporary foreign travellers to Muscovy were amazed at the authority exercised by the Russian tsar, and the servility of even the greatest boyars and merchants before him. Western Europeans were struck by the fact that no Russian had *any* rights before the throne, and that far from complaining over this, Russians bragged about the cruelties of their rulers, the frequent confiscations—even executions—which many of Alexis' predecessors visited upon those who suddenly lapsed into disfavor.

Alexis had a strong sense of the importance of his office. He was particularly fascinated by Ivan the Terrible, the "mad" tsar who a century before liquidated his boyar opponents and vainly struggled to win a port on the Baltic. Alexis was entirely different from Ivan in disposition, and he had the good fortune to rule Russia at a time when Muscovy's power had grown strong enough to win significant victories against the West. Perhaps these dissimilarities were the cause of Alexis' interest in his gloomy predecessor and his times. At any rate, Alexis spent many hours listening to chronicles which dated from the later sixteenth century so that he could ponder the lessons they held for Russians a century later.

For all the power which rested in his hands, Alexis honestly and consistently tried to rule as a Christian prince. No man ever exceeded him in the desire to be a good man as well as a successful sovereign. Alexis once reflected that "God has blessed and made us tsar to rule and judge fairly our people in the East and West, and North and South." On another occasion he expressed the opinion that "it is better to carry out one's tasks with contrition, devotion and humility before God, rather than forcefully and with vain conceit." In a letter to Nikita Odoevsky in 1652 Alexis called upon the prince "to pray daily to the Lord God and His Most Immaculate Mother and all the saints, that the Creator should grant to us, the Great Tsar, and to you, the boyars, to be of one mind and to rule the nation in fairness and justice to all."

Nor were these empty words. A saying common among foreigners in Moscow during Alexis' reign was "All Christian nations would wish to have such a sovereign, but few are so fortunate!" Quotes of this sort would fill a large volume, so we must be satisfied with citing Augustine von Meyerberg, a diplomat who had little reason to be satisfied with the results of his Russian sojourn, but who still opined that Alexis displayed a "combination of goodness, kindness of character, and respect for human dignity that attracted both friend and foe." The Austrian ambassador noted that "we foreigners could never sufficiently admire the fact" that although Alexis wielded "unlimited power over a people which was fully inured to slavery, he made no attempt against the property, life or honor of a single individual." Quite the contrary, Alexis had the reputation of being anxious to restore the properties and rights of Russians unjustly handled by lower courts and crown authorities. Even if Alexis did not always conform to this benevolent image—and he did not, as we shall see in chapter twenty—it still seems that he must have been remarkably kind and sympathetic by the standards of his day.

No tsar could rule his kingdom alone, not even one as dedicated and hardworking as Alexis. The Russian sovereign relied upon a vast hierarchy of soldiers and bureaucrats, men who served the Muscovite prince in their particular capacities in exchange for rewards and privileges—as well as in the hope of being promoted to higher rank. Theoretically, a man could start at the very bottom of the ladder and ascend it (perhaps a rank at a time, perhaps benefiting from royal favor to jump one or several rungs) to the highest rank—boyar. Richard Hellie classifies these gradations of service into "Upper Service Class," "Middle Service Class," and "Lower Service Class." The lowest rank in the last group was *Soldier*, rank-and-file Russian troops in regiments modeled along western lines and officered by foreigners in service to the tsar. *Garrison Soldiers* were assigned to stockades and fortified cities. Still more privileged were the *Artillerymen*, for in addition to their salaries they quickly gained the right to live in suburbs attached to fortified border towns or cities of the interior, where they enjoyed land allotments and, in peacetime, the right to engage in handicrafts and trade. Artillerymen obtained hereditary rank after a certain term of service. In all this they were similar to the still more highly rewarded *Cossacks* and *Musketeers*.

SERVICE RANKS OF THE RUSSIAN STATE UNDER TSAR ALEXIS

Upper Service Class

(Men in the first four ranks were members of the Boyar Council)

Boyar (boyarin)
Lord in Waiting (okol'nichii)   According to Hellie, there were 62 mem-
Council Noble (dumnyi dvoryanin)   bers of these three ranks in 1668, 97 by
Council Secretary (dumnyi d'yak)   the end of the next decade.

Keeper of the Seal (pechatnik)
Master of the Horse (konyushii)
Armorer (oruzheinichii)
Warden (lovchii)
Table Attendant (stol'nik)   500 members of this rank at any
                                           one time (Kotoshikhin)
Servitor (stryapchii)   800 (Kotoshikhin)
Lord of the Bedchamber
    (postel'nichii; also spal'nik)
Moscow Noble (Moskovsky
    dvoryanin)
Resident Noble (zhil'ets)   2,000 at any one time according to Ko-
                                           toshikhin; 1,500 according to Hellie's
                                           evaluation

Middle Service Class

Gentry (dvoryanin)
Junior Boyar (syn boyarsky)

Lower Service Class

(These were service people without aristocratic standing, "service people by contract" [sluzhilye lyudi po priboru] , but their ranks were hereditary by this time)

Musketeer (strelets)
Artilleryman (pushkar')
Cossacks in state service

The military reforms of the 1630s-1650s added to the above ranks

Soldier (soldat) and such mounted ranks as Dragoon (dragun), Lancer (kopeishchik), Hussar (gusar), and ordinary cavalryman (reitar)

Peasants and poor townspeople might enter ranks of the Lower Service Class when a member was removed with no son to follow him. As one document puts it, "When [a serviceman retires] , his son must serve; if he has no son, then a [peasant] recruit [must be furnished to replace him] ."

(*) Based upon Richard Hellie, *Enserfment and Military Change in Muscovy* (Chicago, 1971), especially pages 22-25, 168, 199-200; *Dictionary of Russian Historical Terms from the Eleventh Century to 1917,* compiled by Sergei G. Pushkarev, edited by George Vernadsky and Ralph T. Fisher, Jr. (New Haven, 1970); E.M. Zhukov (Main Editor), *Sovetskaya Istoricheskaya Entsiklopediya* in sixteen volumes (Moscow, 1961-1976).

Members of the "Mid" *[handwritten: Check of Paid]* ⋯ alaries and estates in the provinces w⋯ ⋯ne needed for military service. Equi⋯ ⋯bow and arrow and mounted on small, sturdy horses, these⋯ ⋯rs formed the basis of the Muscovite armed forces at th⋯ ⋯became tsar, Alexis⋯ was fully committed to the "gunpow⋯ ⋯revolution," however, which meant that he was anxious to introduce⋯ Russian regiments trained and armed along western lines. The middle Se⋯ Class thus lost most of its former military significance. But it held⋯ on to its land grants—and even gained increasing hereditary rights ove⋯ ⋯states—in exchange for continued service to the tsar, especially in the royal bureaucracy. The Middle Service Class was comprised of *Junior Boyars* and *Gentry,* groups which formed the two lower social orders of the Russian aristocracy under Tsar Alexis. Hellie estimates that the M̲i̲d̲d̲l̲e̲ ̲S̲e̲rvice Class included some 25,000 men at any one time.

The "Upper Service" nobles lived in Moscow and garnered salaries attached to their bureaucratic posts while also enjoying the incomes of large estates scattered throughout the land. Hellie thinks that some two thousand men were numbered in this group during the entire first half of the seventeenth century. Their ranks began with a group called the *Resident Nobles,* a term deriving from the verb "to dwell" (zhili), indicating that the people in question were commanded to live in Moscow near the tsar to carry out his errands and orders and, in Alexis' case, to accompany him on military campaigns. Above them were the *Moscow Nobles,* a category established a century before Alexis when a thousand of the "best" provincial nobles were placed on choice estates near the capital to be available to perform responsible peacetime duties for the tsar, or constitute his special guards units in war. Some of the Moscow Nobles of Alexis' time were indeed descended from the original thousand families, but most were parvenus elevated to that status through their own accomplishments.

Courtiers of the Bedchamber were subdivided into several orders. The most distinguished supervised the tsar's bedroom and clothing, while others tended him during the night or roused and dressed him in the morning. Most *Servitors* were active in the army or the bureaucracy, although some, as the term would suggest (and as was indeed the case with early holders of the title) actually served the tsar in matters pertaining to food, dress and household, or assisted him at ceremonial occasions and on his travels. *Table Attendants* once performed exactly this function during grand banquets or when the tsar dined privately. By Alexis' time, however, they were important officials in the army, the Moscow bureaus, the provincial bureaucracy and diplomatic service. They did much to formulate policy and administer it. *Wardens* were responsible for the tsar's entertainment at the chase, managing his hunting preserves and stocking them with game. By Alexis' time *Armorers* and *Equerries* were important administrators as well as supervisors of royal weapons and steeds; *Keepers of the Seal* affixed the tsar's seal to edicts.

The four highest ranks enjoyed the supreme honor of membership on the Boyar Council. When the Council was in session, the *Boyars, Lords of the Chamber* and *Council Nobles* sat on benches before the tsar, the exact distance of each man from the sovereign depending upon his council rank and family lineage. The *Council Secretaries* stood and took notes on the deliberations, though sometimes the tsar invited them to take a seat. Kotoshikhin says "the more eminent and more intelligent" boyars took an active part in these discussions and gave "wise answers" to the tsar's inquiries, as did some of the talented junior figures. But "other boyars hold their beards tightly and do not answer, for in many cases the tsar confers boyar rank not for intelligence, but for exalted lineage, and many of these men are unlettered and uneducated."

The three higher ranks of the Boyar Council numbered 62 men in 1668, and with six Council Secretaries of the fourth rank constituted a true power elite. The Council wielded authority second only to that of the tsar himself, and its role in drafting edicts is seen in the characteristic opening formula: "The tsar has decreed and the boyars have assented." Under the Muscovite autocracy, however, agreement of the Council was in no way necessary for laws to take effect, nor did conflicts take place between the tsar and his "slaves" on the Council. "When the tsar speaks his mind on a particular matter," Kotoshikhin notes, "he then orders them, the boyars and council members, to consider and suggest the means" whereby the royal will might be best accomplished.

Under Alexis, members of the Boyar Council also headed most of the state bureaus, the prikazy. Boyars and Lords of the Chamber supervised the larger, more important bureaus, but smaller ones might be handed over to Council Nobles, even Table Attendants or Moscow Nobles. A Council Secretary might direct bureaus as important as the Foreign Office, the Central Office of Military Affairs, or the Service Estates Bureau, and, if successful, might be promoted to Council Noble or higher. The man who formally presided over a Bureau held the title "leading person" (nachal'nyi chelovek), but its actual administration was in the hands of secretaries and the clerks who worked under them. A large bureau was served by as many as 400 secretaries and clerks, a tiny bureau by as few as three.

The rank of bureau clerk might seem inconsequential, but it was an instrument for getting ahead in the Muscovite world. Ninety percent of the senior bureau secretaries of the seventeenth century began their careers in the lower office. Impoverished noble families joined priests, merchants, artisans, and "service people by contract" in scheming and bribing to have their sons appointed bureau clerks. As for the secretaries, their sons often were quite happy to have the opportunity to follow their fathers' paths. The clerks were either of "senior" or "junior" status. The first directed the various "desks" within a bureau, assisted by "junior" colleagues, who copied drafts of documents and memoranda prepared by the "senior" clerks. Service nobles despised bureau secretaries and clerks as low-class underlings, but they were often more highly educated than the haughty nobles, and for this reason earned the respect of foreigners. Actually, secretaries and clerks were sufficiently important in function and few in number also to be considered an elite. Vernadsky says of Leontiev and Griboedov that, "like the majority of diaks (secretareis) in Muscovite administration, [they] were not only industrious and experienced but also intelligent and able;" and, indeed, they were actually the "managing editors" of the new Law Code of 1649. Kotoshikhin estimated that there were "about one hundred secretaries and about one thousand clerks" attached to the bureaus in Moscow and to the officials they sent to the provinces.

"Supernumeraries" formed the lowest order of bureau people. They received no salary and supported themselves "from affairs," that is, through bribes received from people who hoped to expedite favorable handling of their affairs before the bureau. A supernumerary probably hoped to become a junior clerk, and then to ascend further the ladder in his particular bailiwick.

The number of bureaus was constantly changing. Twenty-two existed in 1613, forty-two at the time Kotoshikhin described Russia under Tsar Alexis. About forty prikazy existed long enough during the seventeenth century to be called "permanent;" another forty or so were created for specific tasks and soon disbanded. For example, Alexis organized the Investigatory Bureau in 1648 to liquidate tax-free properties in the suburbs and insure that their new holders were included on the tax roles. Its work speedily accomplished, the bureau was dissolved in 1652. The Historiographical Bureau is another example of a small, short-lived office. Alexis formed it in 1657 to compile a history of his dynasty, and when this was accomplished two years later, in 1659, it was closed. Most of the temporary bureaus had military functions or managed western territories occupied by Russian armies. They shared secretaries and magistrates with the permanent bureaus and were often merged and reorganized during their brief lives.

Some bureaus existed to carry out fiscal tasks. The Treasury, for example, collected direct taxes on trade and handicrafts and issued coins. The Treasury also illustrates the tendency among the bureaus to take on tasks completely unrelated to their original purposes. Sometimes this happened because tsars had confidence in a particular director, and to insure that other important tasks would receive his attention, assigned them to his office, even if the new problems had nothing to do with the bureau's ordinary work. In other cases the bureau chiefs were simply greedy for a maximum range of responsibilities and revenues. Either way, bureaus quickly were transformed into empires whose jurisdictions sprawled, clashed and overlapped in bewildering fashion. Thus, in Alexis' time the Treasury also supervised the Tula iron manufactories, held court hearings there in ownership disputes, purchased and distributed cannon balls for the army—all this despite the fact that none of this had anything to do with the fiscal activities for which the Treasury was created originally.

The most famous bureau was the Foreign Office. Formed in 1549, it operated until 1720, and during the seventeenth century was led by such important figures as Ordin-Nashchokin, Artamon Matveev, Prince Vasily Golitsyn, and L.K. Naryshkin. The Foreign Office received foreign ambassadors and carried on correspondence with foreign states. This made that bureau a highly cosmopolitan place, and foreigners knew that they could find easy employment there as translators or interpreters. Kotoshikhin notes that the fifty translators at the office in the early 1660s earned from fifty to one hundred rubles a year, while seventy interpreters received between fifteen (or less) and forty rubles annually. Paul of Aleppo was begged to remain in Moscow, "to be our interpreter and translator of the Arabic language; for we have interpreters of all languages except the Arabic." But he always answered; "I would not stay if you gave me all Moscow," to which came the good-natured reply, "You are right not to abandon your wife!"

Paul did serve the Foreign Office as an occasional translator, however, and presented it with various memoranda from his father, Patriarch Macarius of Antioch. He tells us that the chief of the Office collected petitions which fell within its jurisdictions and relayed them to Alexis, "who writes upon them what his pleasure is." If the tsar were absent from Moscow, the petitions were presented to his "deputy or lieutenant," for the bureau head "can do nothing of his own authority."

The Foreign Office maintained a library of books and newspapers from Western Europe. Alexis was curious about developments abroad and demanded regular briefings from the Office. This took on a more systematic form after 1665, when the Foreign Office began to issue two news bulletins each month, one copy for the tsar and his leading assistants, another for its own work. This information was regarded as "highly secret," for in addition to current events Alexis wanted to know what the foreign press was saying about Russia. By nature Alexis was secretive and ever anxious to know what was going on behind his back. Collins asserted that Alexis "has his spies in every corner," and even claimed "'tis death for any one to reveal what is spoken in the tsar's palace," where his "sentinels and guards stand silent like statues;" hence, "no noise is heard in the palace, no more than if it were uninhabited." The Foreign Office did what it could to read the mail of foreigners and to learn the secrets of their embassies to Moscow. Once, in 1659, Alexis boasted that as a mark of his great friendship for the king of Denmark, he had *not* opened letters from the king to his envoy which had arrived in Moscow before Oldeland himself. Alexis did ask, though, that news contained in the documents be communicated to him.

Some bureaus had military responsibilities. The Foreigner Bureau, for example, was the office which from 1624 engaged, supervised and paid foreigners in the tsar's service, most of whom were professional soldiers. The Cannon Bureau oversaw the production and import of armaments. Alexis organized the Cavalry Bureau in 1649 to manage his dragoon and infantry regiments of Western type. Other bureaus performed specific functions at least partly indicated by their names. The Monastery Bureau which later caused such friction between himself and Patriarch Nikon was formed in 1649 to oversee the economic affairs of the monasteries, to act as a judicial administration over them and collect revenues from peasants living on their lands. The Pharmaceutical Bureau recruited physicians and specialists in related fields, organized Russia's first medical schools, saw to the cultivation of plants and herbs needed for healing, and maintained a pharmacy in Moscow sufficiently large and magnificent to earn lavish praise from foreign visitors.

The Bureau of the Grand Court was one of the most important departments in the earlier seventeenth century, but it steadily lost Alexis' confidence. It had been the instrument whereby tsars had managed various economic affairs of the Church, but after 1649 most of these tasks were brought under the jurisdiction of the Monastery Bureau. The Bureau of the Grand Court was also responsible for directing the sovereign's estates, his commercial operations and manufacturing activities. But Alexis was so appalled by the office's heavy bureaucracy and general inefficiency that after 1663 he handed the responsibility for increasing

numbers of his lands and enterprises to his Privy Chancellery, the celebrated *Prikaz tainykh del,* or "Bureau of Secret Affairs."

No single institution tells us as much about Tsar Alexis as the Privy
Chancellery. He created it in 1654 as a personal staff to counteract the
notorious sluggishness and incompetency of the other state bureaus. The
tsar was then planning to accompany his armies in battle against the
Poles, and in his absence he wanted an office in Moscow to which even
the poor could deliver petitions with some assurance of sympathetic
consideration. This meant that the Privy Chancellery was to exercise
supervisory powers over even the most powerful bureaus with their officials basking in entrenched powers and revenues. To emphasize the
power and the importance of the Privy Chancellery, Alexis himself was
its minister. It must have been a rather small bureau, though, judging
from the fact that generally it was staffed by no more than fifteen clerks.
Nor did its officials come from the higher ranks of society which provided leadership for other bureaus. The members of the Privy Chancellery rested comfortable in the realization, however, that more than any
other group in the capital they were the tsar's personal agents, and, as
years went by, Alexis himself was increasingly involved in the day-to-day
management of its affairs.

Because the Privy Chancellery was a personal instrument of the tsar,
it tended to his most private concerns. For example, it supervised two
hundred royal falconers who tended 3,000 falcons, gyrfalcons, and
hawks, as well as the 100,000 pigeon nests which were used to feed and
train the birds. The Privy Chancellery kept Alexis' personal cash box
and oversaw the Kremlin Amusement Palace where the tsar was entertained and kept in a fit mood. Much of Alexis' private correspondence
went through the Privy Chancellery, which also handled his alms and
charities, and the distribution of many church books. The affairs of
Alexis' favorite monastery, St. Sabba the Elder, also fell within its pur-
view.

Some contemporaries supposed that Alexis' decision to assign his
economic holdings to the Privy Chancellery would deal an even greater
setback to the Bureau of the Grand Court than creation of the Monastery Bureau in 1649. Much insight is gained into the prikaz system, however, once it is realized that the Bureau of the Grand Court was hardly
affected by these reversals. It simply gained two new rivals, two new in-
stitutions which had to be fought for jurisdictions and incomes, and
undermined in every possible way. Symptomatic of long-range realities
was the fact that the newcomers were abolished speedily when Alexis
died in 1676, whereas the Bureau of the Grand Court survived even
Peter the Great!

The prikaz system suffered from the fact that it was not the rational product of a genuine bureaucratic scheme. Bureaus were created from time to time over the centuries to deal with certain problems, but their duties and competencies were formulated—if at all—in the most general terms. The tsar and his Boyar Council were themselves often at a loss to know where to refer an unprecedented or unusually complex matter, and the solution to such a dilemma often enough was to create yet another bureau, thus adding to the overall confusion. Functions and jurisdictions were hammered out over months and years through a rich intrigue in which the struggle for private advantage was naked, brutal, and unapologetic.

All this created little efficiency or sense of common purpose among those whose highest honor in life was supposedly to serve the tsar.

Chapter Fifteen

ALEXIS THE MILITARY REFORMER

Alexis was interested in military questions. He was personally in the field during two years of crucial fighting against Poland, and carefully observed all aspects of life at the front. Alexis was not so vain as to attempt to direct strategy and tactics in detail, but he did acquire enough experience to fancy himself as something of a military expert. Among the tsar's papers of this period are strategic exercises and a notebook sketching army encampments and positions. Alexis was a more prolific author than any other tsar—indeed few Russian contemporaries of any sort exceeded him in breadth of interest and vigorous style. His numerous and lengthy letters contain graphic eyewitness accounts of sieges and battles, as well as subtle, perceptive accounts of camp life. The tsar was capable of asserting forceful discipline, but his letters and memoranda show that he was also acutely aware of fluctuations in morale among his officers and men. Later in life Alexis spoke of a desire to write his memoirs of the Polish war, though he never accomplished this task.

Alexis knew that the victory of his armies depended upon much more than his encouragement on the battlefield. The Russian armed forces had to be reformed along Western lines. To the credit of Tsar Alexis he did not merely contemplate these needs, nor did he succumb to the xenophobia of churchmen and boyars which would have had him ignore the foreigner and let things Russian remain as they were. Alexis pushed with great personal determination to translate his visions into real life. In an explosion of energy which burned low—but hot and unflickering— for a quarter of a century, Alexis issued a stream of commands (many in his own hand) to recruit mercenaries and foreign military specialists, to buy munitions and supplies in foreign lands, to form new Russian regiments of "foreign" type, to build the first Russian warships, to purchase secret weapons which, if rumors proved but half true, would give the tsar's legions nearly superhuman fighting power. Alexis did not gain all he wanted in these areas, but he accomplished so much that it is hard to imagine how someone else in his time or place could have done better.

Above all, Alexis attacked the traditional Russian *opolchenie*, the "levy" which called the service noble with horse and peasant retainers to active duty. When Russia went to war under Alexis' father in 1632, 26,000 such nobles presented themselves, less than half of whom actually took the field. The training of these men was haphazard, their service reluctant and uninspired, and they showed badly against the Polish legions so justly famed for their training and leadership. The basic problem of the Russian army was that by the seventeenth century its main battles were coming to lie in the west, but for the most part it had been organized and prepared to defend against nomadic and Tatar raids in the south and east. The "levy" of service nobles had been reasonably effective on this terrain, as was the support of its standing reserves: 11,200 service Cossacks, 10,200 Mongols, 8,500 Chuvash and Cheremis tribesmen, according to the army rolls of 1630. But the service nobles, the striking force of the Russian army, were inadequate in every way when used against Poland.

Alexis could discern the future from the fact that the few Russian units which performed well in the disastrous Smolensk campaign of 1633 were the "new model regiments" organized along western lines, trained and commanded by 105 foreign officers. Unfortunately, the Russian government did not have sufficient time to build many such units. When Moscow suddenly decided to attack, it had available a mere six infantry regiments (with 6,118 soldiers), along with a 2,000-man cavalry regiment and an understrength regiment of dragoons. But these units did not break under Polish fire, as did the levy of nobles. Nor did the more highly disciplined soldiers pillage and rape Russian civilians, as did the purely mercenary units of foreigners in "service" to the tsar. Maintenance of the "new model regiments" cost 129,000 rubles a year, however, so they were disbanded after the war.

When Alexis became tsar, then, the only soldiers at his disposal who by any exercise of charity could be called "professional" were the musketeers. They numbered almost 20,000 in 1632, and when created in the days of Ivan the Terrible were a force to be reckoned with. By Alexis' time, however, their military effectiveness had eroded greatly. Not only were the musketeers untrained in new military methods, their equipment was outmoded. Even worse, over the years the government had economized in their support by shifting from cash salaries and the demand that they be on duty full time—vital factors in building a "professional" army—to land grants and trade-artisan "privileges" during peacetime. Alexis' elite musketeer bodyguard impressed Moscow's civilian population when the tsar moved about the city or appeared on ceremonial occasions. But the tsar himself was not fooled. Alexis knew the fighting power of his musketeers was low, and after their performance in the riots of 1648 he no longer even supposed they could be counted upon to protect him from a mob.

During the remainder of his reign Alexis moved to create "new model regiments" of Russian soldiers, units drilled and officered by foreigners. His efforts grew especially energetic after 1651, as the likelihood of war with Poland steadily loomed larger. The Russian army was divided into infantry, cavalry and dragoons. Russians were recruited for these branches through a system whereby each noble estate was obliged to supply an infantryman and a cavalryman for each ten to thirty households—the number varying from year to year and from one corner of the realm to the next. Sometimes entire villages were drafted, especially in the south, where some served as soldiers and cavalry, the remainder as support workers. Well over 100,000 members of the working population were mobilized in this manner between 1654 and 1679. Alexis occasionally even conscripted landless nobles "of scanty means" into the new regiments as ordinary soldiers at a monthly salary, ignoring their complaints that this "degraded" them to the status of peasants and bondsmen.

Alexis' generosity to foreigners able to command these soldiers quickly became so well known that hundreds, even thousands, of commissioned and non-commissioned soldiers flocked to enter his service. They came from as far away as Spain, by sea and overland, with or without prior invitation, accompanied by families though usually travelling alone. Most were lowly corporals and lieutenants, some were captains and colonels. From the outset Alexis engaged Lord Charles Edgard as a "Generalissimo" with the right to promote associates to the rank of lieutenant-colonel. We do not know exactly how many foreigners entered Russian service in these years, but the number must have been considerable. Sources indicate that in 1661 alone 82 officers and 207 non-commissioned officers took up the tsar's colors, including such

eventual celebrities in Russian life as Colonel Crawford, Major Patrick
Gordon and Captain Paul Menezius. Meyerberg noted in 1661 that there
was an "endless multitude" of foreign soldiers in Russia. He personally
knew four generals and more than a hundred colonels alone. Records
show that in 1663, 55,714 Russian soldiers in 55 infantry regiments
were commanded by 2,422 officers, nearly all from Western Europe.
Eighteen thousand Russian cavalrymen were enlisted at that time in
"new" regiments.

Alexis favored Russian regiments of European type as the basis of
the new Russian army, but he also recruited mercenary units for service
in Russia. The tsar was so pleased by the offer of Colonel Fjünberg to
raise regiments abroad that, for example, in November 1660 he allowed
the Dane to recruit four infantry and four cavalry regiments, "trained
people in all respects in full armament, with firearms masters, engineers,
gunners, and all sorts of innovators." Perhaps a quarter of the army of
1663—14,000 men—was comprised of mercenaries, compared with six
percent of the much smaller army raised under Alexis' father in 1632.
The influx of foreign soldiers into Russia made it possible for Alexis to
rely less upon the traditional levy of service nobles. While their number
rose from 26,000 to over 39,000 between 1632 and 1651 (giving them
thirty percent of the army's total effective strength), John Keep's analysis of the Muscovite elite notes that, under the military budget for 1662-
63, the total number of nobles under active military service fell to
21,850, "of whom 14,598 seem to have been mobilized in the traditional way.

Foreign military treatises were at least slightly known in Russia before Alexis came to the throne. The king of Sweden sent Fronsperger's
Kriegsbuch to Russia in 1607, along with an appeal the next year for
the Muscovites to rise up against the "Polish and Lithuanian dogs." In
the next several years treatises of Europe's leading military theoretician,
the Dutch writer Johann Jacobi van Wallhausen, were quickly translated
into foreign languages. Alexis was so eager to tap foreign thinking on the
art of war that between 1647 and 1649 he personally pressed the publication in Holland of a Russian translation of Wallhausen's *Krijghskonst
te Voet* (The Art of Infantry Warfare; 1617). This was the first Russian
infantry drill manual, the first book in Russian to display copper engravings, and but the third secular title in the history of Russian book
publishing. In a burst of optimism Alexis had 1,200 copies printed of
The Study and Craft of the Military Formation of Infantrymen, the
English equivalent of the Russian title of Wallhausen's. This translation
project is an interesting example of how informed Russians of the day

hoped to apply Western learning to Russian problems on an ambitious scale. The *Study* had no direct effect on the Russian army, however, for only 134 were sold in Russia, most of these to civilian readers who were often enough learned priests. Each foreign colonel followed his own drill method to the very end of Alexis' reign—and later.

Western technology greatly fascinated the tsar, and Alexis was determined that Russia must have its finest products. His instructions to agents going abroad continually urge them to obtain the "best" of everything. Thus Alexis instructed Colonel Frantz to travel to Holland in 1658 to recruit "such engineers as have no equal in all Europe," while John Hebdon was dispatched "to foreign lands" to obtain "the best colonels and instructors in military formation," as well as outstanding firearm and grenade makers, and fortification experts.

The instructions given to Frantz and Hebdon were difficult, but at least possible of being executed. In other instances, however, Alexis breezily handed down orders for all sorts of "artful things," "wonders which are not in the Muscovite state" but which he believed were available in the mysterious, technological West. Hebdon once was instructed to buy "a glass such as may be placed under a city so that everything in the city may be seen." Another agent was to fetch back "the very best sappers, who would be able to carry out sapping under a river, and under a lake, and through stone mountains, and upwards through a mountain and through water" by using "such sapping equipment as would enable a man to dig two sazhens [about fourteen feet] in the strongest places, and ten sazhens in easy places in twenty-four hours."

Alexis' agents did indeed report exciting weapons from time to time. Johann van Horn, the tsar's permanent representative in Lübeck, treated the leading merchant Peter Mikiyaev, Alexis' special envoy to the city, to a secret demonstration in 1660 "of high-explosive musket charges which had not been used earlier in the German wars [the Thirty Years War] ; and the cartridge master secretly fired those high-explosive charges for Peter, having taken him to a faraway place from the city. And the charges of that musket went a distance of 80 sazhens." But Mikiyaev explained to Alexis that "Johann did not give him samples without a government order for those high-explosive musket charges."

Alexis often reached for his notebook to sketch out new weapons of his own design. Colonel Nicholas Bauman, an artillery master from Holstein, showed Danish visitors to Moscow in 1659 designs for a cannon which the tsar had invented, and he described weapons tests which Alexis attended. Alexis also relished military reviews on Moscow's Devich'oe field, and for hours cannons, projectiles and regiments passed before their sovereign's admiring eyes. Alexis himself planned many of these parades, and his officials spared no care to make them impressive. A special messenger was dispatched from the Privy Chancellery to the Tula iron works on March 7, 1658 "to take from iron production at Tula one hundred hand grenades and fifty medium [weight grenades] that are pushed by feet, and bring these grenades to Moscow by the 12th day of March, and to give [all this] at Moscow to the Privy Chancellery of our great sovereign, to secretary Dementy Bashmakov."

The four large iron manufactories at Tula were the pride of Russian industry at the time Alexis became tsar. Established by a partnership of Dutch merchants which included Boris Morozov, they were the first major iron works in Russia to use water power and modern European technology. Situated just south of Moscow, at Tula, long a center of iron artisan forges, foreign masters and Russian apprentices labored here after 1637 to supply Russia's armies with barrels for muskets, carbines and pistols, as well as with armor and spiked helmets.

The tsar took strong measures to expand iron manufacturing, and by the end of his reign a dozen new enterprises dotted the Russian land. One of these iron works was built by Morozov after leaving the Tula project, another by Ilya Miloslavsky, seven of the remainder by the crafty entrepreneur Peter Marselis, sometimes in cooperation with his stolid and unimaginative partner, Filimon Akema.

The output of these and other enterprises did much to modernize the equipment of the Russian armies. Besides the traditional matchlock musket, Alexis' infantrymen were supplied with the lighter flintlock musket worked by a striking hammer, and even a few firearms loaded at the breach. Russian cavalry acquired pistols and carbines as reliable as those used by their western counterparts. Cast-iron cannon not only replaced copper pieces, artillery fire in general came to be better coordinated with cavalry charges and infantry movements. Foreigners observing Russian artillery under Tsar Alexis lavishly praised both the quality of the weapons and their use. Alexis and his military assistants consistently assigned talented men to the artillery to serve as gunners, siege-engineers, grenadiers and marksmen. Assigned to border fortresses and the major cities and towns within the empire, these men earned considerable respect from both Russians and European visitors. A Danish envoy to Moscow in 1673, for example, after witnessing an artillery demonstration declared that he had "never seen such good shooting with grenades."

The military authorities also made an effort to strengthen the defenses of cities. The Time of Troubles had demonstrated clearly the inadequacy of the wooden walls and earthen barriers surrounding Russian towns; during the 1630s the government therefore began to employ Dutch engineers to supplement such structures with stone fortifications. Cornelius Claus of Holland was commissioned to work upon the Rostov fortress, while in Alexis' time de Musheron labored to rebuild Astrakhan and Terek after Razin's rebellion made tragically evident the weakness of their defenses. Following the terrible fire at Archangel in 1667, Alexis decided that the city's walls and defense works should be rebuilt in stone. The tsar appointed Peter Marselis to work on this project together with Willem Shapf, who made extensive sketches and began construction the next year. But stone was such a scarce and costly commodity and was so difficult to transport that Alexis was not able to accomplish all that he desired in improving the defenses of Russian towns. Yet he often instructed his agents to engage foreign specialists in "town fortification" for service in Russia.

The project for strengthening Astrakhan included building a war fleet on the Caspian Sea, a flotilla designed to suppress the piracy of "thievish Cossacks" and to foster trade with Persia. The tsar exhibited the good sense to reject proposals for oar-powered ships in favor of sail vessels, reminding his advisers that "when the Holstein diplomats in recent years sailed on a ship to Persia, their [oar-powered] ship was destroyed on the sea." John of Sweden happened to be going abroad on his own business at the time Alexis' naval project was reaching fruition in 1667, and the tsar ordered his merchant friend to engage foreign shipwrights to build and sail the five small craft of the planned fleet. Four European shipwrights labored on the ships at Dedinov from the summer of 1667 until November 1668.

Alexis spent over 9,000 rubles on this venture. The principal vessel was the Eagle, so named because the double-headed eagle was then the symbol of the Russian monarchy. The captain was David Buthler, who with fourteen other Dutch sailors and masters supervised transport of the ships from Dedinov to Astrakhan, where they were launched in early 1670. But disaster befell this first Russian sea-going fleet. Stenka Razin and his rebel forces (which included a flotilla of 200 small boats) took Astrakhan in June. Buthler was fortunate enough to escape with his life, but the insurgents burned the Eagle to a skeleton. The attention Alexis had lavished on all these ships had gone for naught, and Russia was forced to wait another quarter-century, until Peter's masterful Azov campaign, for construction of a permanent ocean-going navy.

Alexis' wars and military preparations imposed a tremendous burden upon Russia. The crown was spending about 275,000 rubles each year on the army during the 1620s; by 1680, four years after Alexis died, the figure had climbed to 700,000 rubles, a tremendous increase even after making allowance for an inflation rate which may have been as high as 25 percent. We do not know the share of government expenditure absorbed by the armed forces in Alexis' time since the first state budget was not drafted until 1680. The army then consumed some 62 percent of the total expenditure of 1,125,323 rubles, compared with 24 percent for court expenses and royal pensions.

In a poor and backward country such as Russia the tax burden fell most heavily upon the peasants—and they could hardly bear the burden. Richard Hellie thinks that crop-to-seed yields in Russia at this time normally were less than three to one, scarcely more than in Western Europe almost a thousand years before. Hellie notes the irony that in the very years in which Alexis attempted modernization of the army, his job was made more difficult by an actual *drop* in yield-ratios, a decline partly caused by unusually severe winters in Eastern Europe between 1651 and 1680. While the peasant forked over additional cash payments for the new army, he also continued to support "the middle service class by payments in kind". The symptoms of distress were clear: taxes were collected with difficulty and remained often in arrears, army salaries were paid erratically and seldom in full, peasants fled their estates or sometimes raised fire and fist against noble landowners. The uprisings in Pskov and Novgorod in 1649 and 1650 were largely protests against crown grain exports, exports which paid for arms imports but also drove up food prices throughout the land. Even royal officials admitted that the tax burden was terrible and unrelenting. Alexis honestly thought of himself as a benevolent father-tsar, but to many modern historians it seems that his army existed as much to control and plunder its own people as to defend the land from foreign enemies.

Some households levied and collected their "share" of taxes through their own elected board of elders. The people of these villages were known as "black peasants," inhabitants of "black lands"—lands belonging to the state. Because their farming villages were directly under crown jurisdiction and not held by monasteries or nobles, these peasants were as close to being "free" as any element of the lower classes in Russia at that time. But most taxes were paid by *serfs*—peasants attached to the lands of monasteries or nobles (including those of the tsar). The only role these households were invited to play in the economic process was to come up with their assessments in money, labor and soldiers as best they could. The district lords and their bailiffs avidly stalked such rubles, along with "donations," "bribes" and "honors"—all of which the desperate, frightened peasants offered in hope of suffering the least harsh treatment possible. Alexis constantly and fiercely admonished his district lords to enforce his edicts justly and not abuse their powers; indeed, he threatened them with the death penalty for doing anything less. Yet the administrative cost of provincial government was held down by continuing the ancient tradition whereby the district lords supplemented their salaries from Moscow by "maintenance" in the provinces—money and "gifts" from the local population—and those who requested such posts commonly included in their petitions the plea "Let me go to *such-and-such-a-place* to feed myself!"

The crown offices in Moscow which held jurisdiction over districts in the provinces might send magistrates and judges to investigate and rectify the worst acts of a district lord; nobles and even commoners also might request investigations. But prospective petitioners knew that they might suffer even more should local officials somehow manage to remain in office after such an "investigation." In any case, dealing with Moscow was slow and frustrating—as we see from the plaintive cry of the service nobles at the Assembly of the Land in 1642 who told Tsar Michael "we are worse afflicted by the red tape of Moscow, Sire, than by the Turks and Tatars." In short, local government under Alexis operated according to the ancient principle that the strong are permitted everything whereas the weak suffer what they must or, as the old Muscovite saying has it, "the wolf is near, and on a cold, dark night the tsar is indeed far away."

The district lord also exercised military responsibilities. His title ("voevoda" or commander) actually originated as a military rank and it was not until the Time of Troubles that the voevoda was dispatched to the provinces as a civilian authority. In Alexis' time the district lord was usually the local official who handled orders to send men and material to Moscow or elsewhere. He might also accompany and command regiments in the field in wartime. Russian armies moved in the formation familiar in the west: advance, left, center, right and rear regiments. The center unit in Russian was called the "Great regiment," and its voevoda, the senior officer, was called the "Great Commander." When Alexis went on campaign he bestowed the honor of his presence upon this regiment.

Alexis' care for the army led him to organize new bureaus to deal with specific military problems. In his first four years as tsar Alexis established the Dragoon Bureau, the Cavalry Bureau, and the Bureau of Artillery Barrel Manufacturing Affairs—each to supervise affairs relevant to its particular branch of the Russian war machine. Alexis once reminded his officers that "people, not grain, make fortresses firm against enemies," but he well understood Napoleon's dictum that, for an army to fight well, it must eat well. And so, at the height of the Thirteen Years War against Poland and Sweden in 1663, Alexis instituted the Grain Bureau to supply the army at the front. The sovereign was actually ahead of his time in pressing for a regular provisioning service, and the Grain Bureau was abolished after his death. A permanent quartermaster corps was established only under Peter the Great.

Alexis also turned his attention to how his armies might best be raised and maintained in areas distant from Moscow. He supplemented the traditional administrative division of Russia into civil districts (volosti) with a new unit, the "military district" (razryad). The Central Office of Military Affairs (razryadnyi prikaz) supervised these military districts, the first of which were created in areas won or regained in war (for example, Smolensk in 1654). Other areas were on the southern or eastern frontier, in Siberia or in the vicinity of Kazan and elsewhere on the Volga, where the object was to strengthen Moscow's hold over areas but loosely defended in the past. The Central Office of Military Affairs tended to military matters in its subject districts and kept careful rolls of service people settled on local estates. Bureau officials periodically revised the records so that the tsar would know the exact quantity of men, horses, and military supplies available throughout the kingdom. The system worked so well that just after Alexis' death military districts were formed in central Russia, too, and in every corner of the land they gained control over revenues once routinely dispatched to the Central Office of Military Affairs at Moscow. Alexis' search for greater administrative efficiency in this case helped stimulate his son Peter to a sweeping redivision of Russia into new administrative units.

The tsar had considerable reason to be pleased with the new army he labored so hard to create. He derived particular satisfaction from the way his legions performed against Poland and Sweden in the early years of the Thirteen Years War. Russian foot soldiers were armed with lighter, more effective weapons than had previously been the case, while the artillery—much improved—did a credible job of supporting infantry movements and cavalry charges. Russia's western foes came to speak respectfully of the "Dutch cleverness" of the Russian forces. If the tsar's armies were not always or in every way the equal of Poland and Sweden, on the whole they fought well enough to enable Muscovite diplomats in the 1660s to wrest concessions which had been out of the question as recently as 1634.

Admirable as Alexis' military reforms were, he was able to sustain an effective "modern" army only so long as Russia was actively at war.

Fiscal pressures were so great that Muscovy could not maintain the fighting machine created with such labor and ingenuity during the Thirteen Years War. When peace was concluded in 1667, the pressure to maintain an army of maximum strength inevitably disappeared. Twenty to twenty-five regiments of Western European type (totaling 25-30,000 soldiers) remained on "active duty," but otherwise the Russian military forces were comprised of units which were not so very different from those which existed at the time Alexis became tsar.

The musketeers, for example, were still poorly trained and equipped. They brooded over the role they might play in the warfare of the future—but not sufficiently to improve themselves as soldiers! The 55,000 men enrolled as musketeers in 1681 treasured their commercial and handicraft privileges more than their military calling. How could it be otherwise when they served a beggarly government which paid them so miserably and irregularly?

The gentry and junior boyars also realized that they were increasingly irrelevant to modern war—and likewise failed to respond creatively, as soldiers, to the challenge. Once the lower service nobles gained permanent control over the peasants on their estates they evaded service on an unprecedented scale, and were even less prepared to fight than before. As the years passed under Tsar Alexis they fell into a mellow, mindless routine of eating and drinking, carousing and celebrating every possible festive occasion. The historian Nikolai Ustryalov portrays an existence wherein "for entire months the carbine and musket would hang peacefully on the wall, covered with rust, and the soldier-service noble busied himself with plow, ground meal, went to the fair and sold what he could. To collect them for a campaign was no less difficult than before." Nor was their service, when claimed, of higher quality.

The "new model regiments" which had been the basis of the Muscovite army during the Thirteen Years War were still effective units, especially when well led. But their full potential was limited by the fact that their "European" characteristics seldom survived for very long. Many of the soldiers turned to small-scale handicrafts and trade, even to farming town plots to supplement their meager, irregularly paid salaries. Thus they were sliding uncomfortably close to the decadent musketeers, especially with the development of the practice whereby the sons of soldiers entered their father's regiments upon reaching manhood.

The quality of foreign officers in Russian service also deteriorated in Alexis' later years. Even at the high point of his military innovations he could commission only those who arrived in his distant, forbidding land, and many of their number were lazy and incompetent. Scotch

Royalists in Russia such as the Drummonds and Hamiltons were among the world's finest soldiers, but Sir Patrick Gordon confided to his diary in 1663 that a "significant part" of the foreign officers who had been arriving in Muscovy in the last two years were "foul, low people," many of whom had not really "served as officers" elsewhere. Schleizing admitted in this period that some "gallant people" were in military service to Alexis, especially those "who were sent for by the tsar from abroad, and who earlier had served the Swedish, Polish, and other kings." But Schleizing had no praise for most of the foreign officers he met in Russia: "Some of them are called old, others new foreigners. The old foreigners were born in Russia [and] the foreign blood in them has vanished; a great part of them have Russian manners, go about in Russian dress and are very poor in the military art, [for they] remember little or even nothing about it. For the best officers, the wretched birds who have landed here are so obnoxious that they are simply splinters in the eye. They have not returned to their homelands because their fathers and grandfathers took eternal citizenship in the [Muscovite] state, and many of the accepted the Russian faith."

Ironically, after many of these foreigners were settled on estates—a practice which relieved the government of the need to pay them cash salaries—they proceeded to take up lives all too similar to those of the Russians: they evaded calls to duty, their service was of terrible quality when it could be had, their aspirations and concerns revolved entirely around their families and lands. They came to Moscow to teach Russians what Russians did not know, but ended by learning how easygoing life in Russia—as led by some Russians—might really be.

Chapter Sixteen

ALEXIS THE BUSINESSMAN

Alexis was the most powerful man in Russia—and the richest. His incredibly diverse economic interests ranged from farming to artisan trades to commercial operations on an international scale. All this fell to the young sovereign as part of his royal inheritance. Unlike other tsars, however, Alexis was a dynamic and innovating entrepreneur. Though not a stormy, combative person such as Peter the Great, Alexis was no more able than his son to leave untouched those worldly affairs which engaged his concern. Earlier tsars collected the profits of their enterprises without playing a role in their management or development. Alexis expanded his holdings in entirely new directions, and with the instincts of a fine businessman tended to even small details in the operation of his economic "empire."

The tsar's lands and enterprises traditionally were managed by the Bureau of the Grand Court. We gain some idea of Alexis' wealth from the fact that when Alexis became tsar the Bureau had royal lands populated by 27,200 serf homesteads under its jurisdiction, compared with 7,012 homesteads held by the next greatest landowner, the tsar's cousin Nikita Romanov. (Two other nobles held estates with 6,000 and 5,000 homesteads, one with nearly 3,000, eight with 2,500 to 1,000 peasant households). The Bureau of the Grand Court also managed trade activities on the tsar's lands. In Moscow alone it supervised eight artisan communities: cauldron makers, lead smelters, smiths, carpenters, tent makers, potters, stove makers, and brick bakers.

But Alexis was displeased by the general inefficiency of the Bureau of the Grand Court. The Bureau, of course, was no worse than other government bureaucracies, its sluggish procedures and heavy paperwork merely reflected established Muscovite practice. But tradition confronted a new spirit in Tsar Alexis. He demanded that difficult tasks be handled, not evaded—and quickly. Above all, he stressed the need for *order* in human affairs, a proper relationship between all parts small and large of an undertaking. He once reflected that "without order nothing will be established and strengthened, without structure things will be lost and nothing will develop." Alexis found symmetry and proportion in all things: a falcon hunt or a winter scene, an army on campaign or a campfire at the front. From his writings it seems he even saw aesthetic qualities in business structures and transactions. But the beauty of all that, for him, hinged upon the "rightness" of the thing. Given this mentality, Alexis was not destined to rely indefinitely upon the Bureau of the Grand Court to manage his economic activities of particular interest.

Alexis found that the Privy Chancellery which he had created in 1654 handled crown affairs with care and dispatch, so he began adding responsibilities. The Privy Chancellery oversaw some 30 towns, as well as a number of agricultural villages and districts by 1664. Alexis assigned it more properties each year, and at the time of his death in 1676 the Privy Chancellery had direct jurisdiction over almost 2,500 peasant homesteads with a tilled area well in excess of 400,000 acres. At that time the Grain Bureau oversaw, under supervision of the Privy Chancellery, royal lands populated by another 14,900 peasant homesteads.

Alexis eventually made it a practice to assign his best lands to the Privy Chancellery. Its secretaries and clerks scurried about Russia in the last dozen years of the tsar's life, reporting to Alexis on the quality of various soils and pasturages, their advantages for farming and other economic activities. The object of this was to add profitable areas to the royal domains, and if the Chancellery decided that a certain area would harmonize well with existing crown operations, it would force even powerful boyars to sell or trade the property. If Alexis were angry at a particular noble, he might order the Privy Chancellery to confiscate his holdings, or force their sale at but a fraction of fair market value. All this made the Privy Chancellery something of a bourgeois praetorian guard, respected for its power, hated for the exercise of it.

The Chancellery also took over properties of special or sentimental concern to Tsar Alexis. The sovereign was a major heir of his childless first cousin Nikita Romanov, and when Nikita died in 1652 certain of his properties went to the tsar. They eventually passed under supervision of the Privy Chancellery, as did a major part of the economic holdings of Boris Morozov, Alexis' brother-in-law, after he and Anna (the sister of Tsarina Maria) died without children. The tsar did not want the village of Pokrovskoe administered indifferently, for Alexis remembered how as a young man he often went there with Morozov, acquiring in this way part of his eventual interest in the entrepreneurial life.

Alexis enjoyed visiting his estates. In the spring and summer he often left the crowded and noisy capital to travel to nearby lands at Preobrazhenskoe, Kolomenskoe, and the Sparrow Hills. Alexis was accompanied by his family—"by the sovereign's entire house," the records put it—by favorite court members and the gray, relentless officials of the Privy Chancellery. Special steps were taken to make the rough lodges and cabins along the way as comfortable as possible. The ladies relished walks through scenes of breath-taking natural beauty while Alexis and the men enjoyed the tsar's favorite sport—falconry. But Alexis mixed pleasure with business. At every stop he received reports and oral briefings on economic activities since his last stay, and, assisted by his Chancellery staff, issued commands to guide his agriculturalists through the remainder of the season. He often inspected on foot the grounds of his estates.

The finest expression of Alexis' interest in agriculture was Izmailovo, a town near Moscow which over the years he built into an amazing agricultural showcase and experimental station. Alexis took the first steps to develop Izmailovo in 1663, when he had rude quarters built there for himself. He also began to relocate peasant families from his other estates to Izmailovo. Specialists were soon hustling about within the settlement's baroque gates and walls, hauling rocks to dam up streams, digging fish ponds, erecting mills and barns as well as threshing floors and bins made of that rarest of Russian building materials, stone.

Alexis began Izmailovo's economic life with farming and fruit orchards, but soon branched out into livestock experiments. His repeated efforts to import Persian sheep were frustrating, for the exotic animals all died under Russian conditions, but the tsar's stables were esteemed throughout the kingdom, as were his superior breeds of cattle, pigs, geese, chickens, and ducks. The thirty-seven fish ponds scattered about Izmailovo teemed with a splashing array of sterlet, perch, pike, pike-perch, bream, ide, crucian, tench, and wild carp. The grounds were speckled with windmills and laced with irrigation canals running to fields so large that at planting time the work force swelled to 700 souls. Other workers tended impressive gardens which boasted some of Russia's finest apples, cherries, pears, currants, gooseberries, raspberries and strawberries. Izmailovo also had two orchards and two kitchen gardens, and a large experimental section where Alexis made efforts (often successfully) over the years to develop Persian grapes and cucumbers, melons from Bukhara, strains of wheat which flourished in the stern valleys of Greece, Astrakhan watermelons, almond trees and pepper plants, "India berries" (indigo?), Caucasus cornel, Hungarian pear trees—as well as various breeds of madder, herbs, date trees, cotton and pumpkins. It seems that Alexis wanted to have anything in his garden which did not yet grow in Russia! Strange plants were brought to Izmailovo from Simbirsk, Astrakhan and Terek. Orders in the tsar's own hand commanded Hebdon to fetch back to Moscow "foreign trees a sazhen in length" (no other specifications!), while among the objectives of an embassy to London in 1662 was to seek out "all sorts of seeds which are expected to grow in the soil of Moscow." Gardeners from Astrakhan and lands further to the east continually visited the tsar and advised him on how to adapt the crops of their climes to Russian conditions.

Alexis also recruited a large number of European specialists to work at Izmailovo. With the tsar's approval, they even carried out various mechanical experiments. For example, the watchmaker Andrew Krik in 1665 brought Alexis a model of a device which would grind grain with water power. Not to be outdone, the Russian watchmaker Moses Teren'ev presented a model of a threshing machine which, when demonstrated, so pleased the tsar that he granted Moses ten rubles on June 17, 1666, to build three other models to illustrate further how his idea would work.

Alexis spared no cost or care in making Izmailovo a success. We see this from the records of but one prikaz, the Gunsmith Bureau (Oruzheinyi prikaz), and for but one item—nails. To cite just a few examples, on September 5, 1669 the tsar ordered the Gunsmith Bureau to send 5,000 nails for the vineyards being erected at Izmailovo, and on royal command the next month the same bureau sent another 5,000 nails to the stables there. A royal edict of May 16, 1670 had the same prikaz forward 2,000 nails for the brick kilns of Izmailovo, and on August 16, 1671, 25,000 nails for the church being built there dedicated to the Festival of the Protection of the Most Holy Mother of God. The Gunsmith Bureau on May 23, 1672 was ordered to send 74,200 nails of various size to Ismailovo for general carpentry work and for a barn at its glass factory. And so on, and so on, for various bureaus and various commodities during the last dozen years of Alexis' reign.

Alexis often resorted to amusing folk practices to improve the farming at Izmailovo. A.I. Zaozersky notes that the tsar once heard that improved harvests were gained by sprinkling fields with vegetable oil and water which had been used to wash the legs and feet of sick monks. Deciding to try this before the sowing that August, Alexis sent instructions in his own hand to the Trinity monastery requesting the father superior to send him "secretly" a dish of butter from the brothers' table, along with water which had washed the feet of those in the infirmary. The abbot was also to go to the well used by St. Sergius the Miracle Worker and, after reading the burial service, to draw three buckets. Alexis then staged a solemn ritual to dispense this butter and water around the fields of Izmailovo. The tsar himself played no role in this ceremony, but he plotted the positions of those who did, and supervised their movements from the sidelines. Alexis often repeated this ritual at grain sowings in May and August.

Foreign and Russian craftsmen were well paid and happy at Izmailovo. The zoo and shady gardened pavilions made its grounds a lovely place to visit. But the peasants who labored at Izmailovo were harshly treated and miserable. For them the place was a prison, complete with walls and observation towers. A government report prepared soon after Alexis died reveals that 481 of the 664 homesteads bound to Izmailovo "in permanent residence" had taken flight, "and almost all of the remainder are ready to flee." Izmailovo exhibited the best science and technique Russia knew under Alexis Romanov, and it also reminds us at whose expense the accomplishments were gained.

Alexis was always interested in manufacturing and production, and, as the years passed, his attentions focused more strongly on these activities. The tsar established a large rope walk to give employment to the "needy" from all parts of the kingdom, and he also operated saltpeter and gunpowder works. Yet all this was insignificant in comparison with the many large royal salt factories and fish processing plants scattered throughout the realm. The tsar's estates also served as centers for the production of potash, flax and hemp. All this provided huge profits, but as the years passed Alexis grew increasingly bored with such "traditional" forms of production. The tsar's thirst was for innovation. During the 1660s, for example, we see Alexis making continual efforts to bring Indian weavers to Moscow to produce fine fabrics in royal workshops. But his agents could not find qualified workers. Attempts to buy mulberry trees at Astrakhan for replanting at Izmailovo failed, as did a project for silk making at Moscow under direction of the Armenian craftsman Larion L'gov in 1665. Alexis made a final effort in 1672 to have his officials "seek in Astrakhan or Terek or abroad for the very best gardeners of mulberry gardens who would be able both to establish a mulberry garden in Moscow and to produce seeds of the mulberry tree and silk worms." These searches also failed entirely.

Alexis' manufacturing experiments included a tannery to produce a higher grade of leather than that otherwise available from Russia's many artisan shops. The Privy Chancellery bought a site on the Yauza River near Moscow, and by March, 1666, began assembling equipment there. Alexis hired a qualified Armenian tanner by the name of Arabit Martynov, assigning him an interpreter and an apprentice. But the shop was poorly located and had to be moved. The tsar spent 158 rubles on a second enterprise, only to have it destroyed by fire in September, 1670. A third shop was organized near the capital, at Vorontsovo field, at a cost of 250 rubles. It was difficult to find qualified craftsmen to run the tannery after Arabit's death, yet the shop was successful enough to be expanded in August, 1672. Yet, when Alexis died, the government closed the tannery, arguing that foreign equivalents of its leather could be imported at a cheaper price.

Alexis was more successful in establishing a glass manufactory in Russia. This was a truly innovative step, for glass was quite unknown to the "old" Russia. Not a single glass item appears in the exhaustive inventory of dishes belonging to the industrialist Maxim Stroganov at the time of his death in 1627. Russian serving dishes were crafted of wood, clay or metal, windows were covered with fish bladders and animal skins. State offices and the homes of the rich sported mica windows, which at their best were extremely sophisticated art works. Russian masters mounted this material into elaborate, multi-colored designs, and sixteenth-century English travellers found that Russian mica passed light better than their own glass. Mica was so valuable in Russia that it was prospected and mined with the same care as precious stones and ores, and Paul of Aleppo reported that the quality product "does not break, but is as pliable as paper."

Alexis' interest in glass was the manufacture of dishes and bottles. When John Hebdon went abroad in 1656 the tsar asked him to obtain the materials and craftsmen to establish a royal glass manufactory in Russia. Nothing came of this project at that time. But a decade later Alexis renewed his interest in glass manufacturing. Perhaps he was encouraged to do this by the technological wonders which now abounded at Ismailovo. At any rate, the tsar decided to locate his glass manufactory there—where a model salt works had also been established—and to pattern his plant on the successful enterprise which a group of Dutchmen and Swedes had established at Dukhanino field near Moscow in the 1630s. Water power for the factory's machinery was provided from Serebryanka stream. The Izmailovo works was finished by early 1669, and was manned by a foreign master and six Russian apprentices Alexis persuaded to leave Dukhanino for his employ.

The eight or more additional "Venetian" craftsmen recruited in future years greatly improved the output of the Izmailovo glass manufactory. As I noted in a book on the origins of Russian industry, Alexis' glass furnaces at Izmailovo churned out bottles ranging in size from eight bushels to a "quarter-bucket," glass jugs large and small, a vast array of table tureens, mugs, cups, goblets (with and without covers), wine glasses, large glasses, small high-rimmed glasses, flat glasses, flasks, dishes, plates and saucers, as well as ink pots, candlesticks and lamp globes. The masters produced sophisticated designs and color patterns. The best of their work went to satisfy the needs of the royal court, or was passed on by the tsar as personal presents to his closest favorites. Apothecary items were bought by the Pharmaceutical Bureau to service its needs. The less exquisite work of the tsar's glass manufactory was offered for sale at Moscow in a special shop which he owned. Records which happen to be available for 1687 indicate the store then had an inventory of 535 dishes. (The factory itself then had 2,512 items on hand.) In all, the Izmailovo factory was a profitable venture which operated at least until 1706. The best of its work was fine enough to be exported to Persia in exchange for silk.

Even so, Alexis' most significant venture in adapting the new technology of the West was in iron manufacturing. In fact, almost half of the manufactories of European type built in Russia before Peter the Great were iron manufactories. The first of these iron works was built by the Stroganov family at Sol-Vychegodsk in the far northeast with the help of English technology in 1583. Still more significant were the four iron manufactories Andrew Vinius and his partners organized at Tula near the end of the 1630s. Twelve similar iron enterprises appeared in Russia during Tsar Alexis' reign, eleven others from the time of his death until the mid-1690s, when Peter the Great launched his own unique program of war and industrialization. In short, Alexis' time saw the relatively intense development of a modern Russian iron industry.

When Alexis sent Ilya Miloslavsky on a diplomatic mission to the Netherlands in 1646, iron manufacturing occupied a surprising amount of his future father-in-law's assignment. The tsar had just settled an ownership squabble among the Dutch iron manufacturers at Tula by confiscating the factories—using the excuse that the foreigners had delivered poor quality cannon to the Russian army (saving the best for export), and had failed to carry out their agreement to instruct Russian workers in advanced stages of the iron manufacturer's art. Miloslavsky justified the tsar's actions by complaining to the Dutch States about "the many unjust things" Marselis and Akema had done at Tula. Miloslavsky also engaged Dutch masters to build other modern iron works in Russia. Ilya hired a family capable of doing this work, and on November 1, 1647 Hendrik van Akken was presented formally to Tsar Alexis. Hendrik built an iron manufactory on the Yauza River just north of Moscow, but he died on April 19, 1650. His widow and two of their four sons wanted to remain in Russia. They admitted they could not operate the enterprise themselves, but Romashka, the eldest, assured Alexis that if he were permitted to go abroad "he would bring to the tsar the same sort of [cannon] master as his father was." Records do not make clear whether Alexis responded favorably to this petition, but soon after this the van Akkens returned to Holland and nothing further is heard of their iron works. By 1651 the Tula works had been returned to Marselis and Akema.

Alexis' own career as a private iron manufacturer began in 1668, when Boris Morozov's widow died and Alexis took her property in escheat, including the iron enterprise Boris had established on his estate at Pavlovskoe in 1651. The tsar's Privy Chancellery decided to expand the scale of operations to include the nearby Zvenigorod district. The Borodnikovsky works was operating here by early 1669. A third enterprise, the Obushkovsky plant, was built in the area in 1672.

The three royal iron manufactories operated successfully throughout Alexis' lifetime. They were not large, however, At the time Alexis died, twenty-eight men tended the blast furnaces, worked the forging hammers and smithies, burned charcoal for fuel, and tended to other skilled or semi-skilled jobs. Musketeers and other specially assigned soldiers labored at the mines, while the serfs of local crown villages transported raw materials and finished products. None of the output was sold on the open market. The dry, factual records of the Privy Chancellery make clear that most of the factories' products went to service Alexis' other economic activities: plows, scythes, axes and other work tools to royal estates at Dedinov, Skopin, Romanov, Izmailovo and Chasnikovo; salt pans, kettles and bar iron to the tsar's salt works at Pereiaslavl and Rostov; angle-iron and sheet iron for the construction and repair of churches in Moscow. Such orders were sometimes written in Alexis' own hand, at other times they were routinely issued in his name by secretaries and clerks at the Privy Chancellery. Sometimes this bureau sent its clerks to stay at the factories for a time to supervise special orders, check the books and inventories, bring money back and forth. The factories were managed from day to day by such well-paid Chancellery officials as Fedor Chertkov, a high-ranking aristocractic Equerry who worked under the personal instruction of the tsar. Cannon were also smelted here after 1672.

When Alexis died and the Privy Chancellery was dissolved, the three manufactories were transferred—predictably—to the Bureau of the Grand Court. The Bureau leased the three iron works to private Russian entrepreneurs in 1686 who closed the aging enterprises and in their place built two larger manufactories, the Sorokinsky and Kezminsky, which employed fifty or more skilled and semi-skilled workers. These enterprises supplied the domestic Russian market, and operated with further changes in ownership until 1705.

Chapter Seventeen

ALEXIS AND HIS MERCHANTS

The Russian past is filled with bold, extravagant figures—and Russia's merchants form no exception. The most famous merchant in his day was Grigory Nikitnikov, son of a humble trader from Yaroslavl. By the time Grigory amassed a fortune and relocated to Moscow in 1622, his trade network extended through Russia and Siberia with connections abroad to Persia and the Middle East. Nikitnikov sold a variety of goods, especially woolen cloth, furs, and fish. He began to invest in salt manufacturing in 1632, and by the end of that decade his thirteen salt works at Solikamsk in central northern Russia employed over 600 free wage-workers. The wily, spirited man built a cathedral at Yaroslavl, a wooden church at Solikamsk, and a magnificent stone church dedicated to the Trinity and his own family near his elegant mansion in Moscow. Nikitnikov's exports through Archangel were occasionally valued at as much as 40,000 rubles annually, and at one point he was able to offer the colossal sum of 90,000 rubles for properties of the troubled Ivan Stroganov, another Muscovite entrepreneur.

When Nikitnikov died in 1651 a new giant had established himself on the horizon. This was Vasily Shorin, rightly called by Samuel H. Baron an "extraordinary" Russian merchant of the seventeenth century. Shorin controlled fisheries, fish processing plants and transport operations, as well as salt works and several estates which enabled him to sell grain on a massive scale. He financed three costly and disastrous trade expeditions to Persia, the first two of which were pillaged at a total loss to its owner. He enjoyed great political influence during Alexis' reign, and by the time he died in 1678 or 1679 he was acclaimed universally as the most important Russian merchant. Crown offices often addressed communications to "Vasily Shorin and his comrades," and in distant England in 1662 merchants still seethed with the memory of how Shorin had collected the tsar's trade duties from them at Archangel: "Should there be more [customs] heads like Vasily Shorin and assistants like Klimshin," they told Russian diplomats who had gone to London to negotiate a loan, "you will succeed in driving away all the foreigners. We have never seen such unfair people anywhere in the world."

Nikitnikov began his career as a "town merchant," the fourth and lowest order into which the Russian crown grouped its merchants. Above them in status stood the clothiers. Vasily Shorin presented a contrast to Nikitnikov in that his was a "family on the rise," and from the beginning he was enrolled among the still more prestigious leading merchants, the *gosti*. About 30 men were enrolled in this order at any one time under Tsar Alexis, including some foreigners. Nikitnikov received this title in 1614, about the same time as Vasily's father Grigory Shorin. Two decades later Tsar Michael elevated Vasily Shorin to that rank.

Leading merchants usually were promoted from the ranks of the merchants' guild. A few members of the merchants' guild, however, were richer than some leading merchants, and we do not know why they were not granted the higher title. Baron thinks that only three leading merchants were wealthier than the merchant guild member Yakim Patokin in 1634. But the most substantial member of that group was Yakov Gruditsyn. He owned fisheries, salt works, numerous stores and forty peasant villages. A modern historian, Lyashchenko, estimates that his capital constituted about one twenty-third of all the capital held by the 158 members of the Merchants Guild. Just below this order of merchants were the clothiers, an archaic and misleading name since by Alexis' time its traders might well have had nothing to do with cloth or clothing. The town merchants were at the bottom of this hierarchy, and must have numbered in the thousands. Registered and bound to the residential areas of their towns, they were subdivided further into "better," "middle," and "junior" people according to wealth and status. A man held one of these merchant titles through royal decree, and at the tsar's pleasure might be elevated, demoted—or dismissed altogether—at any time.

Kotoshikhin, the source of so much interesting and valuable information about Russia at the time of Alexis Mikhailovich, tells us that some leading merchants did an annual business as great as 100,000 rubles. Besides carrying on their own trade they held the right to make beer and vodka, and buy or mortgage patrimonial estates. These privileges were denied the lower merchant orders, though members of the merchants' guild and clothiers could, like the leading merchants, keep liquor in their homes for their own use. At the same time, Kotoshikhin emphasizes the duties which the four merchant orders owed to the crown. The leading merchants served as trusted heads or sworn assistants in the sable treasury, royal customs-houses and liquor stores, and were responsible for collecting special tax levies imposed on the urban population. Members of the merchants guild and clothiers likewise served as sworn assistants, or aided the leading merchants in their services to the realm. Some of the town merchants also were selected each year "to serve the tsar in customs-houses, taverns, and other enterprises as trusted heads and sworn assistants."

Members of any one merchant order were anxious to be elevated to higher rank, and they constantly used their political connections to try to bring this about. The highest honor, of course, was to become a leading merchant. They not only controlled large amounts of capital and did an annual business as great as 100,000 rubles, they gained a slice of the profits connected with supervising the tsar's foreign and domestic trade operations. After appraising foreign imports for customs payment, the leading merchants often purchased what they pleased and released what was left—if anything—for sale to other Russian merchants. Sometimes these purchases were for the leading merchants themselves, but even if they were on behalf of the tsar, they often gained some profit from the transaction. The court connections a leading merchant enjoyed enabled him to steer any number of important crown contracts in his direction, an important consideration in an age of rapidly expanding state expenditures. Leading merchants might import goods and buy and sell anywhere in the land. They paid no customs dues, or did so at a greatly reduced rate, and were not to be "hindered" by local officials. They were also exempt from warehouse taxes.

The status of leading merchants was forcefully enshrined in law. The fine for abusing or dishonoring them was 50 rubles, as opposed to 20 rubles or less for a member of the merchants guild. Courts often took the word of leading merchants as gospel truth if they would but "kiss the cross" in swearing to testimony. Leading merchants held the right to be tried in Moscow by the tsar or one of his close officials, where their court connections would serve them well, even in litigation connected with other cities and towns. Unlike other Russians, leading merchants enjoyed the right to travel in foreign lands, presumably on business.

On balance, however, the hazards of being a leading merchant might well outstrip the benefits. Not only was it difficult, inconvenient, and unpopular to collect customs and taxes for the tsar, the leading merchants were obligated to make up any differences between what the crown expected and what they actually collected. Perhaps it was easy for them to gain loans and credit from the tsar and royal bureaus, but repayment often was demanded at the worst possible times. Moreover, when the crown owed money to the leading merchants, it might force them to accept in settlement goods they did not want, and at greatly inflated prices. From time to time the tsar might assign himself monopolies on certain goods, freezing even the greatest merchants out of trade in those items. After the copper riots of 1662, for example, Alexis decided to compensate the crown for an anticipated decline in revenues by proclaiming sables, hemp and beef fat to be royal monopolies. Shorin and others had to deliver their stores of these goods to the treasury for copper coins, 20 percent of which the government proceeded to recover through a new "fifth" tax on the transactions which had just caused these men to lose their wares. Then the copper coins were repudiated! "No doubt efforts at evasion were plentiful," says Baron of this episode, "but anything turned over was in effect confiscated."

Popular anger also might be visited on the leading merchants. Angry mobs resented their wealth and privileges and seethed with the memory of how avidly they collected taxes and special crown levies while evading—at least according to popular belief—payment of their own "fair" shares of these revenues. Because merchants stored precious goods and liquors in their homes, these buildings were bound to attract rioters, especially if the men in question had a reputation for injustice or helped the government draft unpopular policies. Nikitnikov's mansion was spared in the Moscow riots of 1648, but thirty-six other homes were pillaged—including that of Vasily Shorin who, in Baron's opinion, escaped death only because he then happened to be serving Alexis as customs collector at Archangel. The theft and destruction of Shorin's properties in 1648 hurt him a great deal, though not as much as the Moscow riot of 1662 and Razin's capture of Astrakhan in 1667, coming as did these events at the same time Shorin suffered business setbacks which troubled so greatly the twilight years of his once brilliant career. The Swedish observer Kilburger, writing in 1674, called the leading merchants "a covetous and pernicious fraternity" and suggested that should a riot occur "the rabble will wring the necks of all the leading merchants."

At any rate, the careers of leading merchants were stormy and troubled, and it was a rare experience when Vasily Shorin saw the title kept in his family for a third generation when Alexis made his son Michael a "leading merchant." In a study of Russian-born leading merchants between 1623 and 1710, Baron concludes that 27 families accounted for 75 leading merchants, well over half the total number of 132 in these years. But this does not mean that the families of leading merchants were financially stable. The title was a favor of the tsar, not hereditary, and "only one family in three succeeded in perpetuating itself . . . for more than one generation." Only five families retained the title of "leading merchant" for more than two generations. Three of these lasted three generations, two others for a full four generations, but one of these, the Yuryevs, "appears to have become economically debilitated" by the time Peter the Great was at the point of abolishing the title altogether in 1711. Only the Sverchkov clan succeeded in maintaining its "substance" and "vigor" throughout the period 1623-1710—hardly a spectacular record, and one that shows how difficult it was for large-scale Russian businessmen to nourish success once it had been attained.

Alexis must bear much of the blame for the uneven performance of his fellow entrepreneurs. The advantages and successes he enjoyed as tsar crippled their own activities; even the favors he bestowed upon the leading merchants and others reinforced their subservience to someone else. As if it were not bad enough for the tsar to make their properties and careers uncertain, he also impressed them into the administration of unpopular government policies which made them vulnerable targets of popular resentment when social upheavals finally—inevitably—burst forth.

In another sense, of course, there is a limit to the degree to which
Alexis can be held responsible for the plight of his leading merchants.
He shared the assumptions of an age which held that the entire land was
the tsar's patrimony. The fisheries, forests and furs of the land literally
belonged to the sovereign, even if their use usually was leased to private
people. Russians made no distinction between the tsar and the state. Together they represented a mysterious and awesome higher power before
whom even a mighty individual was but a humble slave. Little wonder
that petitioners of the tsar referred to themselves in humiliating diminu-
tives and self-effacing terms. Thus Vasily Shorin as his star was setting
begged for an easing of the debts of "your plundered and utterly ruined
bondsman, Vaska [Jackie!] Shorin." Even proud foreigners petitioning
Alexis for royal favors called themselves "undeserving slaves," "poor
and defenseless and helpless" orphans dependent upon "thy kind favor
alone."

Russians under Tsar Alexis did not live in an environment which allowed entrepreneurs to be self-reliant and bold, ready to take action with
but slight reference to crown "interests." The merchant in Muscovy enjoyed no independence of the crown, no "rights" against the sovereign
or those who acted in his name. Russians were forced to play the game
on terms set by the crown. A leading merchant collecting revenues for
Alexis one day might unfairly assess a competitor to hurt him, indeed
ruin him, knowing that the next day the roles might be reversed entirely.
It was vital to act boldly against a colleague while the moment was
briefly there! Russians lacked the maturity of entrepreneurial *spirit*
which would have told them that the real interest of each merchant was
best served by joining with his fellows in demanding security of life and
property for all. The leading merchants should have been the ones to
lead in building such *esprit de corps,* but they could not see their interests
in a perspective wide enough even to consider this course of action. En-
countering the entrepreneurial vision of the West, we find the leading
merchants envying its power but never imitating its spirit. Their sole
solution was to beg their "father tsar" to protect them from the "unfair"
competition of foreigners.

The leading merchants resented the duty-free trade privileges bestowed
upon foreign merchants to encourage international trade. Russians also
resented the fact that foreign capital in Russia had grown to the point
of capturing even large blocks of domestic trade. Foreign entrepreneurs
loaned Russians money when it was available from no other source.
Foreigners used smaller Russian merchants to retail their imports within
Russia, and to act as their agents in buying Russian goods for export to

the West. The smaller Russian merchants profited from these relations with foreigners, and had no objection to their activities in Russia. But the leading merchants were appalled to see that foreign capital was coming to dominate the Russian market. Their solution to the problem was simple: curb foreign competitors so that the leading merchants might fill the vacuum thus created.

Strongly-worded petitions submitted to Tsar Michael in 1627 and 1637 demanded that foreigners no longer be permitted to carry on retail trade in Russia. Indeed, foreigners should be expelled from the interior and required to do their wholesale buying for export in the border towns. But Michael's statesmen feared the rupture with the West that such a policy might create, and therefore these petitions were greeted with sympathy but no action. Russian merchants renewed their complaints at the Assembly of the Land in 1642, saying: "And the traders among us, thy slaves, Sovereign, have become much worse in the past few years, because all our trades in Moscow and in other towns have been taken over by many foreigners, Europeans and Central Asians who arrive in Moscow and other towns with all sorts of commodities and sell them." These complaints also were ignored.

When Alexis came to the throne, however, Russian merchants had reason to hope that their demands would at last be met. Not only was Boris Morozov a powerful entrepreneur, he surrounded himself with influential merchants and announced a policy of bringing money into the treasury by promoting both foreign and domestic Russian trade. Another petition was presented to the tsar in 1646 by "your slaves and orphans, the humble leading merchants and lowly trading men of the merchants guild and clothiers," and even by some of the town merchants of Moscow. They complained against "the Dutch merchants and those of the Brabant and Hamburg who came to Moscow to trade," but they singled out the English for particular criticism knowing, perhaps, that Alexis was incensed by London's rebellion against Charles I. Some Russians hoped that if Alexis could be persuaded to take action against English merchants, eventually he might do likewise with regard to other foreigners.

The petitioners grumbled that the English had established warehouses, trade posts and large houses throughout Russia, "and now dwell in the Muscovite state, just as in their own country." They buy Russian goods "and as soon as certain wares grow expensive, they begin to sell those wares; but as for wares which are cheaper and not in demand, they keep those in their warehouses for two or three years, and when the prices of those wares go up, they begin to sell them." They even buy and sell Russian goods among themselves, "conspiring among each other." They send Russian traders into the smaller towns and the countryside, "having concluded loan agreements and made debtors out of many poor and indebted Russians." These goods are then exported without—the plaintiffs pointedly observed—paying trade revenues; "and they cheat you, Sire, out of your customs duties." The petition claimed that the "entire Muscovite state" had been reduced to starvation by foreigners "buying up meat and grain and all kinds of provisions in Moscow and other towns, Sire, and removing them from the Muscovite state to their own land."

But this was the very moment when Alexis wanted to introduce more foreign expertise into Russia. To develop his new army the tsar needed to recruit European officers and obtain weapons manufactured abroad. Alexis knew that Russia would be isolated from the West as it had not been for nearly a century were he to act against foreign merchants as was being demanded in 1646. The tsar therefore decided on a limited range of measures as a means of mollifying Russian critics. He abolished the duty-free trade privileges some foreign merchants enjoyed, decreeing that henceforth they must pay duties one-and-a-half to two percent above the rate for Russian merchants on all goods bought and sold in Russia. This would please Russian chauvinists and at the same time increase state revenues. Many of the tsar's "favorite" foreigners, nonetheless soon were exempted from this provision.

Alexis' decision to expel English merchants from the Russian interior in 1649 had more of a cutting edge, but not much more. The role of the English in Russia was relatively minor by that time and, in any case, Alexis was not acting from economic motives but from indignation over the recent execution of Charles I. The tsar argued that English trade privileges in Russia were transacted through charters which he had granted "to you at the request of your sovereign, the English king Charles, out of brotherly friendship and love." But, as the expulsion edict noted, "the entire English nation has committed a most evil deed, putting to death their sovereign." So, henceforth, while England's merchants might engage in wholesale trade in Archangel, "you may not journey to Moscow and to other towns, either with or without merchandise."

The issue of foreign merchants in Russia flared up again in 1653, when Vasily Shorin and other leading merchants petitioned that traders from Holland and Hamburg be limited, as were the English, to wholesale trade at border towns. But Russia was then moving towards war with Poland and Alexis was even less willing than before to break Russia's few ties with the West. But he was clever enough to take advantage of the petition to issue a Commercial Charter the following year, 1654, a charter which brought new revenues into crown coffers. Alexis suggested cutting the profit margin of foreigners by raising their trade taxes.

Earlier foreigners had been forced to pay five percent on goods bought or sold in border towns. Now, according to the Commercial Charter of 1654, they had to pay eight percent of the value of the imports they sold, and ten percent of the value of Russian goods bought for export. This did nothing to strengthen Shorin and his friends in their competition with foreign capital. Even with spotty enforcement and the inevitable exemptions granted to the tsar's "favorite foreigners," however, this measure raised new revenues and helped finance the Polish war. It also encouraged foreigners to import arms and other needed goods into Russia throughout the Thirteen Years War (1654-67). The goods they bought in Muscovy were so cheap compared to prices similar wares fetched in the West that the entrepreneurs easily compensated themselves for all the trade duties paid in Russia. Alexis' detailed knowledge of international market conditions thus helped him to formulate trade policy calculated to strengthen the crown's finances without harming Russia's trade position abroad.

Even so, as soon as peace was concluded with Poland the most important Russian merchants presented another petition calling for curbs on foreign competition. With Russia now less dependent upon trade with the West, the tsar was willing to consider the arguments presented in the petition more sympathetically. Alexis turned to his good friend, Afanasy Ordin-Nashchokin, to draft the specific details of a new policy which would assure Russians a better share of the future profits generated by foreign trade.

Nashchokin did not intend to drive foreign entrepreneurs from Russia. Although Muscovy no longer had an urgent need for arms and mercenaries after 1667, the country still depended on the West for the further development of domestic manufacturing and foreign trade. Afanasy Lavrentevich knew all this quite well. His attitude towards the West also was conditioned by psychological and intellectual curiosity. "There is no shame in taking what is good, not even from your enemies," the chancellor often declared. Collins claimed that Nashchokin was "the only patron the English have here," and noted that on any number of occasions Afanasy also had defended Peter Marselis from the attacks of jealous Russian rivals.

This man whom Collins described as "sober" and "abstemious," "indefatigable in business," a "great and wise minister of state not inferior peradventure to any one in Europe," was, nonetheless, intensely devoted to the monarchy and to the best interests of Russia. Nashchokin was determined that all economic activity in Russia should strengthen the power of the state, and it was with this conviction that he turned to the question of foreigners trading in Russia. The innovations Nashchokin considered and discussed were so sweeping and comprehensive that in early 1667 Collins declared that the chancellor "is now about reforming the Russian laws and new-modelling all the tsar's empire."

Afanasy Nashchokin had tried his wings as a domestic reformer two years earlier. Alexis had appointed him commander of Pskov at the time Nashchokin was negotiating with the Poles there in 1665. Deciding to reorganize the government of the city, Nashchokin's reforms were broad and ambitious. To handle local judicial affairs, he created a town council whose fifteen members were elected from the various suburbs for three-year terms, five being in active service during any one year. Nashchokin reasoned that such a council would counteract the abuses of power which the tsar's bureaucrats and the wealthier merchants notoriously visited upon the lesser townspeople. Nashchokin also wanted to break the hold which foreign merchants enjoyed there, as elsewhere in Russia.

Under his experiment, the Russian merchants at Pskov were united into a corporate organization which Nashchokin expected to advance the interest of all its members. The more substantial merchants were to extend credit to weaker members through the Town Hall, the building where the town council administered justice and organized tax collections. The smaller Russian traders thus no longer would need to turn to foreigners for loans. Not being indebted to foreigners, neither would such Russians be forced to act as their agents or to sell goods to foreigners at prices so low as to undercut leading merchants, clothiers, and members of the merchant guild. But Nashchokin's reforms would not free the smaller Russian traders from all dependence on others. They would simply come under their Russian "betters." Nashchokin's scheme actually specified that the greater Russian merchants would "accept" their more modest colleagues and share commissions with them on the profits of their joint operations.

Ordin-Nashchokin did not intend to eliminate foreigners altogether from the commercial life of Pskov. But he resented the fact that the Swedes in particular swooped over the border to buy goods at the most "advantageous" times, "cheating" Russian sellers out of a fair profit. According to Nashchokin's reform, foreigners would be invited to Pskov for two annual wholesale fairs lasting a total of four weeks, one beginning on January 6, and the other on May 9. Foreigners might trade there duty free, but a third of the price of the goods they bought would be paid in foreign silver coins (called Joachimsthalers) which the Russian merchants were to exchange for Russian money. In this way the crown would gain the "hard currency" needed to purchase military goods in the West.

Nashchokin's plan was implemented in 1666, and failed immediately. This was small cause for surprise, considering that Nashchokin had been forced to return to Moscow, after which Alexis appointed one of his fiercest opponents, Prince Ivan Khovansky, to serve as commander at Pskov. Khovansky had no interest in backing innovations which lessened the powers of his office. Nor were these reforms much supported by the Pskovites. The wealthier element hoped to persuade the tsar to ban foreigners entirely; the more modest traders had no objection to doing business with foreigners anyhow. Nor did they relish being subordinated to Russians simply because they were Russian.

It was scarcely Nashchokin's nature to abandon an idea simply because it was sabotaged in a particular instance. He continued to meditate on the essence of the Pskov reform, now thinking to apply it on a national scale. Nashchokin's hour of opportunity sounded in January 1667, when, with peace concluded between Russia and Poland, Alexis asked him to draft a set of new statutes regulating trade within the Muscovite state. Nashchokin conferred with Vasily Shorin and other leading merchants, he carefully studied the petitions and complaints which Russian merchants had pressed on the crown in earlier years. The fruit of his labors was the "New Trade Code," which, when proclaimed into law by the tsar on May 7, 1667, replaced all existing tariffs and commercial arrangements.

The New Trade Code limited foreigners to wholesale trade at the border towns, where they would pay six percent customs on goods sold. If they gained permission to transport goods within Russia, they paid an additional ten percent transit fee on their sales, a fee Russians did not have to pay. A third of all their payments to Russian merchants had to be in foreign coin—a measure calculated to bring revenues to the treasury since these coins had to be exchanged promptly for Russian currency. But to encourage the influx of precious metal into Russia, foreigners gained the right to buy and export Russian goods duty free. Foreign monies illegally handled in Russia were fined at ten percent—or confiscated altogether. By law, foreigners could not engage in retail trade in Muscovy, nor could they exchange wares among themselves. The code did not work perfectly, of course. Violations occurred, and, as usual, some foreigners gained partial or complete exemption from the provisions of the New Trade Code. Still, it was the most important piece of seventeenth century Russian trade legislation. It has been estimated that because of the code the trade foreigners carried on in later years was taxed four times as heavily as that conducted by Russians. The New Trade Code of 1667 was a fitting monument to Tsar Alexis and his talented statesman, Afanasy Lavrentevich Ordin-Nashchokin.

PART THREE

MAN AND TSAR

Chapter Eighteen

ALEXIS TURNS ON NIKON

Alexis returned to Moscow in late 1656 quite different from the meek young man who had set out on his first campaign two-and-a-half-years before. Alexis was now twenty-seven years old, and since May 1654 he had spent almost his entire time at the front. He saw bloodshed in these months, rewarded bravery and punished cowardice, disciplined the insubordinate and praised those who struck a good example for others to follow. Alexis had felt the excitement of crucial strategy meetings, he had settled tactical disputes, he had learned to be watchful lest Polish diplomats regain at the conference table what Russian armies had won at such great cost on the battlefield. Alexis experienced all this without falling victim to worldly-wise cynicism, without losing the simple love for his fellow man which impressed so many who knew him. Above all, Alexis returned to the Kremlin a mature young man capable of coping even with the arrogant, overbearing Nikon.

Nikon was now, under the terms of his secret agreement with the tsar, serving his second three-year term as patriarch. The program of church reform he began so quietly with the "correction" of old church books was now culminating in a new liturgy visible for all to see. Historians who display a weak appreciation for the passion spiritual factors can arouse label Nikon's innovations "trivial" and "unimportant." Consequently, the resistance which the reforms triggered is viewed as anger aroused by other, supposedly more "real" issues—serfdom, exploitation, an increasingly autocratic and bureaucratic state, or hostility to the foreigner and his ways. According to this view, religious controversy concealed resentments which were really secular in origin.

Granted, the outlook of the anti-Nikonians was shaped by a variety of elements, some of which had little to do with religious issues. Still, in the final analysis, every piece of evidence suggests that the remarkably intense believers of Alexis' time (and the tsar himself must certainly be included in their ranks) felt religious issues with a passion which, if alien to us, should not be discounted. Russians of that day knew that

NIKON ATTIRED AS PATRIARCH, oil painting by Daniel Füchters about 1660.

Nikon's reforms were meaningful and important. Thanks to Nikon, citizens of the Third Rome now used three fingers to sign themselves with the cross. They addressed God differently in the Lord's Prayer, described the Holy Spirit in the Creed in a new way by omitting "very" from its eighth article, chanted three rather than two hallelujahs during the liturgy. Billington notes that even illiterates could see that the name of Our Lord at familiar places in church now was rendered *Iisus*, not *Isus*.

A man who could barely count knew that five consecrated loaves of bread had replaced the traditional seven during the Offertory, that one loaf rather than several was presented at the altar, while the waters were blessed once rather than twice in observance of the Epiphany. There was no need to be a geographer to observe that church processions now proceeded in the face of the sun rather than with its movement. If some thought these innovations were important enough to be made, others thought they were important enough to be resisted.

Controversial as the changes were, this did not shake Nikon's position as patriarch. Alexis placed the full weight of his office behind every reform. As soon as Nikon brought to Alexis' attention the fact that the blessing of the waters on Epiphany eve was not celebrated at Constantinople, the practice was banned by royal decree. Alexis was thrilled at the church song Nikon introduced from Kiev, and he paid no attention to those who were critical of it. In any case, the fiercest opponents of reform were shuttled off to distant places before they could build a protest movement. Even moderates were pleased when Nikon eliminated the corrupt practice of permitting the mass to be shortened by having several voices read different parts of the liturgy simultaneously. Most church enthusiasts were pleased that Nikon's masses and church processions grew increasingly solemn and theatrical. The patriarch and his assistants appeared in elegant vestments, with cherubim and trim in brocade and pearls. Their newly resplendent mantles, miters, hoods, caps and white latias were all of Greek design. Censers and chalices, candlesticks and candelabra were unprecedentedly dazzling, and seemed to many a fitting demonstration of God's importance to man.

Even Nikon's suggestion that ecclesiastical authority was of a higher order than crown authority was not, as such, displeasing to Tsar Alexis. The Palm Sunday ritual which reenacted Christ's triumphal entry into Jerusalem with the tsar leading the patriarch's horse existed before Nikon, and it survived his fall. Alexis extended this practice outside Moscow, where local governors began to lead the steeds of their bishops and metropolitans. If this tradition seemed to diminish the tsar before his patriarch, Alexis knew full well that after the ceremony the patriarch paid him six rubles for the honor which had just been rendered. Throughout his life Alexis never hesitated to humble himself before churchmen, most of whom stood a great deal lower in his esteem than Nikon. Alexis especially grieved for those who lay in monastery hospitals, and foreign observers were shocked to see the tsar kiss their hands, stroke their brows, and wash their feet.

The sovereign did not quarrel even briefly with Nikon's suggestion that governors and magistrates in the provinces find guidance in canon law as well as in the ordinances of the crown. Alexis knew full well that the tsar was the ultimate source of authority in either realm, and within that framework Alexis believed that Muscovite officials should be receptive to church guidance. Still, even at the height of his influence over Alexis, Nikon could not persuade the tsar to abolish—rather than suspend—those terms of the Law Code of 1649 which offended church interests.

Not even Nikon's supposed greed for power was the cause of his downfall. Quite the contrary, Nikon's first major argument with Alexis came over the patriarch's reluctance to grasp new powers, an episode which marked the beginning of the end for Nikon. This controversy involved the question: who had jurisdiction over the metropolitan of Kiev, the patriarch of Moscow or the patriarch of Constantinople?

When Alexis began his war for the Ukraine (Little Russia) in 1654, he took the title "Tsar of All Great and Little Russia." Similarly, he altered the title of the head of his church to read "Patriarch of All Great and Little Russia." In this as in other cases Nikon was not anxious for a new title, but he did accept it out of deference to his master. Nikon rejected, however, Alexis' notion of the authority contained in this patriarchal title. Thinking in canonical terms, Nikon decided that his relationship to Kiev was merely honorific, that the metropolitan there stood under the authority of Constantinople and would so remain until that patriarch voluntarily transferred his powers over Kiev to the patriarch of Moscow. But from Alexis' viewpoint, the union of the Ukraine with Russia had occurred already, and the Orthodox people of the Ukraine now fell under the same ecclesiastical jurisdiction as other subjects of the Third Rome.

This theoretical dispute became a concrete problem when Metropolitan Silvester Kossov of Kiev died in late 1657. Alexis and his advisers saw an opportunity to solidify Moscow's control over the Ukraine by appointing Kossov's successor. The Ukrainian clergy generally accepted this innovation, and it was not even clear that the patriarch of Constantinople would bother to object. But the ever-principled Nikon decided that he could not consecrate this metropolitan. At one point during the controversy Alexis fell to cursing his patriarch, calling him a "son of a bitch" and yet harsher names. Nikon stood his ground but, hoping to avert a break, invited the tsar to visit the Iversky monastery after Christmas. Alexis agreed to make the trip until, at the urging of his boyars, he demonstrated his dissatisfaction with his "special friend" by not appearing at the cloister.

Nikon's position with the tsar deteriorated in other ways as well. The Swedish war which the patriarch had so loudly demanded went badly from the moment Alexis failed to take Riga in October 1656. War with both Poland and Sweden impoverished the Russian people, the tsar's treasury stood empty, efforts to negotiate loans in Venice and elsewhere were denied unceremoniously. Alexis' military setbacks also brought problems with his fickle Cossack allies. All this, together with the friction over who would designate Metropolitan Kossov's successor—an appointment Alexis felt would strengthen his hand in the volatile Ukraine—left the tsar disillusioned with Nikon and his policies.

Seeing a crack in the friendship between Alexis and Nikon, the boyars intensified their campaign to convince Alexis that the patriarch had abused his authority and posed a danger to the throne. Some claimed that Nikon had agreed with Alexis' decision to take the field so that the patriarch might control Moscow and dominate affairs of state. Alexis chafed at subtle hints that Nikon was more feared and venerated than he. Others called Nikon a plundering thief who in his master's absence transferred royal property to favorite monasteries.

Alexis was struck by the united front which the boyars now presented against the patriarch. Maria had never cared for Nikon, though her opinions were not so much expressed in words as in a quiet refusal to join Alexis and his sisters in their lavish donations to Nikon's beloved Holy Cross and Resurrection monasteries. The jealousy of Maria's father, Ilya Miloslavsky, was aroused when it became clear that Alexis valued Nikon's advice more than his own. The Miloslavskys and Streshnevs (related to Alexis on his mother's side) also frowned upon Nikon, for his origins were even more humble than theirs. They and other court notables now moved in to destroy Nikon. Their memories still blazed over the way Nikon had tyrannized them in the tsar's absence. Before he grew so politically powerful, Nikon and the nobles had dealt simply with each other. Boyars who visited the patriarch entered his palace without the permission of the doorkeepers. When a lord was announced, Nikon greeted him personally; when it came time to leave the patriarch accompanied his guest to the outer door. But Nikon changed as soon as he came to exercise the authority of "Grand Sovereign." Visitors were kept waiting in Nikon's reception room. Then, Paul of Aleppo noted, "they walk into his presence with extreme fear and awe; and having transacted their business standing before him, take their departure as he continues sitting in his place." Even great lords who were tardy in arriving to make their morning reports waited on the stairs in the cold, for the doors were shut at a certain time and Nikon's attendants had orders not to let anyone in. Those who suffered such indignities were eager to avenge themselves as soon as the opportunity appeared.

Alexis no longer chatted with Nikon in a friendly way after 1657, nor did the two men exchange palace banquets. Nikon was not consulted on affairs of state. Alexis even shunned the services Nikon celebrated, preferring now to hear others sing the liturgy in his own private chapels at the Kremlin. Nikon still invited the tsar to attend his masses, and often prolonged the ringing of the bells so that Alexis might be summoned again. But the tsar never came.

The final break between Alexis and Nikon came in July, 1658, at the time the patriarch's second term—as he and the tsar alone knew—was about to expire. At this point King Teimuraz of Georgia was visiting Moscow. Traditionally the patriarch was present when the tsar received such an important guest, and Nikon's attendance in this case seemed especially appropriate since Teimuraz intended to place his people and church under Muscovite protection. Nikon sat in his palace on July 4, wondering why he had not been invited to the royal banquet which was about to begin. He finally sent an assistant, boyar Prince Dmitry Meshchersky, to inquire about the oversight. At the moment Meshchersky arrived at the royal palace the way to the grand stairs was being cleared by Bogdan Khitrovo, a lord of the chamber who was commonly known as the tsar's "whispering favorite" because of his boundless appetite for politics and intrigue. Khitrovo was slapping at the crowd with his staff, and, seeing Meshchersky, leaped towards him and slapped a sharp blow on his head.

"You ought not strike me, Bogdan Matveevich," Dmitry said. "I come here not idly, but on duty!"

"Who are you?" Khitrovo inquired.

"I am the patriarch's servitor and am here on duty," Meshchersky replied.

"Don't make too much of yourself," Khitrovo declared. "Why should we regard the patriarch so highly?" He then hit Meshchersky again on the forehead, wounding him severely this time.

Nikon lodged a written complaint about this episode, telling Alexis that if he would not punish his guilty officer "then we, by the power given us from the Lord God, will punish him as we know how to do to gain justice."

Alexis answered Nikon, promising to investigate and even telling his former friend "I will see you after a while." But the tsar took no action, nor did he grant the patriarch an interview. In fact, in the next four days Alexis deepened the split by refusing to attend two special masses which the patriarch traditionally celebrated in the presence of the tsar. On the last occasion, on July 10, 1658, Alexis sent Prince Yuri

Romodanovsky to the patriarchal palace to tell Nikon that the tsar would not grace this service with his presence, and to proceed without him.

"You condemn and insult the tsar's majesty. You have yourself called Grand Sovereign." Then the prince added: "But you are not a Grand Sovereign; we have only one Sovereign, the tsar!"

"My being called Grand Sovereign was not from my desire," Nikon retorted. "The Grand Sovereign, the tsar, was pleased so to style me both by word of mouth and in writing, and of this I have proof in letters written to me by the tsar's majesty with his own hand."

Romodanovsky stood his ground. "And now the tsar's majesty has commanded me to tell you that he forbids you to refer to yourself as Grand Sovereign in speaking or in writing, and that he does not mean to honor you any more!" With this, Romodanovsky broke off the discussion.

Abused and offended, Nikon now decided to take drastic action. The patriarch sent word to his assistants to begin the morning service. He had his servants place a monk's garb in a bag and bring it to the Cathedral of the Assumption, where he was to celebrate mass. Instead of the traditional closing prayers, however, Nikon read the "Sermon of the Good Shepherd" written by his beloved St. John Chrysostom. The patriarch then told the shocked congregation that because of his sins and the tsar's anger "I can no longer be your shepherd." Vernadsky quotes the high point of this oration, in which Nikon declared,

> I witness before God if the tsar had not sworn in this very temple in the presence of the bishops, the boyars, and the people to keep intact the teachings of the Gospel, of the Apostles and of the Church Fathers, I would not have accepted the patriarchal see. Now, as the Great Sovereign has violated his oath and has unjustly imposed his wrath on me, I have to leave this temple and this city, giving room to the tsar's anger.

An attendant now brought the monastic garb to Nikon, and he theatrically moved to replace his elegant patriarchal headgear and dress with the simple black cloth of a monk. Actually, Nikon had just returned from the Resurrection monastery to be present, he supposed, for the reception of King Teimuraz. Nikon had a special liking for that cloister, for there he could pray and work as a simple monk while supervising the construction of important new buildings. He intended to return there now.

The congregation, however, was in pandemonium. Frantic over Nikon's statement, the people barred the doors of the cathedral so that

THE CATHEDRAL OF THE ASSUMPTION. Built by the Italian architect Rudolfo
Fioravanti (known to the Russians as "Aristotle" Fioravanti because of his learning and wide range of abilities) between 1475 and 1479.

their patriarch might not leave. Nikon scribbled a note to the tsar announcing his departure, and the people—thinking this would bring Alexis
to the church—let a deacon carry it to the Kremlin. Meanwhile Pitirim,
the metropolitan of Krutitsa, and Metropolitan Michael of Serbia, hurried off to tell the tsar what was happening. After a short while Alexis
returned Nikon's letter and announced that he would not appear in the
church. Instead, Alexis sent his trusted boyar, Prince Alexis Trubetskoi,
and one of Nikon's fiercest enemies, Rodion Streshnev. (The tsar's uncle,
Simeon Streshnev, had amused himself and his friends in recent weeks

by teaching a dog he called "Nikon" to sit on his hind quarters and wag his front legs in imitation of Nikon giving the blessing.) By the time the royal messengers arrived, Nikon had donned monk's dress and exchanged the ornate staff of the patriarch for a plain staff.

"The Grand Sovereign commands me to ask why you request a cell," said Trubetskoi. "You have cells of your own in the patriarchal residence."

"Those cells are not mine," Nikon held. "Let the person whom the tsar may place there live in them. As for myself, I only beg the Sovereign to be so kind as to let me go to a monastery."

Trubetskoi left to confer with the tsar, then returned to the cathedral to persuade the patriarch to stay in Moscow. During these exchanges Nikon held firmly to his position: "I have no quarrel nor slanderous words whatsoever against the Grand Sovereign or any one else. I leave my chair knowing my many sins against God, for on account of my sins here in Moscow there have been many plagues and war and all sorts of misfortune. Therefore I leave my chair." Trubetskoi rushed back a second time to the Kremlin, carrying with him the letter Nikon had tried unsuccessfully to have delivered to the tsar earlier that day.

Nikon was not so composed as he appeared. His stern, formal features concealed a highly emotional nature in which fast notions of justice mixed uneasily with strong feelings about people and life. Dark and gloomy thoughts surely passed through Nikon's mind as he sat on the lowest step of the episcopal platform in the middle of the cathedral, gazing at its west doors beyond which stood the tsar's palace. In those moments Nikon perhaps recalled his days of power, and the contrast with his present humiliations must have hurt him deeply. Occasionally he rose to leave the cathedral, only to observe that the weeping people still would not let him pass. Seeing them crying, Nikon likewise burst into tears. And so he waited.

Trubetskoi finally appeared a third time. Again he returned Nikon's letter to Alexis, but this time he added: "The Grand Sovereign has commanded me to tell you to choose for yourself a monastery and cells wherever you wish."

Nikon bowed to the boyar, saying: "I thank the Grand Sovereign for his grace." Then the patriarch strode from the cathedral.

The congregation followed Nikon, begging him not to leave Moscow, undoing the collar of the horse hitched to the patriarch's carriage. Nikon then splashed through the mud of Ivanovsky square, the people in hot pursuit, weeping and groaning that the shepherd was leaving his sheep. The Gates of the Savior were slammed and barred so that the patriarch might not depart the Kremlin, forcing Nikon to sit on a ledge until royal officials appeared to reopen the gates. Nikon now crossed Red Square and followed Ilinsky Street to his palace, the weeping multitude dogging him every step of the way. Nikon turned to the people, blessed them, and entered his residence. At that the crowd dispersed and went home.

Nikon remained in Moscow three days, hoping that Alexis would yet offer a compromise which would make it possible to stay in Moscow. Perhaps Alexis himself wanted that reconciliation. The dramatic episode in the Cathedral of the Assumption had been difficult for him too, and in later years the tsar was to say that in those hours he was asleep with his eyes open, "and saw everything in a dream." In fact, Alexis preferred that Nikon not leave Moscow. But he felt that to confer with Nikon personally, even to accept the letter he wrote in the cathedral, would lend the patriarch an advantage which might well mend the argument on Nikon's terms. The boyars also were determined to prevent such an outcome. They continued their slander against Nikon and urged the tsar to hold firm.

The Novodevichy monastery now sent to the patriarchal palace two open-air basket-work carriages of the sort used in Kiev. Nikon often had passed about Moscow in such vehicles, arousing the ire of conservatives who grumbled over his attachment to "foreign" things. The patriarch's books and most treasured possessions were loaded into one carriage, and he seated himself in the other. In this way, on the morning of July 13, 1658, the patriarch set out for the Resurrection monastery.

Nikon supposed that his flight from Moscow would shock Alexis into realizing that he could not govern without his "special friend." This would force the tsar to meet with Nikon, which would give the two men an opportunity to resolve their differences and work together again. A subtle point should be appreciated: Nikon's dramatic departure revealed that he had supporters, a fact which the patriarch might have hoped would carry some weight with the tsar and boyars in the politically charged atmosphere of the Kremlin.

Was Nikon thinking of earlier times when important Russians had strengthened their positions by suddenly leaving their posts? He probably knew of the cold winter day in 1564 when Ivan the Terrible gathered his personal treasury and favorite icons into a sleigh and journeyed to Alexandrov, forty-five miles east of Moscow. Much as Nikon was doing now, Ivan then thanked the townspeople and commoners for their support, but pleaded that boyar opposition had made it impossible for him to govern—so he must leave. Ivan foresaw what would happen: even his enemies begged him to return! Return he did, but only on the condition that he have absolute power to deal with treason, and the power to effect sweeping reforms.

Another precedent which would have pleased Nikon concerned Metropolitan Geronty, leader of the Russian Church in the later fifteenth century. Geronty was angered when his opponents in a particular struggle gained the support of Grand Prince Ivan the Great. Geronty departed Moscow for the Simonov monastery, threatening to resign his office and live as a simple monk unless Ivan came to settle their differences. When the prince saw that nearly the entire Church supported Geronty, he sent his son to beg the metropolitan to return. This was not sufficient. Ivan himself had to appear before Geronty, declare himself to blame in the dispute, and promise henceforth to listen to the metropolitan "in all things." Only then did the metropolitan return to Moscow. Geronty used this victory to punish those church leaders who earlier had worked successfully against him. Geronty prevailed over his prince on another occasion when he seemed at the point of death and the tsar hastily moved to select a subservient successor as metropolitan. Perhaps Nikon thought of these precedents as he left Moscow.

Hearing of Nikon's departure, Alexis sent Trubetskoi with the heavy, elegant patriarchal carriage, thinking that at least its use would make his friend's trip more comfortable. Although he claimed to hurry as best he could, Trubetskoi reached the monastery only after Nikon already had arrived. The prince tried to leave the carriage, but Nikon refused to accept it. After some bickering on this point, the vehicle ended up at Chernevo, a village owned by the Resurrection monastery. The carriage stood there idle for some time. As for Nikon, he remained at the monastery for eight years. But he was not idle.

Chapter Nineteen

THE COPPER RIOTS

Alexis should not have been surprised when a riot broke out in Moscow in July of 1662.

Moscow was always a dark and brooding place, and the hot, dry summer of that year edged its residents to the very brink of violence. The harvest was poor, bread prices soared, hostile peasants flocked to the capital in search of employment or "charity." They might as well have stayed in their villages, for alms and jobs could scarcely be found on any street or square. Even "tax-paying" craftsmen and the traders in the suburbs were feeling the pain of a sharp depression. They could not sell their retail goods, nor could they carry out wholesale contracts negotiated earlier with the "better" merchants. The humble people suffered and watched the leading merchants speculate in grain and exchange Siberian furs to foreigners for export. The poor could but curse fate and complain that "even bad times brought profit to those in favor with God and the tsar."

Alexis' fiscal policies had aggravated the distress. To help finance the Polish war, he began issuing copper coins which were identical to the familiar silver kopecks. At first this caused no problem, and silver and copper exchanged at par. But rumors soon spread that workers at the mint were using their own copper to counterfeit coins. The scoundrels were said to be in league with the ever-despised Ilya Miloslavsky, as well as Afanasy Matyushkin, the greedy, sinister husband of Alexis' maternal aunt and a member of the Boyar Council. Popular suspicions were aroused by the fact that once-humble people at the mint suddenly grew rich, and (as Klyuchevsky says) squandered money right and left, built magnificent houses, clothed their wives like fine ladies and bought wares in the shops without bothering to haggle over prices. Alexis finally investigated the matter. The guilty parties lost their property, after which the executioner hacked away a hand and a foot and sent his wretched victims into exile. Not that important officials were treated so harshly— and this aroused anger, too. Matyushkin was merely dismissed from the mint, whereas the royal father-in-law suffered nothing worse than still greater disfavor at court. Caught in the worsening financial pinch, the government continued to strike copper coins despite the fact they were falling steadily in value. An old silver kopeck was worth twelve of the new issue at the market place by 1661. Nevertheless Alexis still paid salaries and debts with the new coins.

This cheap money devastated the morale of the Russian soldiers and musketeers. Peasants at home long had been fleeing taxes and conscription; now troops on the Polish front often enough imitated their example, shaking the mud of their regiments from their boots and slipping away. By 1662 the authorities no longer expected that troops still under discipline would help recover those who had practiced the higher logic of desertion. Ugly clashes broke out at Novgorod and Pskov between search parties and deserters. Enmeshed in a maze of fiscal difficulties, Alexis announced measures in the first months of 1662 which darkened the mood of the Russian people still further. In February certain goods were made a crown monopoly in the hope that they could be exported for badly needed foreign money. Potash and resin, shoe leather and hemp, sables and beef tallow—all had to be exchanged at crown agencies for the hated copper coins. Wealthy merchants evaded some of these demands, or used political connections to take care of their interests in other ways. But poorer traders were ruined by such transactions. Alexis also took the fateful step of proclaiming another "fifth" tax, a special levy of 20 percent on trade turnover for an entire year. He stepped up measures to collect taxes in arrears, while ordering that the tax which supported the musketeer regiments be taken in grain rather than in his own copper coins! Then came a disastrous harvest in the spring of 1662. The nation and Moscow bristled with discontent.

Muscovites awoke on July 25, 1662 to see what Kotoshikhin calls "thievish posters" on gates, walls and churches throughout the city. In fiery tones these proclamations attacked high taxes and accused certain officials and merchants of "treason"—sympathy with the king of Poland. One such document quickly drew a crowd on Lubyanka street. As the people were puzzling over its message and murmuring against the "traitors," two crown officials, Semen Larionov and Afanasy Bashmakov, pulled down the notice and rushed towards the Land Bureau, where they worked. A furious crowd demanded that the paper be returned, crying "You're taking that letter to the traitors! The tsar's not in Moscow! That letter's important to us all!"

Larionov and Bashmakov managed to reach the Gates of the Savior, but the mob overtook them before they could enter the Kremlin. The letter was recovered and brought to a church on Lubyanka street, where the musketeer, Kuzma Nagaev, stood on the steps and read it aloud. He "cried out to the people, to all who were standing," a contemporary account tells us.

By now crowds were huddling around similar proclamations on Red Square and at churches throughout the city. The sharp clang of the tocsin from countless churches split the still-cool morning air, giving a sign of stormy moments yet to come. Traders fled their shops, some making for home and safety, others to join a great mob forming around the cry, "To Kolomenskoe!" "To Kolomenskoe!"—the royal vacation lodge near Moscow which Alexis then happened to be visiting.

Royal officials reasoned with the mob but it did no good. Troops refused to fire on the people. Soldier and civilian shared too many common grievances. In fact, men from nearly every regiment in Moscow—including the new model regiments and Tatar detachments on the outskirts of the city—crossed over to the rioters, strengthening their determination to go to Kolomenskoe to force Alexis to hear their problems.

THE ROYAL PALACE AT KOLOMENSKOE. First mentioned in the Testament of Ivan Kalita in 1339, by Alexis' time the buildings and churches of Kolomenskoe (most of which were wooden) formed an impressive, distinctively Russian architectural monument. This engraving by F. Hilferding (1768) suggests the appearance of Kolomenskoe a century after Alexis' time.

Alexis' officials at Moscow were in such confusion that they failed to send him word of the events rocking the capital, and the arrival of the crowd at Kolomenskoe took Alexis completely by surprise. He was at church for morning mass when a surly group of Muscovites approached the boyars and court attendants who were in the courtyard, ordering them to fetch the tsar. Looking out of the church, Alexis "with a cry and an uproar" called these messengers to his side, and—as Gordon's diary tells us—learning the mob's "evil design," ordered the boyars whom the rioters wanted delivered over for punishment to take refuge with the tsarina and the royal children in their apartments. While his family "sat in the palace in great fear and dread," Alexis left the church to confront the rioters.

A tsar was traditionally remote and unapproachable, stately and dignified. The unwashed multitudes saw him mainly on ceremonial occasions, or on his pilgrimages and pleasure excursions. Only a handful of clergy and nobles actually spoke with the tsar, and even their opinions were worded carefully and offered mainly upon his request. Alexis' wife, his sister Irene and the "fools in Christ" with whom he surrounded himself expressed themselves in more direct terms, but even here frankness had its limits. The tsar was "terrible" in the same sense that the ancient Hebrews regarded Yahweh. Yet now, on a summer day in the thirty-third year of his life and the seventeenth of his reign, Alexis found himself staring at angry subjects in no mood for the ceremonials which customarily prevailed.

The mob demanded that Alexis lighten their taxes and deliver over the hated boyars and merchants "for killing." Luke Zhitka passed the tsar his hat containing the letter which had been posted on Lubyanka street with the names of the "traitors." Another townsman, Martin Zhedrinsky, raised a clamor, demanding that the letter be read aloud and that the "traitors" be summoned forthwith. Obscenities and profanities were used before The Tsar of All the Russias as freely as he ordinarily offered prayers to God.

Alexis spoke to the rioters in a quiet way, hoping to calm them and persuade them to leave. He promised after mass to return to Moscow, to conduct a personal investigation, to right all wrongs. Several of the crowd grabbed Alexis by the buttons of his coat, shouting, "Whom do you believe—the traitors or us?" Alexis swore before God that his faith was in his subjects, and one member of the crowd stepped forward to seal this covenant by shaking the tsar's hand.

Meanwhile, back in Moscow, the crowds were busily pillaging the homes of the nobles and merchants thought to be responsible for issuing copper money in the first place. The most hated were Fedor Rtishchev and Vasily Shorin, who the month before had been ordered to collect the special "fifth" tax. Shorin rushed to the Kremlin to take refuge in the home of Prince Cherkassky. Shorin's fifteen-year-old son donned peasant clothes and tried to leave Moscow, but he was recognized and seized. The boy's captors were so proud of their catch that they put him in a wagon and solemnly set out for Kolomenskoe—proof positive (in their minds, anyhow) that his father indeed had fled to the king of Poland with "boyar papers," correspondence which, if found, would demonstrate clearly the treason which had caused the recent defeats of Alexis' armies.

As the rioters were making their way to Kolomenskoe they encountered the Muscovites whom Alexis had just pacified and persuaded to return home. The tale of Shorin and his son stoked a new round of indignation, and a combined group made the fateful decision to go to Kolomenskoe for a second meeting with the tsar to make their case with a force and clarity he could not ignore.

When the crowd again reached Kolomenskoe it found Alexis mounting his horse to return to Moscow. The people renewed their demands that the tsar deliver up the traitors—Ilya Miloslavsky and his nephews Ivan Mikhailovich and Ivan Bogdanovich, as well as Bogdan Khitrovo, Dementy Bashmakov, Rtishchev, Shorin and his fellow leading merchant Semen Zadorin, and others. When Alexis renewed his plea that time was needed to carry out an investigation, the fury of the crowd knew no limits and voices threatened the tsar himself.

At this point the tide turned. Alexis had ordered musketeer regiments to hurry to Moscow and Kolomenskoe. By now Prince Ivan Khovansky's regiment had brought the capital under control, partly through threats of force, also by persuasion and their commander's personal popularity. While Alexis was confronting the mob for the second time he received news that musketeer units commanded by Matveev, Poltev and Solovtsov were entering Kolomenskoe through the rear gates—and that Prince Yuri Romodanovsky, in response to the tsar's orders, had raised foreigners in the Foreign Quarter, some of whom were hurrying to Alexis' aid on horse, others on foot. At this delicate moment, the tsar had 6,000 or more trustworthy troops at Kolomenskoe and now he struck back. Alexis gave the order to attack without mercy, and to take survivors prisoner for more careful punishment later.

Pandemonium broke out among the rioters, who immediately showed themselves to be no match for armed musketeers and soldiers. Fleeing Kolomenskoe in a panic, the people were caught in the narrow space between the walls of the residence and the river. More than a hundred drowned, another 7,000 or so were captured and flogged mercilessly on the spot. But Alexis had only began to take revenge.

When he learned that loyal musketeers had arrested those who pillaged the homes of Shorin and Zadorin, he sent a verbal order to his commander at Moscow, Prince A.N. Trubetskoi, to hang ten or twenty "of these thieves." This was done the same day, July 25. Another eighteen were hanged by the tsar's written order on the following day. The object of this was to frighten the turbulent city and to discourage anyone from further rioting and theft. Gallows were erected at the busiest squares and city streets. According to Kotoshikhin, another

108 insurgents were hanged at Kolomenskoe. In following weeks 1,200 rioters with their families were exiled "for eternal life" to Astrakhan and Siberia. The 10,000 or so who participated in the disorders belonged to Moscow's lower classes, with a generous sprinkling of soldiers and peasants who happened to be in the capital. Unlike the disorders of 1648, the musketeers—whose grain wages had been raised just before July of 1662—were the main force which put the rebellion down. Only thirty-three musketeers joined the rioters, most of them from a single unit.

Again in control of the situation in Moscow, Alexis took positive steps to strengthen his position. The troops who came to his defense received generous bonuses, promotions, and improvements in conditions of service—a clear demonstration of the advantages of supporting the sovereign in a crisis. In later years Alexis often remembered the regiments and commanders who served him so well on that day in July. He and his wife were personally shaken by the riots; indeed, Maria was ill from it for an entire year.

The sovereign was sufficiently wise to make at least minor concessions to the popular mood. He was not able to lighten taxes. In fact, another "fifth" was levied in 1663, and it was so unpopular that the Swedish diplomatic representative to Russia reported that "the mood of the people in Moscow is troubled. They are unhappy over the new tax, . . . murmurings are heard everywhere." But later in 1663 the hated copper coins were recalled and exchanged for silver money. Much as this pleased his own people, Alexis was motivated no less by "larger" considerations. Russian merchants needed silver coin in foreign trade inasmuch as Europeans refused payment in copper, the exchange value of which continued to plummet within Russia on the heels of the 1662 riots.

The Moscow riots of 1648 had forced Alexis to summon an Assembly of the Land and, to win the support of his service nobles, the tsar agreed to a new Law Code which fastened serfdom upon the nation. The copper crisis likewise fostered sentiment for an Assembly to reform the finances of the nation and to deal with the economic crisis. Even before the 1662 riots a conference of nobles at Moscow had discussed the high price of grain, and had ended by politely requesting another Assembly: "We ask the Great Sovereign graciously to order the election of the best men of every rank, and also from the towns, for we do not know what to say about copper coins without such men since that is an affair for the entire state, for all the towns and men of every degree." After the July upheaval the townspeople of Moscow renewed their appeals for an Assembly to hear and redress their grievances.

But on this occasion the service nobles refused to support the call for an Assembly of the Land, and Alexis took advantage of this fact to ignore the demands of his townspeople for another Assembly. The tsar had permitted Assemblies during the 1650s, but these bodies were not broadly elected and were called to give advice solely on matters of foreign policy. An Assembly summoned in the midst of the turbulence of 1662 would have been an entirely different matter. A group elected in the heat of such upheaval and strife would have had a weight which could have been hurled even against the autocratic Russian tsar, perhaps forcing Alexis towards sweeping reforms not at all to his liking.

Worst of all, an Assembly of the Land called in 1662 *might* have forced Alexis to summon Assemblies regularly in the future, to tax and rule the land in partnership with it. True, there was little precedent for this in the Russian tradition and few—if any—Russians seem to have thought of such a radical innovation in 1662. On the other hand, Alexis was fully aware that such frightening new currents were running deep in some parts of the world. As we have seen, G.S. Dokhturov, the Russian ambassador to England, reported to his young master in 1645 that "Parliament instead of the king now governs London and the entire English and Scotch land, . . . and the king has begun to do everything according to its will." Alexis deplored the troubles suffered by his "brother" king, Charles I, and for the next three years supported him with loans and the permission to purchase Russian grain on easy terms. Charles lost the Civil War—and his head. As a consequence, Alexis expelled England's merchants from the Russian interior in the summer of 1649, confining them in the future to wholesale trade in the border towns.

Alexis ignored England's various parliamentary governments in the coming decade, stubbornly supporting instead the "legitimate" power of Charles II. But whereas other European kings extended Charles mere sympathy, Alexis did more. The tsar granted Charles' agents the right to buy furs and grain which the exiled king could sell in the West at a profit which in turn could be used to finance campaigns to regain his throne. The tsar only asked to be repaid later, at the original low prices. In his dealings with the Stuarts in these years Alexis showed himself to be a generous, consistent friend of absolute monarchy, and as a man who viewed the cause of legitimacy in thoroughly international terms.

As England grew increasingly restless under Cromwell and the Puritan dictatorship, sentiment built for a restoration of the monarchy. The Royalist cause was helped by the fact that charming and easy-going Charles II ("I am not eager to resume my travels," he once declared)

promised to forgive nearly all his former enemies and rule England together with Parliament. A group of influential Englishmen negotiated a
series of agreements in early 1660 which made the king's return possible.
When Charles crossed the channel and made his way to London's Whitehall Palace, cheering crowds hailed him the entire way.

Charles wrote to Alexis in May 1661, a few weeks after his coronation, formally announcing his accession to the throne and expressing
gratitude to the tsar for displaying "so remarkable and notorious brotherly kindness to us in the time of our affliction." Alexis in turn congratulated Charles and moved to re-establish full diplomatic relations
with England. A Russian embassy led by Prince Peter Prozorovsky arrived at Gravesend in November 1662 with, one observer noted, "a
great train and much pomp." Charles ordered the Russians received
"with much state," for the tsar had "not only been kind to his Majestie
in his distresse," but also had forbidden "all commerce with our Nation
during the Rebellion." Prozorovsky was received with much ceremony
at Whitehall on December 29, 1662, bearing lavish gifts from Tsar Alexis
to King Charles.

Even so, Russian-English relations remained at a disappointing level
for the next several years. Alexis' main objective was to gain English
support against Poland, particularly in the form of a loan. Charles repaid
his debts to the tsar, but Konovalov notes that for all their grateful
words the English were not interested in an alliance, nor even in a close
friendship with Russia. London's primary purpose in its relations with
Russia was to regain the customs-free trade privileges English merchants
enjoyed before 1649. But this did not happen. Russia no longer depended, as it had so briefly under Ivan the Terrible a century earlier, on
a single nation as a foreign trade partner. No longer was it in the interest
of Muscovy to grant one nation privileges not available to others. Alexis
and Charles often exchanged good wishes, even while failing to establish
concrete commercial ties.

In fact, England enjoyed decreasing contact with Russia as the seventeenth century wore on. M.S. Anderson says that only two English merchants remained in Moscow by 1669, and at the end of the century the
Muscovy Company of London, once such a vigorous exploiter of the
Russian market, numbered no more than twelve or fourteen members.
The English consoled themselves over their declining share of the Russian market by their comfortable certainty of their own superiority over
the inhabitants of Muscovy. In London the Russians were held to be
barbarous and backward, cruel and dishonest, drunken and uncivilized.
Their church, with its cruel fasts and endless veneration of the icons,

struck the English as superstitious and idolatrous. Above all, the tsarist system of government seemed tyrannical and unjust. Sir Roger Manley described Alexis in 1674 as a sovereign "fettered by no law but that of his will, which is as extensive as his pleasure." Another observer held that Russians obeyed their tsar "not as subjects but as slaves," respecting him "not as their prince, but as a God." The wealth of the tsar, the magnificence of his court, the brutality of his punishments, all were proverbial—as was the determination and bravery of the Russian soldier, at least when defending his homeland. But most Englishmen thought that Russians were, by nature, base and servile. Indeed, they did not consider Russia even to be a part of "Europe" but rather a part of the "Orient," which included Persia and Turkey.

Alexis, on the other hand, grasped about England the central lesson it held for him: a powerful Parliament resists the powers of a king. Indeed, after a brief period of good relations, Charles II and Parliament fell into controversies all too similar to those which troubled his father and grandfather. Alexis had no interest in fostering such developments in his own land.

But in dealing with the Assembly of the Land, Alexis did not confront the problem which faced English rulers. Parliament was strong because the gentry and merchants shared economic and social interests, and their representatives in the lower house formed a fairly united front against the king and the lords. A similar alliance in Russia, using the Assembly as its vehicle, would have made the Assembly a vigorous, independent political force which would have undermined absolute monarchy. But the Russian counterpart of the English gentry, the service nobles, were not at all interested in joining other groups in society to dispute the powers and policies of their "good and pious Tsar Alexis." Such a moment came, briefly, in 1648, and it was this which made the Assembly of that year an active, vital force. The townspeople of Moscow would have liked to revive that coalition in 1662. At that point, however, the service nobility was a satisfied, conservative class. Its three central demands of earlier years—that the peasant be bound to the land, that the crown do its best to recover fugitives, that sons inherit the estates of their fathers and continue their service to the tsar—had all been attained by 1662. What did the service noble have to gain from further social upheaval? In fact, if the position of the tsar was weakened or called into question, might not this somehow undermine the concessions which the service nobles had gained with such great difficulty? What could an Assembly of the Land accomplish in 1662 which *really* would improve the position of the service nobility?

In short, Alexis' reign witnessed a compromise between tsar and service noble which was to endure for decades and crush any threat to
autocracy at the source. Just as the service noble demanded absolute
power on his estate, so he recognized the right of the tsar to absolute
power over the state as a whole. Serfdom was the dark crime which
bound tsar and landlord in an unshakeable alliance. Each served the
other, and each respected the proper rights of the other. Popularly-
elected Assemblies of the Land with reform programs and an independent
mentality might threaten the "great compromise." Thus the Assembly
of the Land after a fitful, occasionally brilliant history, withered and
died.

Still, its memory lived on and a ballad sung in the far North makes
Alexis implore his subjects—

> Help your sovereign to think his thoughts.
> He must think hard and take counsel.

This from the tsar who, as Klyuchevsky observed, maintained that "the
community's voice is ever heeded," while bringing the days of the Assembly of the Land to a close.

Chapter Twenty

RECONCILIATION?

Nikon was residing at the Resurrection monastery when the Copper
Riots broke out in Moscow in July 1662. The patriarch had gone to his
favorite cloister four years earlier, at a time when the intrigue of the
boyars against him and the power he exercised with the tsar was reaching a high point. Nikon hoped that his dramatic departure from Moscow
would shock Tsar Alexis into realizing that he did not wish to govern
the Third Rome without his "special friend." In this event, the tsar
would recall the patriarch to Moscow to resume their once-close relationship. But Alexis held firm and such an invitation was never issued.

Confusion reigned over Nikon's status. In the first hectic days of his
departure Nikon made loose, self-mortifying statements to the effect
that he was no longer patriarch. Absence from his duties at Moscow—
destined to last nine years—could be used by hostile boyars to draw the
conclusion that Nikon had resigned his office. On his first day at the monastery Nikon agreed with Alexis' emissaries that until Nikon's successor

was selected, the patriarch's traditional assistant, the metropolitan of Krutitsa, should remain at Moscow to transact the routine affairs of the patriarch's office. Nikon insisted, nonetheless, that larger policies must be referred to him, and that his name should continue to be used in church services and on official documents.

Alexis' dilemma was very real. He loved Nikon as a man and hoped that they might effect a reconciliation. But politically they were at a deadlock. Alexis was totally unwilling to resume the old relationship in which Nikon was a "Grand Sovereign" wielding power within the secular realm. If Nikon were in some way to apologize, or at least revise downward his own estimate of the status of the patriarchate, the possibility lingered that he might return to administer church affairs and preside at traditional festivals and in cathedral services. But many at court worked to sabotage even this solution. The boyars knew well that the strange bond which still existed between the patriarch and the tsar might result in a rebirth of their old relationship. This might dilute the influence of the Kremlin officials, or, as they presented the case to Alexis, the "rightful power" of the sovereign.

Nikon offered several times to resign as patriarch, but this was not satisfactory to Alexis and the boyars. Such a solution would not clarify who was right in Nikon's earlier disputes with Alexis and his officials. Moreover, it was clear that in Nikon's mind resignation would permit him a voice in selecting a new patriarch, and he might demand a candidate inclined to continue his efforts to strengthen the power of the Church over the state. From Alexis' point of view, Nikon should be tried by a church council which would declare him guilty of abusing his powers as patriarch, and would remove him from office. But it took time for Alexis and his sympathizers to formulate a precise case against Nikon; it was even difficult to decide the type of tribunal which should hear a case against a patriarch. Months grew into years as these thorny issues were thrashed out at Moscow.

Meanwhile, at the Resurrection monastery, the fallen patriarch had adopted a routine which could hardly have been improved upon by his worst enemy. Nikon gave himself over to prayer, fasting, and mortification of the flesh. He sometimes slept but three hours a night, and always went about in the painfully heavy iron chains which he wore until his death and finally ordered hung over his tomb. Nikon worked beside the other monks at building the magnificent Church of the Resurrection, carrying bricks on his shoulders and with his hands, sometimes alone, sometimes with his fellows. Nikon also cut wood and hay, helped drain marshes, tended ponds, gardens and orchards, fed the brothers with fish he caught by day and at night. Nikon was the first to begin work and the last to leave it—the first to enter church and the last to depart. Knowing of his friend's routine, Alexis took every possible excuse to send Nikon nourishment and alms, whether the occasion was an important festival day, celebration of a victory, or the name day of a royal relative. Nikon generally passed these gifts on to the other monks, or to pilgrims and visitors, for he subsisted on water and a fare as simple as the tsar's own. Nikon appreciated the attentions of his royal master, however, and soon began to pray for Alexis and his house.

Nikon called the Resurrection monastery the "New Jerusalem," and it clearly showed his vision of the role the Russian Church should play in the world. The numerous churches built at the monastery suggested kinship with important places in the Orthodox East. The Church of the Theophany and the Church of St. Peter and Paul, for example, recalled certain churches at Mount Athos, the famous monastic center of the Christian East. The Church of the Resurrection was reminiscent of the Church of the Lord's Sepulchre in Jerusalem. Five great thrones within stood silent witness to the hope that someday the five fathers of the Eastern Church—the patriarchs of Constantinople, Jerusalem, Alexandria, Antioch and Moscow—would gather here and return thanks to God. Nikon constantly toured the grounds of the Resurrection monastery, mulling over the past, thinking of the future. He carefully supervised building activities which would demonstrate in stone that Russia was indeed the "Third Rome," that the center of the faith had migrated to the distant wilds of a New Jerusalem.

Nikon also took up the pen to develop ideological arguments with a thoroughness not possible in earlier years. His writings now revealed an erudite master of church history and canon law, holy scripture and the church fathers. Nikon's letters and treatises—many addressed to Alexis himself—answered the attacks which pressed on him from every side. His combative instincts thoroughly aroused, Nikon threw himself into battle with the dedication of the martyrs of old.

Alexis ignored Nikon's theoretical arguments, being more concerned to gain control over the Church, and to eliminate as much of Nikon's influence as possible within it. In this Alexis found a most cooperative soul in Pitirim, metropolitan of Krutitsa, a greedy, craven man who long had coveted Nikon's office and was willing to play almost any game to get it. It was now Pitirim whom Alexis led astride a horse on Palm Sunday, symbolizing the entry of Christ into Jerusalem and demonstrating for any who cared to think about it just how empty such ceremonies really can be. Alexis also set about revoking the privileges which Nikon had gained for the monasteries at the high point of his power. Monasteries which recently had been placed under the direct jurisdiction of the patriarch reverted to their local bishops. The Monastery Bureau in Moscow now began to control monastery lands, though Nikon once had used his influence with Alexis to delay implementation of this provision of the Law Code of 1649. A number of patriarchal estates were placed under the Monastery Bureau. Nikon protested all this, and even excommunicated Pitirim when he dared consecrate a new bishop without Nikon's participation. But in the faraway Resurrection monastery Nikon exercised no influence over events, and Vernadsky is quite right in saying that after the patriarch's departure "it was Tsar Aleksei himself who assumed the duties of the head of the church administration."

Yet the problem remained: what to do with Nikon?

When Alexis sent a delegation to the Resurrection monastery on April 1, 1659 to persuade Nikon to resign, the patriarch not only refused, but added: "And I shall not keep silence concerning the proper conduct of church affairs."

Alexis then took steps in 1660 to remove Nikon by summoning a church council (which included three visiting Greek dignitaries) to declare that Nikon already had relinquished the patriarchate and that a new dignitary should be elected in his place. To be sure, the council found against Nikon, but its deliberations were protested on legal grounds by the Kievan monk Epifani Slavinetsky, then living in Moscow and famed for his learning and character. Faced with this challenge, Alexis backed down.

Over the next several years Nikon was harrassed by property lawsuits and countless interrogations. His friends were even more harshly badgered and persecuted. The aim of the government was to collect evidence for yet another trial, this time before a church council of indisputable authority, a council which would include the patriarchs of Constantinople, Alexandria, Jerusalem and Antioch. The architect of this trial was Paisios Ligarides, the oily master of conspiracy and intrigue, a charlatan possessed by an ambition so limitless that at one point he hoped that the events he helped set in motion would install him as patriarch of the Russian Church.

Ligarides' career straddled the seamy side of the Eastern and Western Churches. Of Greek (Levantine) origins, at the age of thirteen he entered a college in Rome which educated clergy for the Greek branch of the Roman Catholic Church, the Uniate Church. He graduated with highest honors at the age of twenty-four in 1636. After carrying on missionary work for Rome at Constantinople and in Moldavia, Ligarides joined the

Greek Orthodox Church in 1651 and took monastic vows. Paisios was given responsible work in the East, and, though he never took up residence in Palestine, he was made metropolitan of Gaza. All this time he remained in the pay of Rome and sent regular reports there to the Congregation for the Propagation of the Faith. In short, Ligarides was a Catholic agent in the East working to reunite the church under Rome—and to gain advantages for himself along the way.

Ironically, it was Nikon who engaged Paisios for service in Moscow, thinking to use his scholarship to revise Russian church literature. By the time Ligarides arrived in Moscow five years later, in 1662, it was more profitable for him to offer his services to Alexis and the boyars. Paisios' task was to structure the evidence against Nikon in such a way as to persuade the other Eastern patriarchs that Nikon had abused his office and should be removed. Hopefully, Ligarides' knowledge of canon law and church practices would be sufficient to bring Nikon's career to a humiliating end.

So that Alexis might follow the details of the case being prepared against Nikon, Ligarides and his assistants were instructed to work through the Privy Chancellery. The tsar felt confident enough of his case by December 1662 to summon a council to try Nikon the following year. On Alexis' orders, Prince Nikita Odoevsky, chairman of the investigating committee, imprisoned Nikon in his cell at the Resurrection monastery on June 23, 1663.

After his break with Nikon, Alexis moved to reconcile the enemies of Nikon's reforms to the established Church. The tsar recalled Avvakum from exile at Dauria in 1660, though it took two years for the document to reach this distant region near Lake Baikal—20,000 versts from Moscow—and the archpriest did not reappear in the capital until February of 1664. Avvakum then was received warmly by Rtishchev, the boyars, and by Alexis himself.

"Are you in good health, archpriest?" the tsar graciously inquired, and added, "God has let me see you again." Avvakum kissed the sovereign's hand, pressed it, and harshly replied: "God lives and my spirit lives, your Majesty! As for what lies before us, that God will ordain." Seeing that exile had not mellowed Avvakum, Alexis simply "sighed softly, and went whither he had need."

Avvakum was lodged in the guesthouse of a monastery in the Kremlin, and when the tsar passed the archpriest, he often greeted him, bowed low, and asked, "Bless me," "Pray for me."

Avvakum was touched by this reception. He likewise hoped for reconciliation, and wrote: "The tsar is set over us by God, . . . so I hoped that little by little he would come to a better mind." Avvakum enjoyed presents and money from the tsarina, was flattered by the attentions of prominent people, and relished friendly disputes with Fedor Rtishchev. He admitted that he appreciated the offer of a position correcting books in the printing house more than the honor of serving as the tsar's confessor. ("I desired something better than the confessional," he later reflected.) At one point he moved into the comfortable mansion of Theodosia Morozova, lady-in-waiting to the tsarina and destined to play a key role in the stormy episodes which lay ahead.

Avvakum lived this happy life for a year, until he concluded that neither he nor the tsar could alter their position. Nikon was no longer in Moscow, but his reforms remained. "I wrote to the tsar many things, saying that he should earnestly seek the ancient piety and defend our common holy mother Church from heresy, and that he should put a shepherd of the Orthodox faith on the patriarchal throne in place of Nikon, wolf and traitor, evildoer and heretic."

Disappointed by this letter, Alexis began to look askance at Avvakum, begging him at least to be silent. But such faintheartedness was entirely foreign to the archpriest's character. So Alexis ordered his old friend exiled again, this time to Pustozersk, in the far North. But here again the tsar displayed the tenderness which was so much a part of his character. The day before Avvakum was to be taken away Alexis journeyed to Kolomenskoe, being unwilling to witness the suffering of a person he loved. Avvakum wrote Alexis in November, telling of the misfortunes which were wracking his family, begging to pass the rest of the winter short of their final destination. Alexis at first refused, but he then relented. Avvakum wintered at Mezen, less than half the distance to his assigned place of exile at Pustozersk.

Disappointed with Avvakum, Alexis now turned to the possibility of reconciliation with Nikon—an episode which showed just how treacherous and weak the tsar could be. In late 1664 Alexis sent Matveev and Ordin-Nashchokin to Nikon's friend, the boyar Nikita Zyuzin, asking him to write a letter to the patriarch arranging a meeting with the tsar. Through these messengers Alexis lamented that Nikon and he "once swore to each other that we would not forsake each other 'til death, but he has now left me alone to contend with my enemies, visible and invisible." Alexis admitted, however, that he feared the wrath which an open meeting would provide from his own bishops and boyars. Hence he suggested that Nikon meet him secretly, at the Cathedral of the Assumption.

In the early hours of December 18, 1664 a sleigh entered Moscow and passed through its guard stations. At each point musketeers called out, "Who goes there?" and received the answer, "Authorities from the St. Sabba Monastery!" The vehicle finally slipped into the Kremlin. A tall, gaunt figure disembarked. Nikon was entering the Cathedral of the Assumption for the first time in more than six years.

Matins were then in progress, celebrated by Metropolitan Jonah of Rostov. The doors of the church clattered as a group of Nikon's monks marched to the altar, followed by a crossbearer and the patriarch himself. Nikon reached the patriarch's section and took up his part in the service. When it had finished, he summoned Jonah, blessed him, and sent him to tell Alexis that his "special friend" was in Moscow.

Jonah found the tsar in a palace chapel, and said: "Patriarch Nikon has arrived at the cathedral church, and is standing at the patriarch's place. He sent us to tell you, the Grand Sovereign, of his arrival."

A clamor immediately erupted. Greatly agitated, Alexis relayed the news he had just received to the attendants who stood about him. The boyars shouted and churchmen shook their heads, repeatedly crying, "Oh, Lord! Oh, Lord!"

A group led by Nikita Odoevsky, Yuri Dolgoruky and Rodion Streshnev rushed to the cathedral. They bitterly reproached Nikon: "You gave up the patriarchal throne voluntarily, you promised to be patriarch no longer, you went to live at a monastery and have already written to the ecumenical patriarchs about this. And now, why have you come to Moscow to the cathedral church without permission of the grand sovereign? Go back to your monastery, as before!"

"I have returned to make peace with the tsar," Nikon replied. "This is my throne, and I do not intend to flee from a council of the ecumenical patriarchs." Then, dramatically, Nikon handed them a letter for the tsar.

Uncertain of what to do, the royal courtiers said: "We are not able to accept a letter without the permission of the tsar; we will now go with news of this to the Grand Sovereign."

They soon returned to say: "The Grand Sovereign has sent us to tell you as before to go back to the Resurrection monastery, and to keep your letter."

Nikon replied: "If my arrival is inconvenient for the Grand Sovereign, then I will go back to the monastery, but I will not leave the church until my letter is delivered." The letter was then brought to Alexis while Nikon waited in the cathedral.

Nikon's letter was short and inconclusive. He wished the tsar well, told of a fast he had just carried on for three days and four nights, after which Peter the Miracle Worker appeared to him in a dream, commanding him to make this trip to the Cathedral of the Assumption. (In fact, it was *Alexis* who had mentioned Peter in the letter he wrote Nikon asking the patriarch to come to Moscow, saying that Peter "will aid our friendship and drive away our enemies." In referring to the saint in this way, then, Nikon was tactfully reminding the tsar that he was here upon Alexis' invitation—and that he had the letter which could prove it.)

For a third time, the courtiers ordered Nikon to leave. Matveev and Dolgoruky followed the patriarch's sleigh to the edge of the city, to Zemlyanoi Gorod. Approaching to take leave of him, Dolgoruky said to Nikon: "The grand sovereign has asked you, most holy patriarch, for your blessings and forgiveness."

Nikon tersely replied: "God will forgive him if this is not the result of trouble he has caused!"

"What trouble?" asked Dolgoruky.

"Well, now, was I not instructed to come?"

When this conversation was relayed to Alexis he realized that Nikon must have been referring to a written communication in which the tsar— through the mediation of Matveev and Ordin-Nashchokin, and finally Zyuzin—had expressed the desire for the meeting which had just nearly taken place. In a panic, Alexis sent four trusted dignitaries to recover the incriminating document. They overtook Nikon at Chernevo. Nikon refused to give up the letter, but after lengthy arguments agreed to send it to the tsar by his own messenger the next day, which he did.

Zyuzin now shouldered the blame—and punishment—for everyone else. He had compromised himself as the sole boyar who still dared to correspond with the fallen Nikon. Under torture Zyuzin confessed to lying about the involvement of Matveev and Ordin-Nashchokin, who in turn, of course, denied any knowledge of the entire affair. The Boyar Duma condemned Zyuzin to death.

Alexis heeded the petitions of Zyuzin's sons, however, and set aside the death penalty. Zyuzin lost his landed properties and was sent to Kazan, where, in compensation for the crown service he was to perform, he was permitted a house and moveable property. But this was not quite the end of the case. "When Zyuzin's wife, a woman of precarious health, received the news of her husband's arrest and torture," Vernadsky notes, "she died of shock." The sovereign handed the Zyuzins' confiscated property over to the Privy Chancellery, the office which, as we know, managed lands having particular significance to Tsar Alexis.

Chapter Twenty-One

NIKON AND AVVAKUM IN THE DOCK

The Church was torn by two disruptive forces as Alexis entered the third decade of his rule. On one side stood Nikon and his supporters, on the other were the opponents of Nikon's reforms, the "Old Believers" led by Avvakum, who wished to restore the former liturgy. Ironically, while each was the other's fiercest enemy, both now stood in utter disgrace in the eyes of the Church. The irony was heightened by the fact that Nikon and Avvakum were old friends of the tsar, and Alexis still had personal feelings for both. In kinder moments Alexis could see why his opponents felt as they did. It seemed to him that the Old Believers, in particular, could and should be restored to harmony with the Church, and throughout 1665 and 1666 he made repeated efforts to bring this about. But reconciliation had to occur on Alexis' terms, for the tsar could never forget that as ruler it was his task to defend the Church and the realm from all enemies, even from those he loved, even from those as well-intentioned as he.

Alexis knew that the fiery and magnetic Avvakum was the heart of much Old Believer activity. In the summer of 1665 the tsar recalled Avvakum and his two sons from Mezen where the archpriest had spent the winter (in the words of his autobiography) "teaching the people of God and denouncing the speckled beasts" of the Nikonian heresy. Avvakum carefully had avoided attacking the tsar in these months, showing that their friendship also meant a great deal to him and that he, too, would like reconciliation, if it could properly occur. Nevertheless, Alexis did not receive the archpriest with an hospitality as great as that shown him on his visit to Moscow the year before. Avvakum was lodged in St. Pafnuti's monastery near Moscow, where he received a letter saying: "Will you vex us longer? Do be reconciled with us, dear old Avvakum!" "But I refused," Avvakum said, "as if they were devils."

Alexis now moved to have both Avvakum and Nikon tried and punished. A church council was convened in late April of 1666 to hear charges against several of the most active Old Believers. Because the parish clergy often sympathized with Avvakum's views, only bishops and abbots of the important monasteries were summoned as judges. Even at that, Alexis personally interrogated each man just to be certain that he approved of Nikon's reforms even while rejecting Nikon himself.

Avvakum was condemned in May for "schism, sedition, and false teach-ings," for "spreading his evil designs and false doctrines orally and in writing," for attacking the "correction of the holy creed, the joining of the first three fingers to make the sign of the cross, the correction and the correctors of church books." Deacon Fedor was condemned also, as was Nikita Dobrynin, a priest from Suzdal who had circulated a peti-tion defending the Old Believers and calling for reconciliation with them. The three men were ordered defrocked and placed in solitary confine-ment. Fedor and Dobrynin soon recanted and signed confessions, which they later withdrew. But Avvakum would not repent in the slightest way.

Alexis then resorted to harsh treatment to break Avvakum. Beginning in the late summer of 1666 the archpriest was shuttled from one monas-tery in the Moscow area to the next, secretly or at night and not along the main roads "but by the marshes and the quagmires, so that people might not see me." Disputations and curses were exchanged, beatings were liberally administered. At St. Nicholas "the tsar came to the mon-astery and visited my prison cell, uttered a groan, and then left the monastery; it appears from this that he was sorry for me, the will of God lay in that."

Finally, Avvakum was shorn in the Cathedral of the Assumption, in the presence of the Tsarina Maria. To the surprise of everyone, "She, sweet lady," raised a tremendous clamor over the shearing "and asked to have me released from prison." But to no avail. To complete Av-vakum's humiliation, he was left only "one forelock, such as the Poles wear on their foreheads." Avvakum then was reimprisoned at St. Pafunti's monastery, so that Alexis now might concentrate his efforts on Nikon's trial.

The inquest against Nikon was proving to be a complicated affair. A Russian council was sufficient to condemn heretical priests, but in try-ing a patriarch Alexis felt the need to broaden the ranks of the judges with foreign dignitaries. Specifically, it seemed necessary to have other patriarchs judge a patriarch, but it was no easy matter to bring this about. At first, Alexis sought support for his anti-Nikonian campaign from the entire Eastern Church, taking advantage of the fact that the four great patriarchates of the East—Constantinople, Alexandria, Jerusa-lem and Antioch—had become impoverished under the Ottoman Turks and needed "alms" from the gracious tsar of Moscow. Alexis had ladled out abundant revenues in the past; he now dangled the hope of further aid before Dionysios, Paisios, Nektarios, and Macarius. The latter, of course, already had been to Moscow with his son, Paul of Aleppo, in 1655, and could testify to Alexis' generosity.

Nevertheless, some of the Eastern patriarchs were sufficiently devoted to principle as to cooperate badly—or not at all—with Tsar Alexis. Ligarides' effort to gain written condemnations of Nikon through carefully worded questions (did Nikon breach his duty in taking the title "Grand Sovereign"? Was he wrong to name his monastery the "New Jerusalem"? May a patriarch depart from church tradition? Leave his throne? In such a case, does he make his church a widow?) was something of a disappointment, considering that Nektarios generally exonerated Nikon and pointedly praised him for defending his church against the crown. The patriarch of Jerusalem also reminded the Muscovites of the "proper" procedures to follow in an inquest against a patriarch, procedures which would surely result in Nikon's acquittal. Nektarios' final recommendation to Alexis was to be reconciled with Nikon. The tsar showed his opinion of Nektarios' letter by clapping its bearer in prison so that its contents would not be known in Moscow.

Dionysios and Nektarios also refused to attend the proposed council, pleading that the Turks would not let them make the journey. This frustrated Alexis all the more because Constantinople and Jerusalem were the most prestigious eastern patriarchates. In the end Paisios and Macarius appeared in Moscow in November of 1666, together with ten other dignitaries of the Eastern Church.

Nikon's trial opened in the grand dining hall of the Kremlin on December 1, 1666. This hearing was an even greater farce than the proceedings recently visited upon Avvakum. Alexis' failure to gain the united support of Nikon's fellow patriarchs was compounded by a new disaster—the discovery on the eve of the inquest that the papers granting Ligarides the powers of Patriarch Dionysios' deputy had been forged. Further communications from Nektarios to Alexis revealed that Ligarides was notorious throughout the East as a Roman agent. Nektarios had anathematized Ligarides as early as 1660, not, the patriarch assured the tsar, for Latinism, but for "unmentionable immorality," a phrase which must have stirred Alexis' curiosity as much as it does ours. We now know that throughout the trial Ligarides received regular orders from the papal nuncio in Poland, while he, in turn, submitted written requests for payments to the Congregation for the Propagation of the Faith in Rome. Nevertheless, Paisios Ligarides was so deeply involved in building the case against Nikon that by the time this news appeared Alexis was forced to suppress and ignore it. But the tsar must have brooded over the advice Nektarios offered concerning Ligarides, advice which could be paraphrased: "Keep him far from the secrets you hold, for when you and he part, he will hurry to Rome to betray everything he knows about your empire!"

The worst for Alexis was yet to come. During the trial it was learned that Dionysios had died. While this patriarch had refused to support Alexis against Nikon, neither did he openly oppose the tsar's case. But Dionysios' successor, Parthenios IV, took a stronger stand. Outraged at the role Macarius and Paisios were playing against a brother patriarch, Parthenios declared their sees vacated, and proceeded to have new patriarchs elected in their stead. This news was likewise suppressed at Moscow, for it made the entire proceedings against Nikon uncanonical and invalid.

Nikon entered the Kremlin dining hall on December 1, 1666 with all the pomp due a patriarch, preceded by a cross-bearer. A Greek patriarch was seated on each side of Alexis' throne. All rose as Nikon bowed three times before Alexis, twice before each patriarch. But Nikon refused to sit because the seat prepared for him was that of a humble defendant, not a chair equal to that of Macarius and Paisios.

Hearts must have skipped a beat when Nikon inquired if the visiting patriarchs were authorized by the patriarch of Constantinople to judge him! Did Nikon know that Dionysios had opposed this inquest? Was he aware that Parthenios had expelled Macarius and Paisios from their offices? Nikon had indeed heard all this from sympathetic Greeks in Moscow, but he may not have felt certain that it was true. The visitors pointed solemnly to documents lying on a table as granting them this authority. Out of respect for canon law and the presumed dignity of the visiting patriarchs, Nikon raised no further objections on this point—an unfortunate move for him.

Alexis personally stated many of the charges against Nikon, and the two engaged in several sharp exchanges. The most serious allegations against the patriarch were that he had abandoned his duties, sowed confusion and division within the church, and attempted to usurp powers which rested only with the tsar. The litigation, of course, was technical and involved. Nikon was permitted to attend the sessions and throughout he conducted himself with great skill and dignity. But from the beginning he had no chance, and he knew this perfectly well.

With his characteristic distaste for difficult moments, Alexis was absent when the council decision was read to Nikon on December 12, 1666. It was decided that Nikon had "offended our long-ruling Tsar, Sovereign, and Grand Prince, Alexis Mikhailovich." Nikon had plunged "the entire Orthodox realm into turmoil, and involved himself in matters unsuitable to patriarchal authority and dignity." After a train of such abuses, Nikon "finally left his throne, and yet he did not leave it, for he craftily would not permit another patriarch" to be selected. The

patriarchs who signed this council statement denied that they were acting "through human passion," but rather because "we have learned that
Nikon lived tyrannically, and not humbly as is becoming to a prelate,
and that he was inclined to iniquity, greed, and tyranny." Nikon also
was convicted of several specific crimes, the worst of which, perhaps,
was entitling himself "patriarch of the New Jerusalem," a reference to
his beloved Resurrection monastery.

Harsh punishment was meted out for all this. The patriarchs and the
council decreed that the tsar's special friend henceforth would be known
as a "common monk named Nikon, and not as the patriarch of Moscow,
that he be assigned a place to remain until the very end of his days, in
some old and suitable monastery, where he may lament his sins in great
silence," which is to say, in solitary confinement. The council ordered
Nikon imprisoned at the Ferapontov monastery in the bleak, frozen region of Belozero, far to the north.

As Nikon left the inquest, he was placed in a sleigh with seven guards.
Lost in thought, the fallen patriarch membled to himself: "Nikon! why
has all this happened to you? If you don't speak the truth, you don't
lose friendship! If you had given them fine banquets and parties, this
would not have happened to you!"

Abbot Sergei rode behind the sleigh, a large crowd of Nikon's sympathizers grimly trudging after him through the snow. When the prisoner
turned to speak to his supporters, Sergei snarled, "Shut up, Nikon!"

Nikon glared at this former acquaintance and spat out: "Look here,
Sergei, let He who has authority come and shut my mouth!"

At that point a steward who was delivering a message of some sort
happened to refer to Nikon as the "most holy patriarch."

"Are you making fun of us," Sergei asked, "calling a simple monk
the patriarch?"

"What are you saying?" shot a voice from the crowd. "The name of
patriarch is given from above, not from you, you arrogant one!" When
Sergei called to the musketeers to grab the impertinent fellow, they
replied that he was already in hand and had been sent to the place he
belonged.

On the morning of the next day, December 13, 1666, Nikon set out
for the Ferapontov monastery. Alexis sent money and a fur coat with a
plea for the former patriarch to bless him and the royal family. Nikon
rejected the tsar's presents. As for a benediction, the fallen patriarch replied: "He loved not blessing, therefore the blessing is for me to go far
away from him."

The large crowd which gathered at the Kremlin in the early hours of
the morning on the following day was informed that Nikon would be

brought down Sretenka street. As the people dashed towards Kitai gorod, Nikon, accompanied by loyal monks, departed the Kremlin by another road. During the eight-day journey to Belozero large crowds turned out to catch a glimpse of Nikon and show him their sympathy.

The council now was called upon to confirm the condemnation of Avvakum, who was—predictably—no more contrite than Nikon. The fiery Avvakum saw his appearance as another test of endurance, another opportunity to stand heroically, and alone, for the true faith. "I spoke of many things in Holy Writ with the patriarchs," Avvakum proudly recalled in later years. "God did open my sinful mouth and Christ put them to shame." Avvakum hotly defended the unique practices of the Russian Church, reminding his listeners that Rome and Constantinople had fallen, so that the orthodoxy of the foreigners in the audience now "is of mongrel breed." "You have become impotent," he cried out defiantly, "and henceforth it is you who should come to us to learn." Bedlam broke lose and insults flowed freely until musketeer guards dragged Avvakum away.

Avvakum's courage won him no mercy. In a ringing statement of May 1667 the council reaffirmed the validity of all Nikon's reforms, as well as "the newly corrected and newly translated printed books" which had been published in the last fifteen years in Moscow. It condemned wholesale the Old Believers, "ignorant men" who "with the help of the devil" had employed false zeal and hollow piety to mislead and confuse, to attack and discredit the loyal clergy. In the opinion of the council these people, "speaking and writing under Satan's inspiration, "were heretics and schismatics" and must be suppressed at all costs.

The condemned men, Avvakum and his co-defendants, were punished three months later. Before Father Lazar and the monk Epifani were exiled to Pustozersk, their tongues were cut from their mouths. Avvakum also was sentenced to exile, but through Alexis' intervention was spared mutilation for blasphemy the others suffered.

As Avvakum was about to set out on his final odyssey, Alexis made a last attempt to reach him. He sent a large company of officials which included Matveev and Dementy Bashmakov to speak to the archpriest. Avvakum later recalled that they conveyed a message to him from the tsar: "Archpriest! I see your life that is pure and undefiled and pleasing to God; me and the tsarina and our children, remember us." The envoy wept as he spoke.

Alexis' last words to Avvakum were: "Wherever you be, do not forget us in your prayers."

"And I, sinful one," the archpriest admitted in his *Life,* "now as much as I may, I do pray to God for him."

Chapter Twenty-Two

A CHURCH UNITED?

With Nikon out of the way, Alexis rushed to strengthen his hold over the Church. It was necessary to elect a new patriarch, of course, one who could be counted upon to serve the tsar slavishly, to lead Christ's flock without again seeking to make it independent of the crown.

Pitirim, rewarded with the metropolitanate of Novgorod as the thirty pieces of silver for his efforts against Nikon, was to present a list of candidates for the patriarchate at the special church council scheduled at Moscow in January 1667. He handed his nominations to Macarius of Antioch, who passed them on to the tsar. The names were read, discussion followed. At length, Joasaph, abbot of the Trinity monastery, was selected. But Joasaph "made many excuses on account of his advanced age, adding that he had neither learning nor capacity" for this high office. All who listened knew he spoke the truth.

Alexis flew into a rage, displaying the pressure he had been under in the closing weeks of the Nikon affair. It would seem that to persuade Joasaph to accept the patriarchate Alexis must praise him and his supposed abilities. Nothing of the sort! Instead, Alexis broke into a harangue against Nikon.

"No single personal foe, however noble, no enemy of any sort has ever troubled or exasperated or alarmed me so much as Nikon," Alexis cried, "that former Patriarch of Moscow who verily appeared to me as a new plague from Egypt!" Nikon's contest was "neither praiseworthy nor admirable," the tsar added, for "it flew in the face of all the good which has been shown him." The tsar closed by saying: "And I mean not that which I myself showed—which was nothing—but that good showed him most abundantly from heaven."

The agitated company applauded this, crying out: "Oh tsar! live forever! Many years to you, new Constantine, great Theodosios, most excellent Justinian, defender and brave champion and helper of the church! May the Lord who strengthens rulers likewise strengthen your empire! Oh Heavenly King! preserve our earthly king who has rendered peace to our church and rescued it from all divisions."

The father superior of the Trinity monastery now was proclaimed Patriarch Joasaph II. But the old man was so unwell on the day scheduled for his consecration (February 3, 1667) that the date was moved to the following Sunday. Palm Sunday of that year was "observed with great pomp," note the chronicles, the patriarch astride a great white horse led by Tsar Alexis in his magnificent robes.

Alexis humbled himself before Joasaph in public, but otherwise the tsar was determined that he, not the patriarch, would wield true power within the Church. He set Ligarides to work to apply to Russian conditions the familiar doctrine of caesaropapism, the argument that a Christian "Caesar" wields final authority over the Church as well as the state. Ligarides' task was made easier by Alexis' well-known religiosity and devotion to the Church. "And the good tsar's heir will be still better," Ligarides confidently intoned of the young Tsarevich Alexis Alexeevich. "He will be both tsar and archbishop."

But Alexis did not have his way easily. Although the theory of caesaropapism may have been even more firmly established in Moscow than in Constantinople, the events of the recent years had stirred many Russian Church leaders to a new concept of their position. Bishops Paul of Krutitsa and Hilarion of Riazan privately agreed with Nikon that the priesthood holds a dignity higher than that of secular authority. Unfortunately, they thought that secretly expressing this sentiment to the visiting Greek patriarchs might advance a compromise with Nikon. But Macarius and Paisios betrayed the confidence, and the offending bishops were dragged before the council in January and suspended. Paul and Hilarion were summoned back to recant and receive pardon on February 3, the same day originally set for the consecration of the ailing Joasaph as patriarch. "And all was gladness now," the council records say of this event. "The mists were entirely dispersed and the full-mooned light of peace shone, the very name of which is sweeter than the honeycomb."

The other fifteen Russian bishops were not as bold as Paul and Hilarion, but in their individual ways most applauded Nikon's belief that the crown must not interfere with ecclesiastical authority and church lands. They knew perfectly well that the Byzantine tradition now being so highly recommended was more complicated than Alexis and his theoreticians were making it out to be. True, caesaropapism in Muscovy had prevented the political conflicts so familiar between Western kings and popes. But in the East as in the West church writers often argued that just as the spirit is of a order higher than matter, so too the spiritual authority ordained by God to guide man on earth is "in principle" loftier than its secular counterpart, the state.

Above all, Byzantine doctrine held that there must be harmony, *symphonia,* between church and state. All authorities agreed on this point. The specific nature of this "harmony" might be interpreted differently by various interest groups, of course. But that was exactly the point. Thanks to Nikon, and even after the humiliation of Paul and Hilarion, many members of the church council in Moscow continued to whisper privately "that the empire is excelled in dignity by the priesthood, because," as the records put it, "the bishop is named first in the Church, and the emperor afterwards." For individuals of such persuasion, "harmony" demanded greater independence for the Church.

Paul and Hilarion and their supporters chose Alexis' name day, March 17, 1667, to stage another attack. Paisios Ligarides argued on that occasion that "our glorious and Christian Emperor Alexis" was supreme over both state and church, that he properly "regulates the ecclesiastical ranks, and legislates for the life and polity of the clergy" just as the Christian emperors of old. Ligarides claimed that "with the single exception of officiating in sacred things, all other episcopal privileges are clearly represented by the emperor, and in respect of them he acts lawfully and canonically."

But the dissidents won their point. Twelve chapters drafted into the council proceedings that spring recognized that the tsar's supremacy was limited to civil affairs. "The tsar is supreme in affairs of state, the patriarch in those of the Church."

The "victory" of the Church went beyond mere words. It was most clearly expressed in political life in the fate of the Monastery Bureau, the government office created in 1649 to oversee monastery lands and limit their growth. Nikon had been able to minimize the functions of this Bureau, but for all his supposed influence with the tsar, Alexis could not be persuaded to abolish it altogether. While Nikon dwelt in self-imposed exile at the Resurrection monastery, the Monastery Bureau grew bolder in exercising its functions. Yet, ironically, during the five-year reign of the subservient Joasaph II the powers of the Monastery Bureau were exercised less and less. Continuing pressure from abbots and bishops prolonged this trend under Pitirim, rewarded at last for his cooperation by being elected patriarch when Joasaph died in February 1672.

When Pitirim died on April 19 of the following year, Joachim became patriarch. As Vernadsky says, Joachim "had no theological education and no true religious spirit." He came from a noble military family and distinguished himself as "a church administrator rather than a church prelate." But Joachim was as zealous as Nikon in defending the property and rights of the church, and finally, in 1675, he persuaded Alexis to abolish the Monastery Bureau altogether.

Joachim proved, in his own way, to be as forceful as the universally deplored Nikon. Indeed, after Alexis' death Joachim (who died fourteen years later, in 1690) played an important political role. But it fell to

Peter the Great to gain the final victory of crown over church by abolishing the patriarchate altogether and placing church leadership within the
structure of the new crown administration he created. Significantly,
Peter reopened the Monastery Bureau with greatly increased powers in
1701.

Chapter Twenty-Three

A CHURCH DIVIDED

Avvakum arrived at his place of confinement in Pustozersk in December
1667. He was accompanied by Father Lazar and Epiphany the Elder,
both of whom must have lost but part of their tongues in Moscow four
months earlier, for by now they had recovered most of their speech.

Pustozersk is a place of legendary cold located near the Arctic Ocean,
on the Pechora River. But its frigid, dreary months did little to lessen
the ardor of the Old Believers exiled there, zealots who were joined in
the spring by Nikifor and Fedor the Deacon. These witnesses to the old
faith mingled freely with their musketeer guards during the two years it
took to build a prison at Pustozersk; they were even able to communicate with their Moscow disciples through epistles and pamphlets. Usually
this literature was distributed secretly, but Alexis received two letters
from Avvakum in which the archpriest defended his teachings and relayed "certain of God's signs which had appeared to me in my prison."
Avvakum also begged the tsar to be merciful, if not to him, at least to
his family confined at Mezen.

The Old Belief had grown by now into something much greater than
a handful of zealots in a remote northern town. Alexis thought that a
speedy condemnation and exile of Avvakum and his compatriots would
prevent their resistance from developing into a true split in the Church.
But the schism had advanced beyond this even before the time of their
trial. Indeed, despite the tsar's vigilant eye it had penetrated the court
itself.

The Moscow Old Believers were led by Theodosia Morozova, a close
friend of the tsarina and the widow of Boris Morozov's brother Gleb.
Morozova was a secret follower of Avvakum, and after Avvakum was
sent to Pustozersk she corresponded extensively with the archpriest,
sending him and his wife badly needed money, keeping him fully posted

on the spiritual life of his sympathizers, among whom some bore such prominent family names as Saltykov, Dolgoruky, Volkonsky, Khovansky and Urusov.

When Alexis learned of Lady Morozova's attachment to Avvakum, he personally tried to win her back to the established Church. When this failed, Alexis sent the future patriarch, Joachim, and a monk to reason with her. The *Life* which describes the brave Theodosia's martyrdom claim that "she strongly resisted them," exposed their false arguments, and "put them to shame." Alexis was so outraged at this that he confiscated half her ancestral estate. The tsar would have done worse but for the intervention of the tsarina, as well as his own fatherly affection for Morozova's handsome son Ivan.

The Moscow Old Believers suffered a severe setback when Tsarina Maria died on March 3, 1669. Though not a schismatic herself, the tsarina always had disliked Nikon, smiled favorably on Avvakum, and in general was attached to ancient Russian ways. Furthermore, Maria's passing brought Artamon Sergeevich Matveev to the fore, and he was as unsympathetic to the Old Believer cause as he was convinced that Russian culture should evolve along Western lines. Above all, Matveev thought it necessary to take strong action against the Old Believers, lest the the schism they were spinning grow still larger.

Alexis also became convinced of this danger when he learned in early 1670 that Avvakum's family and friends at Mezen were helping the Old Believers at Pustozersk spread their views throughout the land. Alexis sent Ivan Elagin, a musketeer captain, to break this nexus of schismatic organization and propaganda. While at Mezen Captain Elagin hanged two of Avvakum's "spiritual children," Theodore, "the fool in Christ," and Luke Lavrentievich. Avvakum's wife Anastasia was buried alive with their sons Ivan and Prokopy. Significantly, the stern archpriest did not honor the death of his sons, calling them "miserable ones" and "weaklings" since, fearing death and (vainly) hoping to escape it, at the end they "submitted" to the Nikonian heresy.

Elagin then made his way to Pustozersk with instructions from the tsar on how to deal with the Old Believers there. Avvakum, Lazar, Fedor and Epiphany were given a final chance to accept the Nikonian reforms and receive pardon and freedom. When they refused, they were led from prison on April 4, 1670, to the place where the block stood as a grim reminder of the work done there. Instruments of torture stood in plain view, the executioner at the ready.

An eyewitness account of this event says that the condemned men "were not the least downcast, but blessed the people together and bade

their farewells with bright and happy faces." To the sympathetic on-
lookers they cried out, "Be not seduced by Nikon's teachings! We suffer
and die for the truth!"

Avvakum first mounted the block, shouting, "Here stands our throne!"

The four good comrades blessed each other and said farewell, thinking they were about to be beheaded. But at this point the tsar's orders
were read. The tongues of Lazar, Fedor and Epiphany were to be cut
from their mouths for blasphemy; their hands were to be hacked from
their arms for making the sign of the cross with two fingers. The sen-
tences were carried out as the people in a state of shock called out,
"Lord have mercy! Lord have mercy!"

Alexis' favor protected Avvakum even now. The archpriest again was
spared the punishment visited upon his friends. Alexis ordered Avvakum
cast into a dank earthen prison, where he would receive small rations of
bread, water and beer bread. "Upon hearing this, the archpriest was
sorely offended," our eyewitness continues. Avvakum spat and declared:
"I spit upon his bread and will die without eating it rather than betray
my faith!"

Even then Avvakum probably knew that as long as Alexis lived, he
would not die. As the executioner worked upon his friends, Avvakum
was dragged back to prison, where he "began to weep and to cry at being
separated from his brothers." Eight days later his mutilated friends persuaded Avvakum to break his hunger strike, to live on so that he might
stand for the true faith yet another day.

Thinking the leaders of the schism were neutralized forever, Alexis
now moved against their followers in Moscow. When "Pilate" returned
to Moscow, Avvakum says of Elagin, "others of us were burned and
baked." Instead of breaking the Old Believer movement in the capital,
however, this persecution stiffened its character and brought new sympathizers. Theodosia Morozova's sister, Princess Urusova, joined the
schism at this very moment. Morozova herself had been left undisturbed
during recent months, and tried to compensate for the artificiality of
Muscovite social life by occupying herself with piety and good deeds.
But she found it increasingly difficult to continue the court routine in
the presence of the tsar and to pretend that all was well. After she
secretly became a nun under the name Theodora on December 6, 1670,
Morozova no longer appeared at court functions. Claiming ill health,
she even refused to attend Alexis' second marriage the following month.

Troubles now showered down upon Morozova's head. Alexis was infuriated by her absence from his wedding and the failure of renewed
efforts to reunite her with the established Church. She and her sister

LADY MOROZOVA ABOUT TO BE TAKEN INTO EXILE. Detail from the celebrated oil canvas of V.I. Surikov (1887). Note that Morozova's hand is raised in the two-fingered salute, reminding the spectators (some of whom are well dressed, suggesting that she had numerous supporters in boyar families) that the Old Believers continued to make the sign of the cross in this way. Horace Dewey says of Alexis' controversy with Morozova: "His behavior seemed indecisive at times, and . . . suggests a reluctance to deal brutally with her on his own initiative; she was, after all, a noblewoman. But he could be vindictive; he appeared more upset by her refusal to attend his wedding than by her schismatic religious views, and his struggle with her had definitely personal undercurrents."

were arrested and tormented. Morozova's son fell ill at home, and though
the tsar sent his own physicians to care for him, Ivan died. Alexis now
confiscated Morozova's entire property, though later he did permit her
and her sister to be attended in prison by maidservants. The sisters' good
friend Maria Danilova suffered even more than they, being subjected
according to Morozova's *Life,* to "vile acts" by the "shameless soldiers"
who were guarding her.

The authorities grew worried over the fact that crowds of noble ladies
and simple folk gathered to watch the three women being dragged forci-
bly to services in the official Church. When Pitirim was elected patriarch
in February 1672, he begged Alexis to release Morozova and Urusova.
The tsar refused but did let Pitirim make another effort to persuade the
women to renounce their heresies. After Morozova fiercely rebuffed the
patriarch, Alexis inquired of him: "Did I not tell you about that woman's
ferocity? You have seen her deeds but once, but I have suffered from
her for years!"

Alexis now ordered the three ladies to be tortured into submission.
More dead than alive, they held to their faith. The tsar then directed
that the women be moved to the Novodevichy monastery, only to be
frightened by the news that noblewomen were flocking there in large
numbers in sympathy with the renowned heretics. The tsar's beloved
sister Irene even spoke up in Morozova's defense, chiding her brother
for having shuttled her so cruelly from place to place. Irene reminded
Alexis of Boris and Gleb, celebrated saints of the eleventh century who
according to tradition meekly submitted to death at the hands of their
half-brother, Prince Svyatopolk, rather than respond to his lust for
power with violence of their own.

Alexis removed his troublesome prisoners in early 1673 to a monastery at Borovsk, some 75 miles southwest of Moscow. Here their treatment grew steadily worse: their books and icons were confiscated, they
were placed with common criminals or in dank holes, they were starved
and would have died but for jailers who disobeyed orders and slipped
the high-born ladies small amounts of fruit, cucumbers and water. Even
so, the heroic women faded quickly. Evdokia Urusova died on September 11, 1675. A last effort by a monk to persuade Theodora Morozova
to recant failed, and she slipped peacefully away on November 2. Maria
Danilova joined her two friends on December 2, 1675.

The Old Believer movement by this time was embracing a considerable
number of people. Brother Lazar had defiantly warned Alexis that this
would happen seven years before, declaring from his place of exile at
Pustozersk: "Do not think we are few. A hundred thousand people in
Russia stand ready to die for the faith of their fathers."

If anything, Lazar's estimate was modest. By 1675 the Swedish agent in Moscow, Lilienthal, was reporting that 6,000 Old Believers had gathered in the forests of Kostroma and near Kazan, where they were seizing and burning the new "Frankish" icons and terrorizing priests bold enough to celebrate the mass as reformed by Patriarch Nikon. Hundreds of thousands of peasants in the next several years fled to other remote regions of the Russian frontier—north to the upper Volga and towards the Arctic Ocean, east to the Don Cossacks, the Urals and Siberia, south to the fertile steppe and the protection of the Zaporozhie Cossacks. A few even made their way to the Baltic region. They came from the heartland, fleeing serfdom and taxes, and hoping to find places where once again they might follow the Old Faith. They came as if in response to the summons Avvakum voiced in one of his finest poems:

> As it is written by the son of Vasily,
> Our venerable father Ephraem:
> > Fly, my dear ones,
> > into the black woods;
> > Take refuge, my dear ones,
> > in the mountains and the caves;
> > Hide, my dear ones,
> > in the depths of the earth.
> Ah, if someone would but build me
> A cell in the heart of the woods,
> Where no man went
> And no bird flew;
> Where only you, O Christ, would dwell
> For the good of our souls;
> And where I would no longer see
> All the scandal of this world.

The Old Believers struggled to understand the calamitous events which had overcome Russia. The doctrine of the Third Rome which was the foundation of their outlook held that there could never be a "fourth" Rome. The Third Rome was to shine more brightly than the sun so long as mankind endured. How was it possible, then, that the Russian Church was rotting from within? Even if one could account for Nikon's reforms, why was it that the tsar continued to support them even after the false patriarch was gone? Truly, the antichrist and his black angels no longer hovered in dark corners but now strode boldly the corridors of power in Moscow and elsewhere in the land.

Behold, the end of the world must be at hand! The Day of Judgment must be rising on the horizon, that heavenly day when earthly things will crumble to dust, when the guilty will be condemned as Christ gathers

His saints to reign with them forever. Seen from this view, the sufferings of today must be to test the believer, to winnow the wheat from the chaff. The tsar's legions and executioners were not to be feared; they come to bestow martyrs' crowns. One lived to die in the name of the true faith!

This apocalyptic moment was foretold even before Alexis took the throne. The deep forests of Yaroslavl and Vladimir had seethed since the 1630s with the impassioned message of Kapiton and his "brothers" and "sisters." These craggy heretics declared that the Holy Spirit had fled the established Church, the crown was totally evil, true Christians must renounce all false attractions to worldly life. Efforts of the authorities to track down these troublemakers merely brought more converts to their ranks, and, paradoxically, by keeping them on the run, the tsar's soldiers distributed new "monasteries" and "convents" over increasingly large areas. By the end of Alexis' reign, Old Believers were mingling with the Kapitonians, exchanging stories, ideas and Biblical quotations, and gaining mutual protection. A column of soldiers led by Avram Lopukhin and Artamon Matveev against these "saints" in the area of Suzdal and Nizhnyi-Novgorod produced nothing more than a few burning huts—and the martyrdom by fire of Vavila the Evangelist. The forest heretics otherwise continued in their ways.

More and more the dissenters came to view the tsar himself as the chief apostle of darkness. When Alexis took the throne in 1645, Michael the Hermit announced from his refuge in the forests of Suzdal that the young tsar was not the true sovereign, but a "horn of the antichrist." The Kapitonians quickly took up the same theme. Avvakum's respect for Alexis and monarchical authority, his hope even of winning Alexis' son Fedor (who reigned from 1676 to 1682) to the Old Faith—all this was completely bypassed by the main thrust of the Old Believer movement. Its opinion increasingly came to be that Alexis was not a poor, wayward Christian, but the antichrist himself, an outlook which left Avvakum—from this perspective—in an uncharacteristically moderate position.

Other Old Believers were even more extreme than Avvakum in their search for martyrdom. Avvakum did not fear tribulation, for he had no desire to save his own life. But neither would Avvakum be the one to take his own life. The forest schismatics increasingly disdained such a passive stance. As early as 1666 we read the first accounts of Old Believers near Nizhnyi-Novgorod burning themselves to death, or, as they called it, attaining "purification by fire." Vasily, a Kapitonian, boasted that his preaching caused a thousand schismatics to seek death by burning, drowning and starvation. By this time the Old Believers had divided into numerous sects, each of which denounced the others for departures from the "true" faith and way.

The high point of the Old Believer struggle in Alexis' time came at the Solovetsky monastery, located on a small frozen island in the Arctic Ocean. For more than two centuries this cloister had been as vital to the spiritual life of its area as the Trinity monastery near Moscow was to the Russian heartland. Pilgrims streamed to the Solovetsky monastery to seek the advice of its monks, to venerate the relics of saints buried within its walls. Books and icons produced at Solovki were spread to the remotest corners of the far North. The economic significance of the monastery was as great as its spiritual influence. The basis of its economy was the sale and manufacture of salt, and by the 1660s it operated 54 salt works. The monks also trapped and fished, hunted for mica and pearls, mined and smelted iron. As many as 700 workers assisted the 350 brothers in these and related tasks.

The growing power of higher authorities threatened Solovki's traditional independence, triggering a mood which made the brothers look nostalgically to an earlier day. The Law Code of 1649, for example, set severe limits to the lands monasteries might acquire in the future. Nikon as metropolitan of Novgorod was able to suspend government interference with the monasteries of this region but he also assumed closer control of their affairs for himself. Bad blood between him and the Solovetsky monastery thickened when he settled a land dispute in favor of another cloister. This tension grew worse when Nikon removed the relics of St. Philip from their original burial place at the Solovetsky monastery to Moscow in 1652.

The proud independence of the Solovki monks was paralleled by staunch conservatism in church affairs. Avvakum's friend and fellow martyr Epiphany recalled that when the news of the reformed liturgy arrived, "the holy fathers and bretheren of the Solovetsky monastery began to lament and to weep bitterly, and to say: 'Brothers, brothers! Alas, alas! Woe, woe! Christ's faith has fallen in Russia as in other lands because of Christ's two enemies, Nikon and Arsenios,'" the latter being a Greek scholar who had been brought to Moscow to "correct" the books and liturgy of the Russian Church. Robert O. Crummey further notes in his book on the Old Believers that Solovki father superior Ilya "refused to use the new books and had them locked up without even inspecting them."

The crisis heightened in 1666 when a local church council dispatched Abbot Sergei of the Yaroslavsky cloister to enforce the new ritual at the Solovetsky monastery. Resistance was strong and Sergei fled without accomplishing his goal. An involved dispute now broke out concerning which of three brothers would be Solovki's father superior. The Old Believer monks here also drafted a series of petitions passionately defending their views to the tsar. In the third letter they declared: "We wish to end our days in that ancient faith in which, after the Lord's will, your sovereign father and other pious tsars and princes spent theirs." They assured Alexis that "we are not rebels against you." But if the tsar would not withdraw the hated innovations, he was begged "to send your sovereign sword and dispatch us from this troubled life to peaceful eternity." With fame of the monastery's defiance of Nikon's reforms spreading far and wide, the government decided to close debate and take firm control over the situation at Solovki. The monastery's lands were confiscated after the dissident monks refused further decrees to submit to Nikon's reforms. A musketeer army under the command of I. Volkhov arrived on June 22, 1668 to begin a siege destined to last for almost eight years.

The rebels were aided by their island location. Also, the peasants of the area showed their sympathy with the insurgents by slipping them food and supplies through the blockade. About 500 people took up the defense of Solovki's strong walls in these years, the ranks of the first rebels being swelled by newcomers determined to fight at their side. Refugee soldiers and peasants, as well as Old Believer monks and laymen, made their way here from every part of the land. At the Solovetsky monastery—as elsewhere in Russia—what began as a controversy over church reform ended in open rebellion against the state. The deserter monk Pakhomy informed the musketeer commander Ivan Meshcherinov in June 1674 that "these thieves do not attend church, nor do they pray for the Grand Sovereign." They speak about the tsar "in words so violent that it is terrifying not only to write, but even to hear them."

Pakhomy also stated that "the monastery has enough bread supplies to last ten or more years, and fats, turnips, and minced food to last for about two years," as well as quantities of mushrooms, garlic and fish. By that time Meshcherinov had under his command a thousand well-equipped musketeers. Yet time and again they were repulsed with heavy casualties.

The turning point came in early 1676 when another deserter, the monk Feoktist, told Meshcherinov of a secret undefended entry through one of the monastery's towers. A small party of musketeers passed through this entrance during a terrible snowstorm on the night of January 22, 1676 and, while the garrison slept, opened the gates from within. The final assault now began. The 200 rebels present at that time fought valiantly, but had no chance. When the fighting stopped, only sixty were still alive. A few were pardoned, some were executed, the others were imprisoned.

Alexis took ill the night the Solovetsky monastery fell. He died a week later. By the time the news of the victory reached Moscow, a new tsar reigned over the land.

Chapter Twenty-Four

REBELLION ON THE DON

While religious dissenters clashed with the tsar's soldiers at the lonely, isolated Solovetsky monastery, an infinitely more serious rebellion broke out in the East. Led by Stenka Razin, this movement began in the region of the Don and Volga rivers. Sweeping west and north, for a time it menaced the government in Moscow itself. Razin's revolt was the greatest peasant war of the seventeenth century, perhaps the greatest lower class movement known to history as of that time. And it presented Tsar Alexis with the greatest challenge of his entire life.

Theoretically the Don was ruled by the tsar. But the proud, self-governing Cossack communities scattered along its wide banks long had resisted the reach of crown authority from Moscow. The tsar paid the Don Cossacks annual sums—fierce arguments raged over how much—to guard their frontiers and protect south central Russia from Tatar attack. The rough, hearty Cossacks traditionally shunned agriculture as a thing which bred social classes and degraded the independence of free men. The Cossacks preferred to raise cattle and horses, hunt and fish, drink and carouse, and plunder their southern neighbors.

Beneath the facade of this robust, happy life, the lands of the Don were undergoing painful social change. Here, as in the Ukraine, the Cossacks traditionally welcomed and protected newcomers in search of freedom. "No man is returned from the Don," it was boasted, a defiance which Moscow was hardly in a position to challenge. Knowing this, runaway serfs flocked to the Don and its tributaries. What in earlier years was a trickle had grown to a stream of tens of thousands during Alexis' time, mostly families fleeing serfdom, taxes, and, in the case of the men, military service. Despite the opposition of more old-fashioned Cossacks, the new arrivals resumed farming. For that matter, a considerable number of Cossacks themselves were learning to use the plow and scythe in these years. Indeed, many of them were as badly off as the peasants of Russia, for most Cossack farmers either worked the land

STENKA RAZIN. From an old German engraving which, unlike many depictions of the subject, attempts to portray the man's more fiendish characteristics.

of others or tilled scraps of ground bought with money borrowed from those Cossacks known, significantly, as "house-owners." The latter families also were coming to control the better fisheries and hunting preserves, and to monopolize positions of political and military authority.

Stephen (Stenka) Timofeevich Razin was born into a "house-owning" family about 1630. All who knew him agreed that he was bright and magnetic, a born organizer and leader of men. Diplomatic missions to Moscow and the Kalmyk tribesmen between 1652 and 1663 gave Razin a grasp of the world lying beyond the comfortable horizons of the Don. In these years Stenka also made two pilgrimages to the Solovetsky monastery, long respected by the Don Cossacks for its shrines and miracle-working relics. It is difficult to say what these pilgrimages meant to

Stenka, for he never revealed himself as a religious man. The trips may have stimulated the rebellious side of his character, however, for in these very years the Solovetsky monks were forming a dissident outlook which ended in an armed uprising at about the same time as Razin's own rebellion. Personal experience may also have turned Razin against the *status quo*. Tradition tells us that Stenka's eldest brother left his detachment on the Polish front for a brief visit home in 1665, but was captured and hanged for treason on the direct orders of Yuri Dolgoruky. Some deny the authenticity of this tale, but if it is true either in whole or in part, it must have made a considerable impact upon Stenka.

Whatever the reasons, Stenka Razin formed a bitter hatred of the wealth and privilege he himself shared as a young man. His dynamic spirit was too restless for an ordinary career of military service. Rather, he turned to the human rabble of the Don, a shabby mixture of fugitive serfs and poor Cossacks, offering to take them on a plundering expedition across the Caspian Sea to Persia. Razin led a party of about a thousand men on 35 flat-bottomed boats down the Volga past Astrakhan in early 1667. The flotilla sailed to the Ural River and seized the town of Yaitsk, robbing, raping and murdering in a fashion all too familiar to the people of the area.

Nonetheless, Razin was distinguished at even this stage of his career by a political vision: he proclaimed death to crown officials and the rich, and offered Cossack freedom to anyone who would join him. This made a tremendous impression. Musketeers guarding caravans and strongpoints refused to fight the Cossacks, local city authorities dared not try to suppress them, but tried to ignore Razin's men in the hope that they would go elsewhere. The bandits moved on to the south Caspian shore in the spring of 1668. Reinforced by Don Cossacks, they spent several months ravaging the Persian coast from Derbent to Baku.

Razin by now had conceived a vision of bringing "Cossack freedom" to the Russian heartland, and moved to form the alliances needed for a broader struggle. Fortunately for him, at this very time Bryukhovetsky, hetman of the Zaporozhie Cossacks of the Eastern bank of the Dnieper River, rose up against Moscow. He called upon "all the knights of the Don" to support him and "Lord Stenka" in a coming struggle for Cossack "liberty" from Moscow. Secret proposals for a merger of forces went out to another malcontent at this time also. Cossack messengers approached Nikon at the Resurrection monastery, offering to force the tsar to restore him to power. Nikon declined the offer. Razin sent another delegation in the spring of 1668 to the fallen patriarch, now imprisoned at the Ferapontov monastery in the far North, to tell him the

THE CAPTURE OF ASTRAKHAN BY RAZIN'S ARMY. Engraving from Jan
Struys' memoirs of Russia published in 1676. Astrakhan was the Russian gateway
to Persia and the East, the political and economic center of the Russian empire in
the southeast. Razin's forces took the city on August 24, 1670 and held it for
seventeen months, well after the collapse of the Razin movement elsewhere in
Russia.

Don Cossacks still looked to him as patriarch. Nikon refused their plea that he escape and join them in the Ukraine.

Nikon was wise in refusing to throw in with the rebels, despite the fact that Razin spent the next two years amassing such impressive victories in the east that by the fall of 1670 the only major strongholds left there in government hands were Simbirsk and Kazan. But Simbirsk was the turning point for Stenka Razin, the engagement which turned his crusade from success to failure. Three times he tried to take Simbirsk in September 1670—and his failure shows the weakness of peasant "wars" such as the one he led. Powerful in the flush of success, once the momentum of a peasant uprising is broken, defeat comes as quickly and irreversibly as the rush of earlier success. In this case, Ivan Miloslavsky and his garrison were unshakeably loyal to each other, and they fought with such valor that Simbirsk held for more than a month—giving Prince Yuri Baryatinsky time to dispatch reinforcements from Kazan. Razin led part of his army in an attempt to intercept Baryatinsky before the prince reached Simbirsk, and in so doing suffered the first major defeat of his career. The siege was broken. Razin and his men fled in all directions.

In late September 1670 Prince Grigory Romodanovsky was inflicting equally great defeats upon Stenka's brother Frolka and a large Don Cossack army he had led towards the Ukraine. Unfortunately for the Razin brothers, Bryukhovetsky's earlier uprising of Zaporozhie Cossacks of the eastern bank of the Dnieper River had failed. The current hetman, Demian Mnogogreshny, not only was loyal to Alexis, he sent a large force northeast to Slobodskaya Ukraine (the region of modern-day Kharkov) to suppress the Cossacks there who had risen in support of Stenka Razin. Thoroughly chastened and with time running out, Frolka emulated his brother in falling back to the Don with whatever forces he could salvage.

Alexis now beamed with the prospect of victory. In earlier months he had devoted much personal attention to training and mobilizing forces against the rebels. He inspected and blessed the armies which streamed from the capital during the summer and fall of 1670, and he followed anxiously the progress of his soldiers in the field. Fortunately, the tsar was well served by such commanders as Miloslavsky and Baryatinsky at Simbirsk, Yuri Dolgoruky in the Volga area, and Romodanovsky just east of the Ukraine. It so happened that Alexis was able to raise additional forces just after the turning of the tide at Simbirsk, when in eight days alone 61,000 men passed before the tsar's admiring eyes at Devichoe field on their way to the front. Razin's movement showed strength in the Volga region throughout early 1671, but the insurgents won no further battles and were slowly coming to realize that they had little hope of victory. Razin in defeat was shunned by cities which had opened their gates to him in victory. He fell back to the Don, where he tried to form new alliances and raise more armies. Despite hopeful moments and signs, his cause was quickly fading, and in April 1671 Stenka and Frolka were arrested by loyal "house-owning" Cossacks, and delivered to the authorities. For several months Alexis' armies visited incredible tortures and executions upon Razin's followers. A contemporary source estimated that whereas 100,000 had fallen in battle, another 100,000 fell victim to the executioner. Perhaps these figures are exaggerated; nevertheless they still give an idea of the carnage inflicted upon the people of the border lands.

Razin had always hoped to see the tsar. And he did. But Stenka did not come to Moscow as the victor, and his hopes for royal leniency were in vain. Brought to the capital in June 1671, Alexis personally questioned his prisoner, and then ordered him tortured and executed. According to sources used by Paul Avrich, Razin was flogged, his limbs were pulled from their sockets, "a hot iron was passed over his body, and the crown of his head was shaved and cold water poured on it drop by drop, 'which they say causeth very much pain.' " On June 6, 1671, Stenka finally fell to the executioner on Red Square without a cry or a plea for mercy. Razin's head and limbs were displayed on staves, his body cast to the dogs.

Frolka Razin was brought to Moscow with his brother, but for some reason he was not executed for another five years. Perhaps he compromised with the authorities in some way. Stenka's mother and uncle, on the other hand, were tortured and executed for their role in his rebellion.

Astrakhan remained in the hands of Razin's men throughout the spring of 1671. The rebels there even tried to stage an offensive up the Volga in May, 1671, but fell back when they realized the strength of the tsar's armies at Simbirsk. Ivan Bogdanovich Miloslavsky finally laid siege to Astrakhan in August with a large army of 30,000 men. The rebels surrendered on November 26, 1671. Miloslavsky had promised clemency to the rebels if they would surrender, and even the ringleaders were left to roam and even leave the city for over six months. All this changed, however, when Alexis sent Yakov Odoevsky to Astrakhan as the new governor in the summer of 1672. The prince had been governor there earlier, in the 1660s, and he believed that a firm hand was needed to pacify the city. Several of the leaders were hanged or burned at the stake, others were exiled or pressed into the tsar's service in bleak and distant places.

With the fall of Astrakhan the Razin rebellion was at an end, and a grateful Tsar Alexis was as lavish in rewarding his most effective supporters as he was firm in punishing those whose indecisiveness and mistakes contributed to the initial success of Razin's movement. Officers were promoted, soldiers were paid bounties. The tsar was especially kind to those who were wounded and disabled in the field. Avrich notes that Alexis received Dolgoruky and Baryatinsky in the Kremlin, showering them with money and gifts. Ivan Bogdanovich Miloslavsky regained political influence as well as lands and peasants. On the other hand, Alexis confiscated the estates of soldiers who shunned service at the moment of crisis, while officers and officials who responded poorly to the rebel challenge were stripped of their posts and languished in disfavor. Fortunately, however, Alexis had to deal with only a few men who might actually be called traitors. Unlike earlier peasant revolts, the Razin uprising attracted only a few nobles, officers and officials, an important sign of the growing power of the Muscovite state.

Razin's movement was weakest in the central, southern and northern regions, strongest in the eastern lands of the Volga and the Don. The result of the rebellion was to strengthen the crown and the nobles in all these areas. Landowners regulated their serfs and lands with greater care after 1670. The central government took advantage of its military operations in the east to extend an authority there which would have been out of the question before Razin's peasant war. The Don Cossacks retained some elements of self-government, at least for a time. But, like the Cossacks of the Ukraine, increasingly they were absorbed into the Muscovite realm. The Don Cossacks swore oaths of allegiance to the tsar after 1671; they paid taxes to the tsar's officials and felt the pressure of royal edicts and crown courts. The "house-owning" Cossacks supported these trends, which also strengthened their own social position. Agriculture, that occupation which some said threatened the ways of a free man, grew ever more common on the sweeping, beautiful lands of the Don.

In the long run it was Stenka Razin who gained the greatest glory from that moment in history which we remember through his name. Razin passed into folklore and popular culture as a glorious hero— champion of the downtrodden, foe of the ruling few. Stenka has been celebrated in story and song more than any other Russian national figure, praised as the man who repelled bullets, passed through prison walls, eluded pursuers, bravely endured torture and execution and somehow never really died. The legends are contradictory, of course, and the idealization of Stenka Razin is extremely paradoxical. His movement was more devoted to murder, plunder and rape than glorious ideology, and even in terms of the latter Soviet historians admit that the social forces which might have permitted the erection of a "classless society" did not exist in Russia at that time. Marxists join with monarchists in declaring that the historic task of this time was to "build the centralized Russian state," a state which would be capable, among other things, of crushing peasant uprisings.

The folklore surrounding Razin and his movement does demonstrate how sharply Russia was divided along class lines at the time of Tsar Alexis. The people clearly saw that on one side stood the tsar and his nobles, his officials and merchants, his bishops and armies—while on the other side were Razin and many of the Cossacks, the poor of the towns, the exploited peasants and the impoverished village clergy who flocked to Razin's horsetail flag. Popular folklore offered no praise for Tsar Alexis and his followers at this moment, even though it was they who actually were laying the foundations of Russian greatness and power.

Chapter Twenty-Five

ALEXIS TAKES A NEW WIFE

Alexis was very contented in his family life. His relations with his father and mother had been warm and uncomplicated, and when left an orphan at the age of fifteen Alexis easily passed under the gentle influence of his beloved sister Irene. The tsar's marriage at seventeen was rare by upper-class Russian standards of the period: Alexis was madly in love with his beautiful bride, and he remained generally happy with her throughout their twenty-one years together. The marriage was blessed with thirteen children—five sons and eight daughters. But in this Alexis was not so fortunate. To put it simply, death stalked the royal nursery. Not even the wisest physicians and best care seemed able to do much about it.

Alexis' first son, Dmitry, was born on October 22, 1648. His parents never celebrated his first birthday; the infant died on October 6 of the following year. Maria hoped to soon bear another male heir, but produced a daughter, Eudocia, on February 18, 1650. Troubled days now followed, with the royal couple praying for a son and undertaking various solemn pilgrimages to help bring it about. Despite this and numerous predictions of a son, another daughter, Martha, was born on August 26, 1652. This put a severe strain on Alexis' marriage, and de Rodes reported that another daughter could well mean a convent for Maria. Then came joyous news on February 5, 1654. A male heir was born, and in honor of his father was named "Alexis, son of Alexis," or, as the Russians say, *Alexis Alexeevich.*

Young Alexis was born just as Russia was going to war with Poland over the Ukraine, and three months before his father was to leave Moscow with his armies. Family concerns made these anxious months for the tsar. He might win lands for Russia and glory for himself on the battlefield, but the security of his dynasty demanded more sons, for Alexis could die on campaign and Alexis Alexeevich easily might follow his deceased brother to a premature grave. This would leave the four-year-old Eudocia in succession to the throne. A woman had never reigned in Moscow, and though this would happen in time, the possibility of a female sovereign was not favorably regarded at the Kremlin at this time. Alexis was thrilled to learn, then, that Maria had become pregnant just before he left Moscow with his troops on May 18, 1654. (This child, Anna, was born on January 23, 1655.)

Maria and the family passed through a terrible crisis that summer. Nikon's attack on the "Frankish" icons shook the people of Moscow to the core. A few days later, in July, a terrible plague descended on the capital. Finally, as if to confirm God's harsh judgment upon the people, an eclipse occurred on the afternoon of August 12. The frightened, suffering people of Moscow flew into a panic.

Alexis ordered Nikon to bring the royal family to a safe place. The pregnant Maria set out for the Trinity monastery with her children and the tsar's sisters Irene, Anna and Tatiana. But even here they were not safe! The royal party was forced to flee the plague again, now intending to travel north all the way to Novgorod. By the time they reached Viazma in late September, however, the plague suddenly subsided, and the next month Alexis came to spend the winter with his family at this city. Maria delivered her fifth child here, a daughter, Anna, on January 3, 1655. In February they returned to Moscow and home.

Alexis rushed back to the front on March 11 to lead his troops on campaign west of Smolensk. From then until he abandoned the field in late 1656, Alexis and Maria were separated more than they were united. With her husband settled back in the Kremlin, Maria again attempted to produce a male heir, but only with the greatest frustration.

In the next three years she bore three children, all girls—Sophia (September 17, 1657), Ekaterina (November 27, 1658) and Maria (January 18, 1660)—making four in a series from the time Anna was born. Moscow buzzed with rumors that the convent again loomed before a tsarina so seemingly barren of sons.

Alexis loved his wife and daughters, but as tsar he had special responsibilities he could not ignore. One of the greatest tragedies he suffered in these years was the death of Anna. The tsar was beside himself with worry when the little girl took sick and hovered at the point of death. His old friend Bogdan Khitrovo sent Alexis an astrologer monk, a man criticized by Nikon but widely esteemed for his success in predicting the future. When the tsar asked if Anna would die or recover, the sad answer came that she would pass from this life. Alexis asked the frank soothsayer to remain at Moscow's Chudov monastery to be near at hand when the tragedy ended. Anna breathed her last on May 8, 1659.

Alexis and Maria were more successful at bearing sons in the next five years. Fedor was born on May 30, 1661, a daughter, Theodosia, on May 28, 1662. Alexis was so fortunate as to have three male heirs by the time Simeon was born on April 3, 1665, and he celebrated the occasion with festivities appropriate for the birth of a tsarevich. Alexis held a banquet in his personal apartments in the Terem Palace, in the antechamber and Room of the Cross, on April 10. Sixty poor people were his guests, and Alexis handed each a ruble at the end of the festivities. A second banquet for another sixty indigents was held in the same place on July 18. The tsar again bestowed a ruble on each guest, and two rubles to one fortunate soul who then was ushered into Maria's chambers and presented with over a hundred rubles by the entire royal family. Such banquets symbolized the unity which existed between the sovereign and his people, and demonstrated the charity and humility demanded by the Christian faith. They marked happy occasions such as the birth of a royal child, as well as solemn memorial days for relatives who were ailing or deceased. The tsarina also might host such banquets in her chambers. And Maria was in a festive mood in these years, for on August 27, 1666 she gave birth to yet another son, Ivan.

Ivan soon displayed symptoms of chronic sickness and mental retardation. Alexis and Maria were not much disturbed by this, however, for their eldest son, Alexis Alexeevich was then a bright, sturdy twelve-year-old lad. He would clearly make a fine ruler in his time. Proud parents showered him with gifts, the loveliest of which was an elaborate artificial garden adorned with delicate silk roses, festive dolls, colorful animals and birds. The tsarevich also delighted in elegant boxes and cases, mirrors, combs, silverware, an inkwell with various pens, a silver aromatic spray, silver toothpicks, balsam for headache, and two measures of soil from the Savior's grave.

No father loved a son more than Alexis loved Alexis Alexeevich. The tsar was particularly zealous in celebrating his tsarevich's birthdays. On February 12, 1667, for example, after mass the patriarch and bishops ceremonially entered the tsarina's apartments in the Terem Palace, where young Alexis, his mother and sisters were all awaiting. An appropriate prayer and blessing were offered. The young prince gave out festival cakes to all, and then joined his father in the great "heaven-roofed banquet hall" of the Kremlin palace. Paul of Aleppo says that Alexis "of his joy made birthday presents and no end of celebration to the three patriarchs."

As the Russian New Year approached on September 1, 1667, Alexis made ready to present his son to the people. The night before the presentation, at 8:00 on September 5, the tsarevich personally fed thirty poor people in the antechamber and Room of the Cross of his father's apartment, and after the feast gave each guest two rubles. Truly the young man was learning to follow in his father's steps!

Alexis Alexeevich's presentation the next morning took place on a railed and carpeted spot in the Kremlin court, on a place some 300 paces in circumference. The platform within was thirty feet long, four feet high, twelve feet wide, and was festooned in bright velvet cloth and fine silk carpets. About 9:00 in the morning Alexis emerged from the palace, followed by his heir—each attended on all sides by nobles and dignitaries. The tsar and tsarevich were clad in red, the boy's colors respectfully being of a slightly lighter shade. The three patriarchs left the Cathedral of the Assumption and mounted the platform on the left, while the tsar and his son ascended its stairs form the right. The patriarchs sat down "with their Crownes on their heads, the Emperor and Prince being bare-headed" out of respect. After mass and devotions, all descended from the platform. Alexis first spoke to the assembled people, then to the tsarevich, and finally, in turn, to the patriarchs, clergy, and nobles. Patrick Gordon says the foreigners ("who had a particular place appointed them") and the "commonality" then congratulated the tsar, who was so overcome with joy that he "graced us [foreigners] all with a months means besides our pay." The ceremony lasted two hours.

But tragedy soon descended upon the royal house. It began when Alexis' thirteenth child (and eighth daughter) was born on February 26, 1669, and, after struggling two days, passed away. The tsarina then died on March 4, Simeon joined his mother during the early morning hours of June 19, 1669, and was attended at his funeral in the Cathedral of the Archangel by Patriarch Paisios of Alexandria, who had arrived in Moscow to take part in the trial of Nikon. The tsar was only slightly comforted by the tears of his distinguished guest. But the heaviest blow came when Alexis Alexeevich died on January 17, 1670, less than a month before his sixteenth birthday.

By this time Alexis had collected in addition to a good deal of worldly wisdom—a goodly gaggle of female relatives and in-laws, his sisters Irene, Anna and Tatiana (all of whom, incidently survived to bury him six years later), six daughters, and two pitiful sons: Fedor, almost nine, by no means a stupid child and extremely kind in disposition, though sickly and bedridden; and Ivan, just over three and now displaying advanced states of blindness, speech disorder, epilepsy, and mental retardation. Hardly a family situation to cheer a tsar!

Little wonder, then, that the young tsar—Alexis was just forty when Maria died—turned to livelier people for consolation and cheer. In fact, after two decades of sedate marriage and family life, Alexis now seems to have sought adventurous female company. At least an enigmatic source which textological analysis suggests is from a contemporary Englishman (who may not be entirely reliable, of course) tells us that in addition to the children Maria bore, Alexis had "a *natural* son, whom he created a kniaz [prince], and whose mother he married to a nobleman named Moushin-Poushkin; but when the tsar married his second wife, this lady having through jealousy dropped some injurious expressions against the new tsaritsa, both she and her son were sent to Astrachan, where they died." William Palmer incorrectly attributes these words to Olearius and concludes that this "illicit" romance must have occurred between Maria's death on March 4, 1669, and Alexis' second marriage on January 22, 1671—though it is also possible, if seemingly out of character for the pious tsar, that this affair could have taken place while Maria was still alive.

Alexis' second marriage was quite different from his first. The tsar's first wedding reflected the stern influences of the Zealots of Piety. Music was prohibited, festivities were held to a minimum. The flame of religious revival in Moscow died down in later years, however, while a new force, westernization, manifested itself ever more insidiously and strongly. Efforts to drive the foreigners from Russia, or at least to restrict their contacts with Russians by crowding them into special "foreign quarters," failed miserably. The foreigner seemed to be everywhere in Russia by 1670—leading Russian troops on the drill-field, haggling with native merchants in town squares, serving in government bureaus and counting houses. Russian nationalists deplored this presence, and indeed they were right in predicting that in the long run it was bound to affect Russian life. A small but important segment of Moscow's ruling elite began to imitate life as it was imagined to exist in the West. These people dabbled in foreign languages and ideas, surrounded themselves with European art objects and furnishings, clothed themselves in strange garb, shaved their beards and trimmed their heads, and affected strange manners and customs, not the least of which was taking snuff and smoking tobacco.

The boldest "westernized" Russian of this period was Artamon Sergeevich Matveev, a complex, still enigmatic figure who after 1670 exercised great influence over the tsar. At that time, however, Matveev was by no means a "new" favorite. He and Alexis had been friends from early adult years. Artamon's father, Sergei, was a secretary in the Foreign Office who was sent on a diplomatic mission to Turkey and Persia in the 1630s. As a reward for Sergei's success there, his thirteen-year-old son Artamon was enrolled in the ranks of the "junior boyars" in 1638. This was indeed good fortune for such a young man for, given but a moderate combination of ability and luck, Artamon Sergeevich would have many years in which to work his way up the Muscovite hierarchy. Indeed, he soon came to the attention of Tsar Michael, who in 1642 appointed Artamon servitor to his son, Tsarevich Alexis. Young Matveev became a captain of musketeers in the following year, 1643. Artamon Sergeevich was made a table attendant when Alexis took the throne three years later, and then was promoted to colonel of the musketeers.

Artamon Sergeevich's ascendency in the next two decades was outwardly unspectacular. Miloslavsky had him escort Pomerening to the border in 1651, after a disturbance in Moscow almost took the Swedish diplomat's life. Later that same year, Matveev was dispatched with hostages and tribute to the Crimea. Alexis rewarded Matveev handsomely in 1654 for accompanying Buturlin with 300,000 rubles to Khmelnitsky, and for returning with the glad tidings that the Cossack hetman had taken an oath of allegiance to the tsar. On May 17 of that year the sumptuously attired Matveev led 3,000 musketeers from Moscow on a western campaign which was soon to include Alexis himself. In June 1655 foreign diplomats in Moscow reported that "Colonel Artamon Sergewitz" Matveev, "highly esteemed by H.Z. Maj., as one of his best soldiers," was slain at the front. The report, of course, was false. Matveev's brilliant career was not to end so soon nor in that way. He returned to the Ukraine in 1656 and succeeded in detaching the now wavering Khmelnitsky from dangerous negotiations with the Swedes and Transylvanians. When Khmelnitsky died the next year, 1657, Matveev rushed

ARTAMON SERGEEVICH MATVEEV. Copy of an oil portrait done by an unknown master after the boyar's death.

back to the Ukraine and uncovered the treason of the new Cossack hetman, Ivan Vygovsky. Other successful missions in these years established Matveev as a rising, if still secondary star in the galaxy of Muscovite luminaries.

Matveev's greatest distinction at this time was his famous home in Moscow. He had married Lady Hamilton, daughter of a Scotch mercenary who ended in Russia under service to the tsar. The lady was baptized into the Russian church as Eudocia (Evdokaya) Grigorievna, and with her husband's enthusiastic approval introduced a thoroughly western style of life into their house. The Matveev's simple but spacious home was decorated tastefully in the European manner with elaborate ceiling murals, imported furniture and rugs, timepieces and art objects. Lady Matveev did not seclude herself in the Russian manner, but greeted her company and played the role of an active hostess, finally joining her guests at the supper table. Nor did Artamon use these occasions to load his companions with the typically Russian overdoses of food and liquor. Rather, the Matveevs offered serious conversations along with Western musical and theatrical performances. Alexis enjoyed visiting the Matveev's house, and after Maria's death his attendance at Matveev's evenings became still more frequent.

During one of these evenings Lady Matveev and a young girl approached the tsar with refreshments of vodka and caviar, smoked herring and pickled mushrooms. Alexis was downcast, but delightedly took note of the twenty-year-old Natalya Naryshkina, a tall, stately beauty with generous breasts, black hair, and sparkling bright, black eyes. Alexis had a fine time that night, chatting merrily and taking much food and drink. The young lady cheered him with her modest talk and shy, gentle smile. Alexis learned that her father, Cyril Naryshkin, had formed a close friendship with Matveev in the service, and that Lady Matveev's niece had married Natalya's uncle, Fedor Naryshkin. Artamon Sergeevich had assumed the responsibility for rearing Natalya.

"I will find you a suitable mate, Little Pigeon!" Alexis declared as he left the house that night. Was the tsar then already considering her for his own wife?

As it happened Alexis was then in the midst of marriage plans. Sixty daughters of good families throughout the land were to be assembled on February 11, 1670 for the traditional "selection of the bride." The tsar himself would then choose the lucky one from the ranks of the semi-finalists on April 28. But Alexis was so impressed with Natalya that he made clear to Matveev that he would have only her. True to character, Matveev was not excessively eager to seize this opportunity to advance his ward, and with her, his own interests. He begged Alexis to go through the customary procedure.

News leaked out that Natalya was already the favorite, creating a scandal among Alexis' own family since his eldest daughter, Eudocia, was but a year older than her proposed step-mother. Moreover, the Miloslavsky family—facing eclipse on any other terms—hoped to advance a family under their influence, whereas the Naryshkins were clearly within the orbit of that cunning, long-distance runner, Artamon Sergeevich Matveev.

Four days after Natalya Naryshkina was formally chosen to be the tsar's bride, the opposition mounted an anonymous counter-offensive typical of those who sense they are losing a political struggle and resort to desperate, self-defeating strategies. Notes found in the vicinity of the royal palace charged that Matveev was a warlock, that he used drugs and incantations to cast a spell over the tsar and make him choose Natalya as his spouse. Moscow buzzed over this for the next several days. A full-scale investigation (and a liberal use of torture) failed to incriminate Matveev or the Naryshkins or other members of their faction. The marriage was slightly delayed, but the controversy in no way shook the close relationship between Alexis and Artamon Sergeevich, who, along with Cyril Naryshkin, was advanced from table attendant to council noble, the third of the four ranks on the Boyar Council, on November 27, 1670. In that month Alexis also had Ivan Saltykov begin painting the ceilings of the tsarina's palace chambers in preparation for its anticipated new occupant.

Alexis and Natalya were finally married on January 22, 1671, before a great company in the Cathedral of the Annunciation. One of the guests, Jacob Reitenfels of Courland, Rome's envoy to Moscow in these years, described the bride as "blooming with youth and beauty, well-formed, black-eyed, with a high forehead, an agreeable smile on her lips, a sweet melodious voice, and an enchanting grace in all her gestures and movements." Unlike Alexis' first marriage ceremony, this event was celebrated throughout Moscow in festive style. The wedding reception in the Kremlin lasted most of the night, and was attended by much music, food and drink. The new tsarina made clear in the next several days that she would not remain attached to the ancient ritual which so severely separated men from women, relegating the latter to obscure, uneventful lives.

Natalya's strongest weapon in getting her way was an affectionate husband who himself was anxious to loosen the strict order of Kremlin life. Observers were struck at how pleased Alexis was with his new bride. The tsar of forty-two and the bride half his age were seemingly inseparable. Alexis even took Natalya on once-private excursions to Sokolniki and other falconing preserves. The tsar's children celebrated the warmth of spring by accompanying the royal couple to various lodges near the capital. On the surface, at least, Natalya and her step-children were completely cordial. For the moment, all was tranquility and smiles.

Chapter Twenty-Six

A NEW FAMILY

Alexis and Natalya were quickly blessed with children. The new tsarina became pregnant after seven months of marriage, and on May 30, 1672, two and a half hours before daylight, she delivered a son who was named Peter and is known to history as "Peter the Great." Alexis heard the customary thanksgiving service in his private chapel. At its conclusion a public procession to mark the glad day left the Kremlin palace, the clergy in front clad in elegant robes, crosses and banners and swinging censers held high. Then came court dignitaries, army commanders and the royal family, the women lumbering along for privacy within their canopies and padded screens. A large number of "joyful" merchants, artisans and ordinary townspeople brought up the rear. Winding its way along the Kremlin courtyard, the procession entered the Cathedral of the Assumption. After a short service, long speeches and many congratulations, the procession resumed, making its way to other churches and monasteries before ending at the Cathedral of the Annunciation—where the royal family observed its weddings, births and deaths—for a full mass.

Later that day, Alexis held a festive banquet in the Kremlin's grand dining hall. The proud father personally served his guests and exchanged the pleasant greetings which only a new father can know. That evening Alexis held a supper for the boyars and high officials in the Golden Room of his apartments at the Terem Palace. Alexis delayed his son's baptism until a cycle of church fasts then under way was completed. When the christening finally occurred in June, it was marked by further public celebrations and private banquets, Alexis receiving his guests in in his chambers, Natalya her company in hers.

The joy Alexis felt over his sturdy new boy was increased all the more when his wife bore him two daughters in the next two years, Natalya (named in her mother's honor) and Theodora. The Miloslavskys congratulated Alexis and Natalya on these happy occasions, but privately they looked on in great fear. The Miloslavsky clan already was eclipsed by Matveev and the Naryshkins, and the prospect now loomed that Fedor and Ivan, the sickly sons who survived Alexis' marriage to Maria Miloslavskaya, would never be permitted to reign. Alexis was only forty-five when Natalya presented him with their third child; surely the tsar and his twenty-three-year-old wife had time to produce more heirs?

ALEXIS AND NATALYA. Medal struck to commemorate the birth of their son Peter on May 30, 1672.

   Collins said of Maria that she was "a tolerable beauty" who was "adorned with the precious jewels of modesty, industry, and religion." Natalya possessed equal industry, more beauty, but a good deal less modesty and religion—and she insisted on a life of freedom which would have shocked the pious Maria. No sooner had Natalya married Alexis than she caused a scandal by parting her coach's curtains to have a peek at the crowd assembled to see her pass. The hubbub from all this forced her to behave as tradition dictated for a time. But not for long. Natalya's strongest accomplice in shelving the old social forms was Alexis himself, who for some time had been equally bored with Muscovite restraint. Three children in less than four years gave Natalya more than enough leverage to have her own way. Eventually she was to go about unveiled in an open carriage, appear in male company, and attend mass unsecluded. Ambassadorial reports tell us that on Palm Sunday in the year 1675, as Alexis led Patriarch Joachim on his white horse across the

Kremlin square, the patriarch turned and blessed Natalya and her children who were standing at the windows of the Kremlin dining hall.

Alexis also permitted—even insisted—that his children be exposed to a freer, "Westernized" upbringing. Actually, the children of the tsars for the last hundred years had been reared in increasingly westernized ways, a progression which symbolized the increasing influence of the West over Russia as a whole. Alexis himself had German toys and books, and he witnessed foreign amusements in German clothes. The children Maria bore were still more immersed in western things. Alexis Alexeevich, for example, had an incendiary lens, two copper sun clocks, a spyglass, and every variety of clever mechanical contraption, especially a German clock whose crashing cymbals merrily sounded the hours. But Alexis visited a still more important influence upon his children. He insisted that the Muscovite learning which had served as his main fare be supplemented for them by foreign learning.

Alexis entrusted the education of his children to Simeon of Polotsk, a brilliant scholar, astrologer, orator, writer, and poet. Simeon had studied in Polish academies and at the academy in Kiev before becoming a monk at Polotsk in 1656. Alexis met Simeon in that city while on campaign that year, and was completely taken with his learning and character. Alexis persuaded Simeon to settle in Moscow in 1664. Simeon opened a school at the Zaikonospassky monastery and accepted Alexis' command to tutor Alexis Alexeevich, Fedor, and significantly, one of the girls, Sophia, destined to rule as "regent" for two younger brothers. Moscow was jealous of Simeon's high standing with the royal family, and suspicious of his "Catholic" learning. But Alexis defended him from every attack, going so far as to insist that Simeon live in the Kremlin.

Simeon and other scholars taught the royal children Polish and Latin. Simeon especially was a warm, interesting teacher with a flair for expounding difficult material to children. Fedor studied mathematics and some natural science, all three youngsters were tutored in theology and syllabic versification. Simeon also taught the youngsters political philosophy, emphasizing the duty of a ruler to love his people and tend to their welfare and prosperity.

Moscow and the court had grown quite receptive to Western ways by the time Natalya became tsarina. More than mere whimsy caused Alexis to rennovate his widow's dark, stuffy quarters in the Terem Palace in November 1670, before his marriage to Natalya. The tsar knew that these apartments would not suit a young bride accustomed to the Matveev house. Alexis put Ivan Saltykov to painting scenes on the ceilings of the tsarina's chambers, while other masters redecorated other features of these rooms. Alexis had his own bedroom redone in 1674. Among the new ornaments were three parable scenes from Moses, Esther, and John painted on boards and affixed to the ceilings by carved gilded frames.

Alexis was equally enthusiastic over Western canvas art. The German painter Daniel Füchters presented him in 1667 with works entitled "The Capture of Jerusalem," "The City of Jericho," and a scene from the life of Alexander the Great, who exercised a never-ending fascination upon Alexis. Saltanov painted "The Birth of Alexander the Great" and two scenes of Constantine viewing the fiery cross which led him to the Christian faith. Alexis also delighted in paintings called "The Sense of Touch" and a depiction of "The Five Senses." The tsar's residence at Kolomenskoe displayed a work entitled "A Coat of Arms of the Sovereign and of all His Earthly Kingdoms," and portraits of Darius, Alexander the Great and Julius Caesar.

Alexis' sponsorship of the theater is well known, but it deserves to be told in more detail. Nothing shows more clearly the simple, honest enthusiasm of this kindly tsar for western ways. The Polish campaign had stirred Alexis' interest in the fine arts of the West, including drama, and after his return in 1656 he ordered John Hebdon to obtain "a carriage like the one in which the kings of Spain and France and the Emperor go about, craftsmen who make birds that sing, people who play on trumpets, and craftsmen who make plays." A comedy was given at the English embassy in the Foreign Quarter in 1664, while as early as 1660 Matveev was offering plays and concerts for his guests, which included the tsar. Matveev's example fired Alexis with the desire to have his own theater, as did vivid descriptions by Simeon of Polotsk of plays he had seen in Poland and the Ukraine. Natalya, of course, was eager to have more exciting entertainments at court, but Alexis was not certain that it was proper for him to establish a theater. His Ukrainian father confessor, Andrey Savinovich, assured him this would not be wrong, for if Byzantine emperors and western kings had court theaters, why not the regal Tsar of all the Russias?

Celebrations of Tsarevich Peter's birth included establishment of the theater Alexis had contemplated for so long. Alexis dispatched Nicholas von Staden to recruit actors in the West in early 1672, but the colonel returned with merely five musicians and two "craftsmen." (Perhaps the latter were what today would be called scene designers.) Alexis was in a blaze of enthusiasm for drama now, however, and would have no further delay. If Europe could not provide what was wanted it must be found at home. The question was, who could do it?

Matveev's contacts in the Foreign Quarter recommended Johann Gottfried Gregory, a bright German Lutheran pastor who arrived in Moscow in 1658. Rinhuber, who assisted him in this project, recalled ten years later that no one else dared come to Alexis' aid, but "willy-nilly" Gregory set to it, "either hoping for the Tsar's mercy or fearful of the danger of not doing so. So he associated himself with me and wrote the tragi-comedy of Ahasuerus and Esther." While Gregory worked on the production of the play, Rinhuber spent three months rehearsing sixty-four boys hastily recruited from families residing in Moscow's Foreign Quarter.

A theater was set up at the royal palace at Preobrazhenskoe. Bertha Malnick notes that this small auditorium "was built of wood, and enclosed by a wall with folding doors. Raised benches were built . . . , and the stage was provided with grooves for the scenery. The Tsar's seat was in front and upholstered in red cloth. The rest of the audience sat on plain wooden benches. The stage was separated from the auditorium by a balustrade and a curtain moved from the sides. Both the stage and the auditorium were lit by large wax candles." The Dutch artist Peter Engels, celebrated by contemporaries as "a master of perspective painting," left Matveev's theater to build the scenery for Preobrazhenskoe. Alexis was at first reluctant to have music on the stage, but Jacob Reitenfels recalls that it was pointed out to him "that it is as impossible to have a chorus without music as it is for dancers to dance without legs." Thereupon the tsar rather reluctantly left the matter to others' judgement. The orchestra was made up of Matveev's men from the Foreign Quarter, and, when they arrived, Staden's musicians. Extremely elaborate costumes were made ready for opening night.

Esther had its gala premier on October 17, 1672. Only the highest officials were admitted to this special performance, Reitenfels says, and they were permitted the honor of standing on the stage itself. (Natalya and the children viewed everything through peep-holes in a specially partitioned room.) Rinhuber, the assistant director of the project, was relieved to note that Alexis was "astonished at this play, and gazed at it without moving for nine hours." To show his pleasure, Alexis at the end gave Reverend Gregory a generous gift of sables.

Alexis was so delighted with theater that he had the home of his deceased father-in-law Ilya Miloslavsky remodelled so that it might house plays during the winter at the Kremlin. The first performance here occurred in February 1673. In the following months the actors and their theatrical properties were shuttled between the Kremlin and Preobrazhenskoe according to the tsar's movements in winter and in spring.

During this first theater season Alexis saw productions of *Judith* (presented by 63 actors in seven acts and 29 scenes); *The Little Comedy of Joseph; Adam and Eve;* a farce entitled *Bacchus and Venus;* and a version of Marlowe's *Tamburlaine the Great,* which in Russian was called *The Deeds of Temir-Aksakovo.* The plays were Biblical or took their themes from the ancient world—except for the last, and even here the Mongol warrior stepped on Russian boards as a zealous defender of Christianity. The plays were heavily moralistic and abounded with piteous executions, hair-raising battles and cannonades. Even the tragedies featured the buffoon and a great deal of comic relief. The subjects were sometimes allegorical: in *Esther,* Ahasuerus and Esther represented Alexis and Natalya, Mordecai depicted Matveev, Haman was reminiscent of the corrupt Miloslavskys, and so on. Monarchy was always praised in the strongest tones. Simeon of Polotsk's *Nebuchadnezzar,* for example, opens and closes with lavish tributes to Alexis. William Palmer translated the entire piece, and renders its Epilogue:

> "O most illustrious and religious Tsar,
> Thou God-crown'd and Christ-loving autocrat,
> We give thee thanks for this thy graciousness,
> That thou hast deign'd to hear our acting through.
> Thy penetrating eye has justly scann'd
> This our performance of the Comedy.
> If we have not in every point succeeded,
> Nor satisfied, for want of skill, thy judgment,
> Our lack of wit doth naturally offend,
> But thy rich mind can well afford to pardon.
> Therefore most humbly at thy feet we fall,
> For all shortcomings pardon to entreat,
> And we in turn will pray the Lord for thee,
> Through Thee also He may all forgive,
> And grant thee happily in peace to reign,
> And speedily thy foes to overcome,
> And add unto thee many years of life,
> And give thee after all the heavenly crown.
> Many years!
>
> *Music plays: that is, they sing in chorus the
> Polychronion with musical accompaniments."*

Alexis and his guests were not bothered by the fact that the amateurs delivered their lines in a mixture of German and almost equally unintelligible Russian! The action and sets could be enjoyed easily as could the songs and instrumental music which accompanied and followed performances. The spectators did not mind if a performance lasted five, six or nine hours, for they feasted and belched away into the wee hours of the morning.

The Russian theater was off to a fine start. Certainly no enterprise ever had a more enthusiastic and steady patron than Tsar Alexis. Under his instructions, Gregory took twenty-six boys from the families of Moscow merchants and officials to be trained as professional actors. Apparently they did not make their debut until the performance of the *Little Comedy of Joseph* in 1675, when the Prologue begged the audience to excuse this "children's act." (The actors in the Prologue to *Tamburlaine,* performed later that year, referred to themselves as "untrained and unskilled children.")

Alexis sponsored ballet along with theater. Jacob Reitenfels saw a spectacle at Moscow during Shrovetide of 1673 in which Orpheus danced "a pas de trois between two pyramids; then Orpheus and the others, magnificently dressed, performed some foreign national dances." Another ballet performed at Preobrazhenskoe that year dramatized the Persian King Artaxerxes' cruel hanging of Haman. The ever-versatile Gregory also trained some of Matveev's servants who "played viols, organs, and other instruments, and danced" for the pleasure of Tsar Alexis.

Alexis and the court were making up for the time lost while the first tsarina was alive. Alexis remained pious and rigorous in his devotions to the church calendar, but the tsar's evenings grew wild and raucous as his days with Natalya passed. Even the court father confessor was drawn into this devil's snare. On the night of October 21, 1674, for instance, Alexis gave a banquet in the Amusement Hall for the members of the Boyar Council. The event was "without places"—which is to say that to encourage an informal mood, the customary seating by rank was ignored—and Alexis' personal chaplain was invited. After supper, a German played the organ and the clarion, while others "trumpeted with trumpets, and played on clarionets and on cymbals and drums." The tsar ladled out drinks for the merry crew "till he had made them all drunk, and they went away at the eleventh hour of the night."

Music and theater and other Western delights were reserved for the Russian elite in these days. Only the most favored people at court saw the royal theater; indeed its very existence was secret from the nation as a whole. Technically, it was even against the law, considering that edicts issued when Alexis was a young man had forbidden musical instruments and "profane" entertainments, and these measures remained on the books until the day Alexis died.

But Alexis hugely enjoyed what the law denied others. Even while under the influence of the Zealots Alexis had not forsaken animal shows and the hunt, and as the years passed his passion for these activities grew. Reitenfels describes royal hunting parties "merrily pursuing wild beasts in the forests, either with beaters or trained hounds or swift-flying falcons, or with bows or muskets." The papal envoy recalled that in Alexis' last years, on a Saturday just before Lent, Alexis organized "a fight on the frozen Moscow river between huge dogs of English and other breeds and white bears from the Samoyed region. This was most entertaining, for both the bears and dogs often slided and fell on the icy surface." Entertaining, and illegal.

Alexis' life included still other interests in later years which reveal the gap between what the law prohibited and what he and his friends enjoyed anyhow. In 1672, for instance, Alexis issued an edict stating that "no one is to keep printed Polish and Latin books either secretly or openly in his home, but is to bring such books and surrender them to the governor." Yet Alexis himself—to say nothing of Matveev and others—was frantic to acquire such books, and the very languages mentioned in this edict were the ones he particularly wanted his children to know. Only a year before, in 1671, the Ukrainian educator Lazar Bara-novich had observed that the Boyar Council of "His Royal and Most Radiant Majesty does not disdain the Polish language, but reads Polish books with delight."

Similar tension between law and life was to be seen in dress at court. On August 6, 1675, less than half a year before he died, Alexis issued a reminder to his nobles "that they may not imitate the customs of Germans and other foreigners and cut their hair and wear costumes, coats and hats of foreign type, or allow their servants to wear such." Offenders doing this "will suffer the anger of the great sovereign, and will be demoted from higher to lower rank." Alexis issued such edicts to please churchmen, perhaps even to deceive them into thinking he was on their side in the righteous struggle against western influences in Russia. But the edicts were not enforced, and westernization moved ahead.

The most serious challenge the West offered Russia under Tsar Alexis was not in the realm of amusements, but in military science and technical skills. Alexis' lively mind, his thirst for new experiences, his desire to make Russia a more powerful state, caused him to sponsor innovations in all these areas. Despite some progress, a great gap remained in the field of higher education. Paisios Ligarides joined those lamenting the absence of popular schools and libraries in Russia, declaring: "If you were to ask me: what are the pillars of the state? I would answer:

first, schools; second, schools; and third, schools! " Ligarides was in Moscow from 1662 until his death in 1678. Respected as he was, his advice had little immediate effect. Russia did not have a school equal to an average institution of higher learning in the West until 1689, when the Slavic-Latin-Greek Academy finally opened its doors in Moscow.

Alexis deserves credit, even so, for bringing scholars to Russia and making them and their work prestigious. Epiphany Slavinetsky was perhaps the most remarkable of these men. Like so many of the learned foreigners in Russia in these years, Slavinetsky was a Ukrainian monk engaged to correct church books, and to translate and edit other works. During Slavinetsky's two decades in Moscow he argued that Russian education should be modelled upon the Catholic, "Latin" curriculum. A sensitive, withdrawn figure, Epiphany was esteemed highly for character and scholarship. Alexis had such respect for him that when Slavinetsky spoke out against the proposal that a Russian church council try Nikon in 1660, the tsar backed down and laid different plans to rid himself of the now unwanted patriarch. Slavinetsky carried on scholarly work and taught theology and related subjects at the Monastery of the Miracle.

One of the strongest bonds between Alexis and Epiphany Slavinetsky was the interest each had in the natural sciences, an interest which was certainly not common in Moscow and says something about the quality of Alexis' intellect. The tsar was fascinated with geography. Knowing this, the Dutch States presented him with the huge globe which now stands in Moscow's Historical Museum; the king of Sweden included two globes with presents sent to the Kremlin in 1655. While in Moscow, Slavinetsky translated a geographical treatise on Europe and Asia. Three ceiling panels in a room of the palace at Kolomenskoe depicted Europe, Africa and Asia, as well as a scene of Solomon as judge.

Alexis was still more intrigued by astronomy. A vast ceiling fresco painted in the Kremlin Dining Hall in 1662 was described as follows by Adolph Lyseck in 1675:

"The walls of the hall were covered with expensive cloths; heavenly bodies, wandering comets and motionless stars were depicted on the ceiling. Each body had its sphere with appropriate deviations from its eliptic. The intervals of the 12 heavenly symbols (the sign of the zodiac) were so measured that even the paths of the planets were shown with gold tropics and by such colures as equinoxes and turning points of the sun in spring, winter, summer and fall."

Admittedly this account is not entirely clear, but it seems to indicate that the cosmological scheme was Ptolemaic, that is, following the

ancient Greek astronomer Ptolemy in teaching that the earth was sta-
tionary in the center of the universe, the planets revolving around it in
circular orbits at uniform rates. Most educated Russians of Alexis' time
probably accepted Ptolemy's system—but some evidence suggests that
Alexis was a "modern" follower of Copernicus and Galileo in holding
that the sun was the center about which the other planets moved. Indeed,
the tsar apparently went so far as to suggest to Epiphany Slavinetsky
that he translate the 1645 edition of Wilhelm and Johann Blaeu's *Atlas
novus* in 1661, the year before the Kremlin scene was painted. This was
the first work to appear in Russia which referred favorably to Copernicus' theories. The tsar's farsighted position on the heliocentric theory
of the universe may be judged from the fact that Simeon of Polotsk and
other south Russian scholars were then still attacking Copernicus, and
even Slavinetsky's manuscript was not published until the second decade
of the following century.

The Ptolemaic scheme painted on the ceiling of the Kremlin dining
room, then, provides no clear indication of Alexis' notions about the
universe. At any rate, an entirely different depiction was painted at the
tsar's vacation residence at Kolomenskoe. The historian Raikov notes
that this ceiling fresco fixes the sun at the center of the solar system,
the twelve signs of the Zodiac forming an outer circle while the four
seasons were displayed in the form of female figures.

Astronomy in this period was closely related to astrology. Simeon of
Polotsk and his pupil Silvester Medvedev pored learnedly over the fate
which the stars foretold for men, a science of no less concern to their
royal master, the tsar. The oldest surviving Russian astrological calendar
is a manuscript prepared in 1670. Entitled *A Yearly and Monthly
Schedule*, it is not surprisingly devoted to the tsar himself. Translated
from a Polish work, the Russian *Schedule* occupies 21 pages. According
to B.E. Raikov, ordinary calendar information is contained in the first
fourteen pages, while pages 15 through 20 present badly garbled astrological forecasts. The manuscript ended in the hands of Peter the Great,
who likewise was eager to learn his fate through the stars.

Alexis was interested in western medical knowledge. The tsar encouraged Slavinetsky to translate Vesalius' *De humani corporis fabrica*
(1543), thus taking for Russia a first step towards a scientific understanding of anatomy. Alexis was tended by a dozen or more physicians
over the years, men who included such skilled healers as Andrew Engel-
hart, Johann Rosenburg (both Senior and Junior), Lawrence Rinhuber,
Lawrence Blumentrost, and Stephen von Hagen. The last two remained
permanently in Russia, the others served the terms of their contracts

and returned home. Samuel Collins of England was especially distinguished. Studying medicine at Cambridge and Oxford, he was invited to
Russia in 1659 and stayed there until the summer of 1666. The first
edition of his valuable *The Present State of Russia* was published in
London in 1671. One of the doctors in Moscow in 1674 was Daniel
Jeflowitz, a Jew who became a Catholic, then a Protestant, and finally
a member of the Russian Orthodox Church.

European physicians in Russia were paid high salaries and honored in
every way. They were always impressed with the royal Apothecary,
where Russians and foreigners made "European" medicines from herbs
and materials fetched from every corner of the empire. Prescriptions
here, like the services of the physicians themselves, were available to
boyars and court personages only after petitioning Alexis—and what was
granted was a sign of his personal favor. Alexis did loosen this system
when he built a "New Apothecary" in Moscow in March 1672 "for the
sale [of medicine] to all ranks of people," which is to say to other
members of the elite, since the great mass of the Russian people continued to treat themselves with folk remedies and traditional herb con-
coctions. After 1677 physicians were permitted to remain in Russia
after their contracts with the tsar expired, and to treat patients without
royal dispensation.

But Alexis and his family were cautious in exposing themselves to
western medical science. A contemporary account tells us that "30 or
40 or even more lords" sampled the tsar's medicines before they ended
in the royal patient. While the younger Rosenburg was at court a pre-
scription was prepared badly, and the lady boyar who tasted it took
sick. The good doctor extricated himself from this scandal only with
great difficulty.

Tsars before Alexis had imported physicians, surgeons and pharma-
cists. Alexis was again unique in going beyond tradition: he made efforts
to train Russians in all these arts. As war with Poland grew imminent,
the tsar ordered the Apothecary Bureau in late 1653 (or early 1654)
to take immediate steps to organize a medical school, using the children
of musketeer families and others as pupils. The school was located in
the Kremlin, on the premises of the Apothecary Bureau. The teachers
were foreigners assisted by four interpreters. Hand-written books were
used for instruction. Of thirty people trained the first year, twenty-five
saw field service. Yet another school was opened to send "surgeons who
repair bones" and their assistants to the front in February 1655. When
war with Sweden broke out in 1656, twenty-eight Russian physicians
and surgeons rushed to the combat zone. Medical education declined in

Russia as the Thirteen Years War drew to a close, however, and it was left to Peter the Great to establish the first permanent Russian medical schools.

The medical skills of the West might heal the tsar's flesh, but only divine intervention could cure a royal toothache. Alexis often took pilgrimages in honor of St. Antipas the Great, venerated as the healer of toothache, on April 11, his feast day. Ivan the Terrible was said to have possessed one of Antipas' teeth, and to have encased it in silver. When Alexis journeyed to pray to Antipas at Kolymazhnyi dvor on August 30, 1646, he placed on the saint's shrine two silver teeth purchased in Moscow. Maria often venerated the image of the miracle-working saint in her chambers, and dedicated services to him.

Alexis similarly venerated the relics of other miracle-working saints. He once brought Patriarch Macarius of Antioch to the Shrine of St. Sabba the Younger, located in the tsar's beloved monastery of that name. Opening the shrine, Alexis pointed to the saint's relics and exclaimed: "See the beautiful color of the skull, which is verily of true natural yellow and hardness!" Reflecting a moment, the tsar added: "When I took this holy body from the ground to place it in this shrine, I noticed that one of its teeth had been lost. I did not give up my search until I found it. I had a toothache in the interval, but when I found the lost tooth, I rubbed mine with it—and the pain instantly ceased."

Chapter Twenty-Seven

NEW FAVORITES

An old Russian proverb says that as a man grows older he either loses his friends or his friends lose him. Tsars are no exception to this truth, and as Alexis reached middle age, death began to claim those he loved. Except for his parents, the greatest of these losses was Boris Morozov. Spared by the Moscow rioters in 1648 through the tsar's personal appeal, Morozov never regained the power he once enjoyed. He had to share the tsar's confidence with a host of "new" men, some of whom Morozov himself had helped raise to power—Miloslavsky and Nikon, Dolgoruky and Trubetskoi—as well as Alexis' childhood friend, the increasingly influential Bogdan Khitrovo, and such older families as his mother's relatives, the Streshnevs.

Morozov's powers also declined as Alexis grew in self-confidence, especially after the Polish campaigns, and because of Morozov's increasing infirmities. But Alexis never abandoned his friendship with Morozov, and he paid the old boyar a high honor in October 1661. As his friend lay sick and near death, Alexis visited Morozov's home to comfort him and say goodbye. Morozov asked the tsar to write Nikon on his behalf to ask the exiled patriarch to forgive and bless him. Alexis swallowed his pride, and wrote Nikon as requested. Nikon graciously replied that he knew of no injury to him for which Morozov should worry, but that anything which might be on Morozov's conscience was freely forgiven. Morozov never knew of Nikon's reconciliation, however, for he died on November 1, 1661, before the fallen patriarch's answer could arrive in Moscow.

By this time the fortunes of the Miloslavskys were deteriorating rapidly. Ilya Miloslavsky fell into total disgrace with Alexis when the rumor was bruited about Moscow that the tsar's elderly father-in-law had counterfeited 120,000 rubles in copper money. The copper riots which broke in July 1662 largely were directed at this family, and, as we have seen, the crowds at Kolomenskoe demanded that Alexis hand over Ilya and his greedy nephews, Ivan Mikhailovich and Ivan Bogdanovich. Alexis refused to do this, of course, and his wife's influence kept the Miloslavskys in power and wealth. But Alexis never respected his father-in-law. After Ilya's death in 1668 the family's interests were represented mainly by Ivan Bogdanovich. But his career faltered in 1671. Alexis took new favorites along with a new wife, and later that same year he sent Ivan Bogdanovich to serve as governor of Astrakhan. This appointment was honorable—and profitable—but it kept its recipient from the Kremlin and the rich opportunities available there.

Alexis Nikitich Trubetskoi was another unsteady star in the Muscovite heavens. A member of an old, famous aristocratic family, he became a boyar in the same year Alexis became tsar. Trubetskoi was involved in diplomatic negotiations with Sweden, Poland, and Bogdan Khmelnitsky during the years in which Russia was moving towards war for the Ukraine. He won brilliant victories from 1654 to 1656, but also presided over one of the most humiliating defeats ever suffered by a Russian general. This came at Konotop, in the Ukraine, on June 28, 1659, when the Crimean Tatars and Vygovsky's Cossacks massacred a large force of seasoned Russian cavalry—including most of the 5,000 men taken prisoner. Trubetskoi managed to lead his infantry and artillery back to Putivl, the Poles and their allies in hot pursuit. The once-brilliant commander now became famous only for his defeats. He found it easier to put down the copper rioters in Moscow in 1662—and to use royal favor to accumulate lands and peasants. Alexis Trubetskoi remained a close friend of the tsar, however, and in 1672 stood godfather to Tsarevich Peter. Trubetskoi outlived Tsar Alexis, dying in 1680.

Alexis' close friend Nikita Ivanovich Odoevsky was a member of a prominent princely family and one of the wealthiest men of the realm. He became a boyar in 1640, before Alexis took the throne, and on the day Alexis was married was advanced to a still greater honor, *blizhnyi boyarin*, "privy boyar," one of the boyars entitled to attend the tsar in his most intimate chambers. Odoevsky was the principal commander of the forces on Russia's vital southern frontier during 1646 and 1647, and after the Moscow uprising of 1648 he came to Moscow and assumed leadership of the committee which produced the new Law Code the following year. Odoevsky was a field commander during the early stages of the Thirteen Years War, and in later years was busy with diplomatic assignments.

Bad luck dogged Nikita Odoevsky in his family life. While he was serving as governor of Astrakhan, his eldest son Michael took ill with a fever on November 1, 1652. Michael and his brother Fedor had entertained Alexis at their house that day, and had accompanied the tsar to Pokrovskoe for supper. Michael died nineteen days later. Alexis expressed condolences to the prince on November 21, the day his son was buried, in a letter filled with the tenderest expressions of friendship and love. Alexis assured the unfortunate father that his dead son's family was being cared for, and that all at home was as well as could be expected under the circumstances. In a postscript Alexis declared: "Prince Nikita Ivanovich! Do not grieve overmuch; only trust in God and rely upon me." Fedor was made a boyar in 1655 and, with a brilliant career awaiting him, died the following year. In December 1665, Nikita lost his third son, Alexis. When Nikita Odoevsky died on February 12, 1689, he had seen his surviving son Yakov become a boyar and his grandchildren move into various important positions. But Nikita himself had reached the high point of his power much earlier, in 1668, when he simultaneously presided over the Treasury, the Land Office and the Cavalry Bureau. From that time on his influence with the tsar declined, and at the time of Alexis' death Nikita Ivanovich perched no longer near the top of Moscow's pyramid of power.

Alexis' most talented statesman was certainly Afanasy Lavrentevich Ordin-Nashchokin. Much of Nashchokin's promise was blocked, however, by his narrow views and inflexibility in dealing with colleagues. The economic reforms Nashchokin attempted at Pskov and carried out on a nation-wide scale two years later, in 1665, were as bold and brilliant as his diplomacy. But Nashchokin won the respect of negotiators on the other side of the conference table more easily than the support of his fellow Russian diplomats. He once complained to Alexis that Russians "favor a cause or oppose it not because of the cause itself, but because of the man who advocates it; I am not liked, therefore, my cause is shunned." Time and again Alexis needed to intervene in such situations to support Afanasy Lavrentevich, to settle disputes in his favor. Nashchokin, in turn, was fanatically loyal to monarchy in principle and to Alexis in particular. He stalled and disrupted any number of diplomatic proceedings because the other side had not "correctly" stated the tsar's titles and possessions or in other ways had failed to accord the Muscovite sovereign "proper" honor. But Nashchokin knew that such haggling scarcely represented the true substance of national power. On that level he stressed the need for a vigorous economy harnessed to the needs of the crown, a vision which led him to work for trade with Persia and India as well as with the West. The postal service he labored to create was as efficient as any in the world at that time. Above all, Nashchokin backed Alexis' policy of military reform. He knew the importance of a trained professional infantry and cavalry, he knew the traditional noble *ad hoc* levies had no place in the warfare of the future, and Nashchokin consistently pressed the need for innovation in this sphere upon a willing tsar.

Nashchokin's foreign policy was predictable, perhaps, for one who came from the commercially dynamic Pskov region. For Nashchokin the primary thrust of Russian expansion must be to the Baltic; the warm water ports which would put Russia in full and easy contact with western trade lay in that region. Secondarily, Russia must become master of the Crimea. The first policy would place Russia at odds with Sweden, the second with the Crimean Tatars and the Ottoman Turks. Either option necessitated peace—even close relations—with Poland, which in turn meant that Russia must not seek to expand in the Ukraine.

Like Nashchokin, Alexis saw the value of the Baltic for the future of Russian economic development. But Alexis finally sided with those who argued that acquisition of the Ukraine and Belorussia for the moment must remain Russia's primary task. Logical as Nashchokin's arguments were, most Russians doubted that Russia could expand in the northwest to the Baltic while Muscovy's "rear," the Ukraine, remained open to Tatar raids from the Crimea. It seemed necessary to Alexis to settle things in the Ukraine, where so much already had been committed, before pressing ventures elsewhere. The war with Sweden had been a "mistake," a hasty move taken in 1656 when it seemed that Poland already had collapsed. But Poland recovered, and, in that country's strange fashion, even flourished. Hence peace with Sweden was now the order of the day for this would free Russia from the disadvantages of a two-front war and perhaps win Sweden's support for Russia's continuing struggle with Poland.

Nashchokin clearly was dragging his feet in negotiations with Sweden in early 1661, hoping the talks would collapse. Therefore Alexis recalled Nashchokin, replacing him with Prince Ivan Semenovich Prozorovsky, Ivan Pronchishchev and others. They quickly concluded and signed the Treaty of Kardis in June, 1661. According to this agreement, Alexis surrendered the lands won from Sweden at such great cost by his armies five years before. The Swedish-Russian border specified by the old Stolbovo Peace of 1617 was restored. Sweden's grip on the Baltic remained, and a Russian breakthrough here was not to occur until a half century later, at the time of Peter the Great.

Russian expectations of a rapid victory over Poland now failed to materialize. The Copper Riots in Moscow the following year—1662—made evident that the tsar could hope no longer that his people would endure economic distress without protest. His armies were demoralized, and peasant flight from taxes and conscription was assuming ever more threatening proportions. Moreover, the situation in the Ukraine had grown steadily more difficult and confusing. After Khmelnitsky's death in 1659 many of the Cossacks and their leaders turned to Poland, not to the tsar, making a quick, decisive Russian victory there increasingly unlikely. It seemed impossible to break Poland's grip over the Western Ukraine (the west bank of the Dnieper River), though the east bank Cossacks, led by Hetman Ivan Bryukhovetsky, returned to the banner of Tsar Alexis.

Since Poland was as badly off as Russia and no more willing to surrender its interests in the Ukraine, a truce was clearly in order. After lengthy negotiations at Andrusovo, Nashchokin finally signed a treaty for the Russian side on January 30, 1667. According to this agreement, Russia recovered Smolensk and other important towns and lands in west Russia. Poland recognized the Russian acquisition of the Ukraine to the east of the Dnieper, while the king of Poland retained the west bank and Belorussia. The southern region known as the "Zaporozhian Host" was to be ruled jointly by Russia and Poland. Kiev, which is situated on the east bank of the Dnieper, was to be held by Russia until 1669. The truce itself was to last thirteen years and six months.

Nashchokin hoped to gain time through the Andrusovo agreement to engineer the lasting, firm arrangement with Poland which he insisted must be the foundation of Russia's foreign policy. O'Brien's study of Nashchokin's views on Eastern Europe notes that over the years he often referred to Poland as "a great Slavonic nation," and to the Poles as "our neighbors," "our relatives," "our brethren." Nashchokin personally disliked Catholicism and thought of the Poles as "treaty breakers," "cunning," and "untrustworthy." Yet he continued to hope for an alliance with Poland. The childless John II Casimir was almost 58 when the Andrusovo treaty was signed, and Nashchokin hoped to secure the election of Alexis or a relative to the Polish throne. This would unite the two great Slavic empires, and perhaps even their churches. Nashchokin even tried to demonstrate the advantages of such a union to Polish diplomats, who, characteristically, remained suspicious and unmoved. (They called Nashchokin "incomparably cunning" and found him a man to deal with cautiously, for "he manages to swindle splendidly.")

After arguing the advantages of a Russian-Polish union to all who would listen, Nashchokin prepared a definitive memorandum on the matter for Alexis' consideration in 1668. O'Brien observes that almost every one of the 32 paragraphs in this report opens with the phrase, "it is necessary for Russia to have an alliance with Poland." Nashchokin was in effect saying that centuries of hostility between the two great Slavic empires (Russia fought eleven wars with Poland-Lithuania between 1487 and 1667) had weakened both and profited neither. He was arguing for a sober reassessment of their mutual needs, for a future policy dedicated to what Nashchokin, at least, held was their mutual benefit.

Ordin-Nashchokin's hopes, unfortunately, received no encouragement from the Polish side. Alexis was quite willing to see himself or another Russian elected to the Polish throne, but it grew steadily more apparent that this was but an empty dream. Such being the case, Alexis made the crucial decision in the early spring of 1669 not to surrender Kiev, as called for in the Andrusovo agreement. Artamon Matveev rushed to the city with an army. To prevent a renewed outbreak of hostilities, Alexis offered to pay 160,000 rubles to retain Kiev another five years. Pending final agreement on that point, the Poles agreed in May to extend the Russian occupation of Kiev for another six months.

Nashchokin's final, desperate effort to save his policy came during the spring of 1670, when he attempted to negotiate an alliance with Poland and Denmark against Sweden. (Had this diplomatic initiative succeeded, Russia would have joined a system which also included France and the Holy Roman Empire, and would have been arrayed against Sweden's allies of the moment, England and the Netherlands.) The Polish king, John Casimir, was sympathetic to Nashchokin's overtures, but was sabotaged by his own Diet. "That was Nashchokin's trouble," Ellersieck observes. "He had built his policy around cooperation with a country which could not make up its mind"—or at least could not persuade itself to support Russia and Nashchokin's schemes.

Nashchokin's influence began to decline in the late 1660s, and, smelling blood, the chancellor's enemies rushed in for the kill. For years Nashchokin had been resented by the old aristocratic figures at court. Nashchokin's family was obscure, his wealth was new, his character was harsh and abrasive, and above all, he was hardworking and humorless! The men of affairs who were rising in the Kremlin hierarchy in the 1660s disliked Afanasy Lavrentevich quite as much as did the established bluebloods, all the more when they were forced to work under him. Ivan Pronchishchev, for example, was one of Moscow's leading experts on Swedish affairs, and it was often he who negotiated with the Swedes. Yet, as Ellersieck notes, time and again he found it necessary to subordinate his pro-Swedish policy to the "demands of Nashchokin's Polish policy."

Alexis constantly defended Ordin-Nashchokin against his detractors. When Pronchishchev accused Nashchokin in 1665 of friendship with Nikon, Alexis ordered Pronchishchev briefly imprisoned and forced him to pay a fine for defaming the chancellor. Matveev's father-in-law, Almaz Ivanov, produced evidence in 1666 that Nashchokin's behavior at Pskov was not what Alexis had been told. Nashchokin and Ivanov exchanged insults in the Kremlin and almost came to blows. Again, Alexis disregarded the allegations. In fact, Nashchokin was made a boyar the following year, 1667, and, when appointed to head the Foreign Office, became Almaz's direct superior.

Alexis' friendship for Nashchokin was not shaken even by the defection of Afanasy's son, Voin, to the West. As in so many instances when his friends were suffering tragedy and disappointment, Alexis took it upon himself to console the afflicted person. The sovereign praised Afanasy as "one who loves Christ, peace, the poor, and hard work," and assured Nashchokin that he sympathized with him and his wife in their "great sorrow and tribulation." Least of all did Alexis accept Ordin-Nashchokin's demand that he be dismissed for his son's disgrace— nor did he punish Voin when he finally returned to Russia.

But the attacks upon Ordin-Nashchokin and the failure of his policies began to undermine his position in 1669. In January of that year Gerasim Dokhturov, Alexis' ambassador to England two decades earlier and slated in time to occupy an important place in the Foreign Office and

Boyar Council, engaged in a shouting match with Nashchokin in the very presence of the tsar. Dokhturov convinced Alexis that Nashchokin had not always been truthful in the information he conveyed to him. Nashchokin countered by accusing Dokhturov of taking bribes, an offense which certainly bothered Alexis less than the charge levelled against Nashchokin.

Ellersieck cites another clash between Dokhturov and Nashchokin which occurred in May 1670, an episode which suggests the old chancellor's visible decline in influence. Nashchokin wrote a letter which he sealed with wax and dispatched to Dokhturov at the Foreign Office to be stamped with the official seal and mailed. Dokhturov refused to do this, saying that his instructions required him to read a letter before he could seal it. Nashchokin returned the letter by a senior secretary with the demand that it be sent unopened. Dokhturov loudly and contemptuously stood his ground, forcing the furious Nashchokin to bring his case to Alexis himself. "The upshot was as indicative as anything could be of the way the wind was blowing." Dokhturov was imprisoned for an hour, and then restored to his duties.

Ordin-Nashchokin's eclipse was paralleled by the rise of Artamon Sergeevich Matveev. Alexis had married Matveev's ward, Natalya Naryshkina, on January 22, 1671; Matveev replaced Nashchokin as head of the Foreign Office a month later, on February 22. The official reason for the change was that Nashchokin soon would be sent as ambassador to Poland. But it was not long before he was removed from even this position, then reinstated, and finally dismissed again. As Nashchokin saw his followers purged from the diplomatic office, he begged to retire to a monastery, but Alexis prevailed upon him to say in service for a time.

Then came what Ellersieck calls the "final crisis." Polish diplomats sent to the border were surprised to see that their "good friend" did not head the Russian negotiators. They travelled to Moscow and asked to deal with Ordin-Nashchokin. The authorities there informed the Poles that Afanasy Lavrentevich had died. Muscovite officials then took advantage of his "death" to blame Nashchokin for misunderstandings which had arisen from the Andrusovo peace, above all the Russian failure to evacuate Kiev. The city never went back to Poland, for Alexis knew full well that if he surrendered Kiev he would lose the allegiance of the east bank Cossacks—and if this happened, Moscow's war for the Ukraine would have ended as a complete fiasco. The Russians charged that Poland was too weak to defend Kiev from the Tatars and Turks, and on these grounds refused to return the city. Kiev remained as a bone of contention between Russian and Polish diplomats, but its status did not lead to renewed warfare. Poland recognized in the later "Eternal Peace" of 1686 that Kiev would remain with Russia forever, and in this way justified Alexis' Polish-Ukrainian policy. By that time Nashchokin had been dead for six years. He had finally entered a monastery at Pskov in 1672, as Brother Antony. But Alexis still solicited Afanasy's advice, and Nashchokin was called from the cloister when negotiations with Poland demanded his special insight and skill.

Artamon Sergeevich Matveev was the leading minister during the last five years of Alexis' reign. Yet Matveev's rise had been slow and unspectacular, even after the tsar took Natalya as his second wife. Matveev was not promoted to lord of the chamber until May 30, 1672, in connection with the birth of Alexis' son, Peter. He became a boyar on October 22, 1674, when Alexis' third child, Theodora, was baptized, and soon after this was said to hold some thirty offices at a single time, a record exceeding even that of Morozov and Ilya Miloslavsky. Scandinavian reports suggest that in February 1676 Matveev was accused of reaping more than 20,000 "ecus" yearly from the "Office of Taverns" alone. The new chief minister demonstrated his special position by conducting the most sensitive diplomatic negotiations not at the Foreign Office, but in his now-famous home.

Few people were strong enough to stand in Matveev's way. Only Bogdan Khitrovo and crochety old Yuri Dolgoruky dared attack him openly before the tsar, Dolgoruky's continuing influence being demonstrated by the fact that whenever Alexis vacationed outside Moscow, Matveev and Dolgoruky jointly administered state affairs. But the Miloslavskys, Ivan Bogdanovich and Ivan Mikhailovich, were shuttled off to various assignments far from Moscow, while others not connected with Matveev's faction were weeded from office or transferred to undesirable situations. The power Matveev wielded in public affairs was carried over into a private life which was capricious and completely open to his whims. Thus when Paisios Ligarides left Moscow on a visit to Jerusalem in the summer of 1672, he was charged with obtaining a dispensation from the patriarch there which would permit Matveev to live legally with his fourth wife.

Matveev's foreign policy was cut from the cloth of his entire life— bold, cheerful, and thoroughly opportunistic. Such statesmen as Ordin-Nashchokin and Alexis brought a degree of principle to diplomacy. Nashchokin honorably sought to fuse Polish-Russian power and interests, while Alexis sincerely felt it was his duty to liberate his fellow Orthodox from the yoke of Islam and Rome. Matveev, by contrast, was guided by no grand overriding concerns, nor did he display even the bare minimum of honesty which diplomats expect in dealing with each other. For example, Matveev encouraged Poland to move against the Sultan by suggesting that Moscow was about to provide aid, but Russian support was limited to attempts to rally support for Poland's Turkish campaigns in other lands. This gave Russia something of a favorable image in the West while permitting Matveev to soothe Poland's anger with the plea that it was not Matveev's fault if France and others remained indifferent to their cause. In this Moscow enjoyed the added advantage that, with Poland actively pitted against Turkey, it was easier for Russia to consolidate its hold on the eastern Ukraine. Matveev could also refuse to return Kiev to Poland by claiming that Russia was better able to defend the city against their mutual enemy, the Turks. Russian imperialism could thus be presented as Moscow's contribution to the defense of Christianity in the east.

In dealing with Sweden Matveev alternated between suggestions of friendship or even alliance and threats of joining Denmark, Brandenburg, Holland, and the Holy Roman Empire in an international coalition against Stockholm. Matveev's object in all this, of course, was to keep Sweden from joining Poland (or others) to block Russian expansion in the Ukraine. A measure of good relations with Sweden also weakened the ability of Poland to take a stand against Russian ambitions in this area.

Matveev's dexterity might appear impressive except for the fact that as years passed he found it increasingly difficult to make his policies work, and in the end Russia angered all of its neighbors and gained— except for Kiev—no tangible benefits. But Matveev's diplomacy was fairly successful in his own time. Artamon Sergeevich's larger problem was that as soon as he attained a high point of power, his royal master Tsar Alexis Mikhailovich was unexpectedly approaching death. It was no secret that Matveev's position was tied to Natalya Naryshkina's marriage to the tsar and the heirs she produced. But what would happen to Natalya and Matveev if Alexis passed from the scene?

Chapter Twenty-Eight

DEATH OF A TSAR

Alexis was delighted by the new family Natalya had produced. In little more than three years of marriage she had presented him with three children. Peter was a special joy, for he was not only a male heir, but even as an infant showed himself to be bright, sturdy and eager. The surviving sons of Alexis' first marriage, by contrast, suffered from incredibly bad health. This was a particular disappointment in the case of Fedor, who in so many ways reminded people of his father. Like Alexis, Fedor was gentle and pious, loved to fast and pray, gladly took part in public ceremonies and the pilgrimages expected of a tsar. Fedor was even similar to Alexis in his passion for coarse entertainment, as if in this both found the relief needed to sustain such demanding religious devotions. Fedor was intelligent and educated, and his personality easily won the admiration of those near him.

But Fedor was not expected to live long, being often so ill that he could neither stand nor sit. The tsarevich took his sufferings silently and well, as if to say that if it pleased God to make his life difficult, it pleased him too. Coping with bodily infirmities developed a certain strength of character, but the constant confinement to his sick room, the perpetual bleedings and "cures," left Fedor sheltered and immature. He certainly was not assertive or forceful in dealing with others.

Nevertheless, according to Russian tradition, a tsar's eldest son was his heir. And so, on the New Year's Day which fell in his thirteenth year, it was time for Fedor's formal presentation as Alexis' rightful successor. The ceremony followed the customary ritual on Red Square on the morning of September 1, 1674. In a trembling voice, the tsarevich wished his father and the patriarch a happy New Year and then spoke to his future subjects. Irascible old Yuri Dolgoruky then delivered a flowery oration. When the festivities were behind them, Alexis led his son through one of the Kremlin's most beautiful gardens to join Natalya and the entire royal family in her chambers. All Moscow was celebrating by now. Later that same day Fedor appeared at the Cathedral of the Archangel to receive the foreign residents and diplomats present in the capital. Bogdan Khitrovo announced Fedor to this assembly, and on Alexis' orders said: "You see for yourselves the sovereign tsarevich, bright-eyed and well grown; write of this by courier to your courts!"

But what every one expected—that the seemingly healthy Alexis would outlive his sickly son, Fedor—did not come to pass. While attending a comedy and concert in the Kremlin on a bright day in January 1676, the tsar felt sick, took leave of his guests, and went to bed. Alexis' doctors were disturbed to see his ailment grow progressively worse in the next ten days. The tsar was two months short of his forty-seventh birthday and had seemed to be in good health, but his condition deteriorated so badly that Alexis began to prepare for the end. From his deathbed the tsar asked Nikon for pardon and absolution, addressing him as "Grand Sovereign, most holy hierarch and blessed pastor." In the will Alexis now dictated he reflected upon his life, his accomplishments and his weaknesses, and directed that he be buried at the foot of his father's tomb in the Cathedral of the Archangel. He conveyed the sovereign rulership of the realm to Fedor, instructing his younger sons to obey their brother, the new tsar, in all things. Above all, Alexis worried about Natalya, predicting that "her days of adversity are now at hand." "I would never have married," Alexis lamented, "had I known that my time would be so brief. If I had known that, I would not have taken upon myself double tears."

As the bells of the Kremlin churches tolled the fourth hour on Saturday evening, January 29, 1676, Alexis Romanov passed peacefully away.

Alexis was survived by his sisters Irene, Anna and Tatyana. His living children from his first marriage to Maria Miloslavskaya were, in addition to Fedor, his son Ivan and daughters Eudocia, Martha, Sophia, Catherine, Maria and Feodosia. The children Natalya Naryshkina bore Alexis were Peter, Natalya and Feodora.

Moscow buzzed with rumors in the days following Alexis' death. Russian officials and foreign diplomats openly wondered if Matveev would succeed in maintaining his grasp over national affairs. The chancellor's position had depended largely upon his connections with Natalya, who was roundly detested by the Miloslavskys. Suddenly Fedor, a Miloslavsky, was tsar! Despite this setback, the ever-resourceful Matveev managed to engineer an agreement whereby Natalya would countersign Fedor's decrees, making her in effect his co-ruler and opening the possibility that Artamon Sergeevich would continue as the power behind the throne. But Fedor insisted that his mother's kin return from the distant assignments Matveev had devised so carefully over the years to keep them from Moscow. If Fedor were to come to rely upon the "advice" of the Miloslavskys, what would be the fate of Matveev and his friends?

The stars were not long in decreeing Matveev's fate. With Alexis in the grave scarcely three weeks, Artamon Sergeevich was attacked for

TSAR FEDOR ALEXISEEVICH. Born in 1661, Fedor reigned as tsar from 1676 until his death in 1682. The lad's frail and charming qualities are well captured in this painting by I. Saltanov in 1685. Above the tsar is Simon Ushakov's famous icon, "The Savior's Face Imprinted on the Veil of King Abgar of Edessa," known in Russian as the *"Nerukotvorennyi spas,"* painted in 1673.

corruption and abuse of power, and by mid-February 1676 had been stripped of all offices except directorship of the Foreign Office. But even here everyone knew that Yury Dolgoruky wielded true power, and anyone who was displeased with a decision from Matveev could rush to the old general and have it overturned.

Matveev finally was haled before a solemn assembly in the Kremlin in early July 1676 to be tried—and convicted—by a court which included Tsar Fedor and high court officials. Fedor had insisted from the beginning of his reign that he loved Matveev and wished him no harm, but a well-directed campaign which accused Matveev of abusing his powers and defrauding the poor shook the idealistic young tsar, and manipulated him into a position of hostility to his late father's last favorite. Fedor personally paid the claims of petitioners against Matveev, and in July announced that the fallen statesman would be sent, along with his family and closest supporters, into exile at Verkhoturie. Not even Natalya's pleas for Matveev could change his fate, and so Artamon Sergeevich and his party set out for Siberia in the early morning of July 14, 1676.

Not content with their victory, Matveev's enemies had him stopped on the way and showered with new accusations. Matveev was charged with plotting to overthrow the new tsar, to which end he supposedly summoned evil spirits. Artamon Sergeevich was also held to practice sorcery and black magic, the evidence for these charges being a book which Matveev composed for his son's education, a book which contained anatomical diagrams, medical advice, Arabic numerals and algebraic exercises. Convicted on the spot, Matveev was stripped of all lands and properties except for a thousand rubles. His assignment as governor at Verkhoturie was cancelled. Instead, Artamon Sergeevich was to be exiled to Pustozersk where, in earlier days as an officer of musketeers he had brought Avvakum and other Old Believers. Now Matveev was to mingle at Pustozersk with these and other dissenters, while the local garrison had the ironic task of guarding the man who had once been their commander. Natalya's brothers Afanasy and Ivan Naryshkin also were deprived of their property and honors and exiled, as were Peter Saltykov, his three sons, and other once-powerful minions of Matveev's faction.

Matveev's downfall led to a broader campaign against the western "innovations" which came—rightly or not—to be associated with his name. The Russians who customarily dealt with foreign diplomats suddenly grew hostile, as if to suggest that Matveev had excessively imitated them and their ways. The theater which Alexis organized and patronized no longer gave performances, and a decree issued in Fedor's name in December 1676 ordered the facilities, along with the acting school, closed. Alexis' father confessor Andrey Savinovich was now in disgrace for approving drama in the first place. Patriarch Joachim charged the Ukrainian priest with insubordination and disgraceful conduct, after which Savinovich was tried, convicted, and exiled to a monastery.

Yet the spread of western culture in Russia was not much disrupted by such developments, shocking and dramatic as they were for a brief period. Russia was so deeply immeshed in European trade and diplomacy by this time that it was simply impossible to root out western life as a whole. (*) The very nobles who led the campaign against Matveev and his "innovations" no more desired an end to the fruits of the West than did he. The Miloslavskys, for example, were as avid as any other Russian of the day in their love of foreign goods and European ways.

The tsar himself reflected the presence of the West in Russia at this time. Fedor had a good knowledge of Latin and was fluent in Polish. His first wife (and first cousin) Agatha Grushetskaya was a celebrated "progressive," and was among the first Muscovites to demand that men shave their beards. Conservatives at court were shocked that the tsar permitted Agatha to appear in public, and indeed helped her to and from their carriage with his own hands. Fedor even wore Polish clothes in public. Churchmen deplored these influences and prayed that Russia and the West might again be separated, but their views were lost in the flood. Many shook their heads and dispairingly wondered whether Moscow was really still the Third Rome. The wisest of the churchmen recalled that the decadence had begun years earlier, during the reign of the pious Tsar Alexis.

Fedor's frail health collapsed entirely in the winter of 1681, and everyone knew that death would soon come to claim him. Yet Fedor survived the winter and lingered weakly into spring, sick, unconscious for long periods, and unable to rally himself sufficiently to name a successor. In the absence of royal leadership the court fell into several factions. Some gathered around the "legal" successor to the throne,

(*) One is reminded here of the eloquent and perceptive passages of "The Communist Manifesto" where Karl Marx notes that "The need of a constantly expanding market for its products chases the bourgeoisie over the whole surface of the globe. It must nestle everywhere, settle everywhere, establish connections everywhere. . . . [It] draws all, even the most barbarian, nations into civilization. The cheap prices of its commodities are the heavy artillery with which it batters down all Chinese walls, with which it forces the barbarians' intensely obstinate hatred of foreigners to capitulate. It compels all nations, on pain of extinction, . . . to introduce what it calls civilization into their midst, *i.e.,* to become bourgeois themselves. In one word, it creates a world after its own image."

Fedor's thoroughly invalid brother, Ivan, while others hoped to make his robust half-brother Peter the next tsar. The Miloslavskys and their allies looked to Ivan, the Naryshkins urged Peter's candidacy.

Fedor died on the afternoon of April 27, 1682, the bells of the Tower of Ivan the Great announcing the news to anxious, troubled Muscovites. As the tsar's body lay in state, Patriarch Joachim summoned a secret conclave of nobles and churchmen to press the case for Tsarevich Peter. Several days later the matter was referred to a larger body of notables, a group which claimed the defunct but still apparently prestigious title "Assembly of the Land." O'Brien notes that the will of the Assembly was clear. The cry rang out on every side: "Let Peter be tsar! Let Tsar Peter be the sole autocrat of All Russia!" The few who hoped for Ivan's "election" were shouted down as a delegation hurried to the Kremlin to inform a confused, uncertain nine-year-old boy that he was the new ruler. A Council secretary finally stepped out on the Red Balcony to proclaim Peter's accession to the cheering throng below.

The first decree issued in Peter's name "ordered" Matveev to return to Moscow to serve as chief counselor to the tsar and his mother, Tsarina Natalya Naryshkina. Within a few days Artamon Sergeevich received the news of these momentous developments in Moscow, and he well understood that he would soon return to the capital to hold forth as the most powerful boyar of the land. But Artamon Sergeevich said quite simply— and with more foresight than he probably knew—"I am ready to lay down my life for the tsar."

If Matveev felt that trouble awaited him in the capital, he evidently took but few precautions to deal with it. Departing his place of exile, he travelled in leisurely fashion to Moscow, lingering on the way to visit his old rival Yury Dolgoruky, and to receive the congratulations of the people who now stepped forward as his eager supporters. By the time Matveev arrived at the capital on May 12, his enemies had been given sufficient time to field a well-organized campaign against him. Indeed, he and the Naryshkins stood at the top of a list of 46 men slated for immediate extermination.

The Miloslavskys were the organizers of the plan, which was led by Tsarevna Sophia. The dynamic, determined twenty-four-year-old girl was Alexis' fourth daughter by his marriage to Maria Miloslavskaya. The tutoring she had received along with her brothers awakened in Sophia an interest in power and politics which had grown steadily over the years. In fact, Fedor had relied heavily upon his older sister's advice, and her attentions to him during his final illness were both lavish and publicly displayed. Breaking with the tradition which excluded royal women

THE MUSKETEER UPRISING OF MAY 14, 1682. Miniature from Peter Krekshin's (d. 1763) *History of Peter the Great.* Matveev's bloody death is depicted in the lower scene.

from funeral processions and services, she followed her brother's casket to the cathedral, bewailing his passing and calling out in every direction that he had been murdered—"poisoned by evil-wishing enemies." For a woman as calculating and in control of her emotions as Sophia, this was surely a planned performance. It demonstrated her closeness to the still popular Fedor, and tested public sentiment for her brother Ivan. Try as Sophia did, however, she could not prevent him being set aside in favor of Tsarevich Peter.

The surly, restless mood of the musketeers stationed at the capital gave the Miloslavskys the means to stage their coup. The musketeers were paid erratically and were resentful over the new regiments of Russian soldiers trained and officered by foreigners. Above all, the musketeers smarted over recent efforts by their officers to impose stricter discipline. Natalya foolishly hoped to pacify them by delivering two hated colonels over for public flogging, but this (and payment of a large sum of money) merely made the musketeers bolder in their demands. Now they wanted their commander, Yury Dolgoruky! An impossible demand, this, but still, if the musketeers could be held off for a time, the conspirators might bend them to their own ends: to make Ivan at least co-ruler so that his relatives could dominate the throne.

The Miloslavskys struck on the morning of May 15, 1682. As the bells sounded sonorously throughout Moscow, the musketeers fell into formation. Messengers soon appeared to inform them that "Tsar" Ivan had been strangled. The tolling of the bells now grew mournful as if, O'Brien suggests, to confirm the announcement. The regiments took up arms and rushed to the Kremlin. It so happened that the leaders of the Naryshkin party had just ended a conference with its leader, Matveev, in the Palace of Facets. Artamon was at the point of leaving for home. His orders to close the gates of the Kremlin came too late. The musketeers were already within the courtyard, streaming towards the Grand Palace.

The mob gathered at the foot of the Red Staircase, opposite the Cathedral of the Annunciation, demanding that the murderers of Tsar Ivan be delivered up. Natalya demonstrated that Ivan was still alive by producing him—but even this failed to quiet the crowd. "Give us the traitors! Give them to us!" came the cry.

A group of musketeers clambered up the stairs, seized Dolgoruky's son Michael, and flung him onto the pikes of their comrades waiting below, where he was chopped apart with halberds. Matveev then rushed to young Peter's side, perhaps to protect him, perhaps to gain some sort of safety in being so close to the new tsar. Either hope was in vain. A group of screaming musketeers dragged Matveev away and flung him to a bloody death on the square below.

Musketeers surged through Moscow during the next several hours in search of "traitors" against Ivan, the "rightful" tsar. Generals Yury Dolgoruky and Grigory Romodanovsky were killed in their homes. Three of the Naryshkins were taken and slain, one with a fiendish application of torture. In all, by sundown, some seventy members of Peter's abortive government were dead.

Political negotiations and further mob scenes now followed, until, on May 26, 1682, a hastily summoned, sham "Assembly of the Land" proclaimed a dual monarchy, Ivan being the "first" tsar, Peter the "second." Sophia was to "serve" and "protect" them as regent, though the young woman was already a sufficient master of political intrigue not to rely overly upon titles to bring security. She knew full well that the musketeers were capable of further disorders, and that her position would not be safe until they were brought under control. Cleverly she isolated their "commander," Ivan Khovanski, trying him for high treason and bringing about his execution on September 17, 1682. In the following weeks twelve of the nineteen musketeer regiments in Moscow were removed from the city on various pretexts, finally ending as border guards who were themselves carefully watched for signs of further political ambition. With this breathing spell arranged, Sophia was able to consolidate her position as the first female to rule Russia since Ivan the Terrible's mother, Elena Glinskaya, assumed authority upon the death of her husband Vasily III in 1533.

Sophia as regent was the *de facto* ruler of Russia during the next seven years. Her portraits in this period often show her in the tsar's regalia, holding the orb and staff which symbolized the sovereign's office and power. Likewise, her name appeared with that of her brothers in royal decrees and state documents, Sophia signing herself "Sovereign Princess of All Russia."

Sophia was a competent ruler who relied heavily upon Vasily Golitsyn, her lover and chief minister and one of the most enlightened Russians of his time. Although the Sophia-Golitsyn period (1682-1689) might seem to be a bit beyond the scope of a biography of Tsar Alexis, it deserves at least a brief discussion since many of the problems Alexis confronted before 1676 continued to occupy Russian statesmen in the following decade. It is also true that at least a few of these problems were solved in the 1680s.

Golitsyn himself was one of Alexis' proteges. The tsar made Golitsyn a boyar in 1676 and appointed him to a military position in the Ukraine which carried with it sweeping political powers. For his part, Golitsyn consistently pursued policies calculated to increase the power of the throne. Just before the 1682 uprising which brought Sophia to power, Golitsyn headed the Commission for the Reorganization of Military Service which recommended that *mestnichestvo* be abolished. This "place system" dictated that the tsar would appoint certain families (and certain individuals within a family) to leading positions in the army and state, insuring that "new men" and lesser nobles, even if they had greater ability, always would serve their "betters" in a junior capacity. Tsars long had evaded this system in various ways, but the legality of it remained and insured illustrious incompetents of at least some important positions while making the advance of fresh talent more difficult than was healthy for the country. Golitsyn and his commission recommended that the system be eliminated, strengthening the trend towards greater royal authority which Alexis fostered and which reached a high point under his son, Peter the Great. Significantly, the genealogical records which supported *mestnichestvo* were burned in 1682. Golitsyn was also interested in making the bureaucracy work with greater unity and effectiveness, and, as head of the Foreign Office under Sophia, he brought under its authority eight other major bureaus which governed various provinces or administered military affairs.

Golitsyn as a man was similar to other statesmen who attained high office under Tsar Alexis. He was similar to Matveev in his admiration of the West. Golitsyn's home also was built and furnished along Western lines, complete with mirrors, chiming clocks, rugs and art works. But Golitsyn was a more cultivated and far-seeing individual than the other seventeenth-century "Westernizers," for he knew Polish, Latin and German, gathered a large library and contemplated sweeping reforms which would have ended serfdom and established universal literacy. In this Golitsyn foretold a type of Russian who would become all too familiar to later generations: the well-intentioned, idealistic official who desired much but collided with a harsh Russian reality and accomplished little. As it was, Golitsyn modified some of the harshest features of the penal code, but did not remain in power long enough to attempt more. On the other hand, his years did see an important development in Russian higher education when a merger of two earlier schools in Moscow produced the Slavonic-Greek-Latin Academy in 1687. This academy was headed by Greek monks, signifying that Greek learning had prevailed over the Latin orientation which Silvester Medvedev and other scholars of Alexis' time had demanded as a means of acquainting Russia with modern Catholic thought. The Russian press during the 1670s and 1680s

provided some of the secular works long familiar in the West, though
science and technology had yet to wait for the enthusiastic patronage
of Peter the Great.

Sophia gave Golitsyn a free hand to pursue a foreign policy which
was friendly to Sweden and Poland. Golitsyn reassured Sweden that
Russia had no designs on the Baltic and he moved to solidify Poland's
support for Russian expansion to the south. His objective was to expand
towards the Black Sea, where the Crimean Tatars continued to harass
Muscovy with "slave catching" expeditions and other daring depreda-
tions. Even so, the "Eternal Peace" which Golitsyn negotiated and signed
with Poland in 1686 did not surrender Alexis' gains in the Ukraine,
which was the price Ordin-Nashchokin had been prepared to pay for
Poland's good will. The decline of the Polish kingdom had proceeded so
quickly that the Polish negotiators finally agreed that in exchange for
146,000 rubles Russia might retain Kiev, as well as the western bank of
the Dnieper River, the Zaporozhie region, the Sever area with Chernigov
and Starodub, and Smolensk. These provisions made the treaty of 1687
one of Russia's most successful seventeenth-century diplomatic achieve-
ments, and represented a marked advance over the Andrusovo Treaty
negotiated under Alexis in 1667. Russia also gained Poland's promise
that neither party would conclude a separate peace with the Sultan, who
was "protector" of the Crimean Tatars. Through this agreement Russia
joined an anti-Ottoman bloc which included Poland, the Holy Roman
Empire, and Hungary. Sadly for him and for Russia, Golitsyn pledged
a military campaign against the Crimea, a move destined to topple Sophia
and her entire clique.

Golitsyn himself led the disastrous expeditions of 1687 and 1689.
The failure of the second, especially, weakened Sophia's hold on national
affairs, though she greeted Golitsyn at Moscow as a victor and tried to
make light of his setbacks. Peter himself now ventured into politics
against Sophia, exploiting the fact that important factions of the government were growing restless under the rule of Sophia and the Miloslavsky
clan. Sophia tried to engineer another musketeer uprising to remove
Peter from the scene in the summer of 1689, but key musketeer commanders sided with Peter, so now it was Sophia's turn to taste defeat.
Expelled as regent in September 1689, she was sent a week later to the
Novodevichy monastery. Peter and the Naryshkins returned to power,
though Peter continued as "co-ruler" with Ivan V until his sickly brother,
now half-paralyzed and long afflicted with feeble-mindedness, poor eye-
sight and scurvy, breathed his last in January of 1696. Sophia was not
really involved in the musketeer uprising which attempted to depose

Peter in her favor two years later, in 1698. But Peter was determined that his shrewd half-sister would not threaten him again. Sophia was shorn "Sister Susannah" and imprisoned for life in a convent under a military guard. Peter had triumphed over all his enemies, and he now proceeded to grasp the bridle of the Russian state.

As we look back on the life of Alexis Mikhailovich, we are struck by how kindly history has smiled on this gracious, talented man. If Alexis lacked the brilliance of Ivan the Terrible and the dynamism of Peter the Great, he was nevertheless one of the most successful Russian tsars. Alexis' wars were costly and sometimes poorly conceived, but they had the cumulative effect of increasing the lands—and presumably the power—of the Russian state. Though Alexis left Peter the task of forcing an opening to the Baltic, he did strengthen Russia's hold over Siberia and took giant steps towards the total reconquest of Belorussia and the Ukraine. Above all, Russia eclipsed Poland as the dominant power in Eastern Europe, making it increasingly hazardous for western powers to ignore Muscovy in their diplomatic calculations.

Meanwhile, within Russia the awesome power of centralized government unfolded with a precision and certainty which won the envy of other European states. The Russian tsar, for example, was not accountable to any earthly group after Alexis relegated the Assembly of the Land to the museum of antiquities. One could make too much of the Assembly, of course. We are not certain that it ever hoped to limit the tsar's authority or to force anything like a "constitution" upon him—but it did provide a channel through which, in times of unusual stress, some social groups could press for a change of crown policy. Granted that we should not overestimate the weight of this challenge, the Assembly of the Land did seem to worry the tsar sufficiently for him to shunt it aside in favor of an expanding bureaucracy which brought the largest kingdom on earth a bit more closely under the control of its reigning sovereign.

Soviet historians smile upon this growth of the tsar's authority, applauding the "building of the centralized state" as a "progressive" development. And in a sense it was, for in this period we observe Russian commerce and industry developing, establishing international connections—and enriching Tsar Alexis who was, as we have seen at length, an avid businessman. The new armaments and military forces which grew up at the same time also gave Russia a novel ability to resist foreign aggression and, in fact, to encroach on the borders of declining neighbors. Russian peasants and artisans were the ones who paid the price of this "progress," of course, being taxed mercilessly and robbed of all freedom.

Serfdom haltered the peasants to the land and townspeople to their trades and locales. The nobles "served" the crown in exchange for their social and economic privileges, though it took the stern hand of Peter the Great to standardize this service and extract it in a great volume.

The lower classes did not take their situations gladly, so Alexis' reign was marked by sharp social conflicts. The Moscow riots of 1648 and 1662 and the Razin movement of 1667 were the most dramatic examples of the population's distress, and in each case for at least a brief moment Alexis' government might have seemed to be approaching collapse. The crown was able to prevail, of course, because of the army and because the ruling elite rallied to the support of their tsar—as did, for that matter, the bulk of the lower classes, a fact which Marxist historians are reluctant to investigate. The split in the Church was more problematical for Alexis. The resistance to Patriarch Nikon's efforts to reform the liturgy and bring Russia into the mainstream of the Orthodox Church was so firm and widespread that the schismatics, the "Old Believers," could be martyred but not subdued. In fact, the schism deepened and solidified after Alexis passed from the scene and presents an interesting spectacle in the USSR today. The "official" Russian Orthodox Church has arrived at an accommodation with the Soviet state such as to render it passive and innocuous, but the sects burn with the holy fire of Kapiton and Avvakum, and this leads them to protest state policy, to evangelize, to suffer, and to grow. When Nikon sent a faction of his church back to the catacombs, could he have imagined that its people and those to follow them would endure for a full three hundred years and more?

Alexis was as devoted to Christianity as any person in the land, of course. From childhood he developed an excellent knowledge of liturgy and church music, and was zealous in pilgrimages, fasts, and religious devotions. Alexis' religion went beyond mere outward display, and in him we see one of the finest representatives of Russian spirituality. His religious feeling, his love and devotion, were what made him so free of narrowness and fanaticism, so curious about the world and ready to learn from it. Alexis would take from the West anything which delighted him as a person and seemed likely to strengthen Russia as a state.

In fact, with all of his weaknesses—of which the greatest was his weakness, his excessive tolerance for the wishes of his "friends"—Alexis stands out as one of the most appealing Russians of the entire century. He was a literate, reflective man who was open to his fellows and drew many of them to him in a sympathetic bond which often transcended controversy and death. Nevertheless, Alexis was not skilfull in dealing with difficult people. His support for Nikon shows that he could be manipulated by someone who knew how to appeal properly to his vanity, which in this case was to become the political leader of the Christian East. And his rupture with Nikon illustrates that others could control Alexis by playing to other aspects of this vanity, an inability to endure the suggestion that another Russian might be more powerful and esteemed than he. Alexis dreaded conflict and "scenes." Unfortunately, Alexis found it difficult to understand that some people valued principle more than his friendship. But he would try again and again to make peace even with such trying people as Nikon and Avvakum which is why, significantly, he never lost their love.

People called Alexis the "little monk," or *tishaishii* ("the most quiet one"), a complex word which suggests a man of peaceful manner, someone who is kind, humble and serene. Considering Alexis' genuine piety and idealism, the continual favor he showed to the poor and the afflicted, it is depressing to realize how great was the suffering in Russia during the three decades of his rule. This is not said to discredit Alexis or to suggest that he was a hypocrite. After all, it is a universal human characteristic to separate high ideals from day-to-day actions, though many who do this truly strive to live according to their principles, and some in fact succeed to a high degree. In the case of Tsar Alexis, he seems to have had a tremendous ability to dissociate his personal Christian life from the policies he felt forced to follow as tsar. Alexis the man held banquets for the poor, rose early on feast mornings to visit prisoners in jail, wiped tears from the eyes of those who suffered and wept. Alexis the tsar taxed his people, conscripted men into the army where their sufferings were of no interest to anyone; he cared not a bit that the peasants were exploited, he did nothing to alleviate their distress.

And yet, he was the Father Tsar. "God has appointed us," he often said to the leading members of his court, "to rule the land with justice, to defend the widow, to bring justice to orphans and the lowly. Let us rule, boyars, with compassion and a kind heart!" He said this many times yet apparently saw no need to change the policies he enacted and administered every day. This was not a tender age, to be sure, not a time when statesmen worried about "social injustice" or waged wars on poverty. This was an age of power, a time of expansion, an era of war. Judged by these standards, Alexis was not only an accomplished ruler, but a far more successful statesman than European contemporaries who in their own time were thought to be more illustrious than the Tsar of Holy Russia. Russia was still an unknown quality in Alexis' time, a rising force, a phenomenon whose nature was fluid and in the process of being shaped and determined. But Western Europe would soon know what Russia represented, it would quickly come to respect the power of the Romanovs. And for this Alexis' descendents were in large part indebted to him.

SELECTED BIBLIOGRAPHY

Abbreviations (most common places of publication)

L.	–	Leningrad	P. –	Petrograd
M.	–	Moscow	St.P. –	St. Petersburg
N.Y.	–	New York City		

Abbreviations (most common journals and series listed below)

CASS   –   *Canadian-American Slavic Studies*
CSS   –   *California Slavic Studies*
FoG   –   *Forschungen zur osteuropäischen Geschichte*
ISS   –   *Indiana Slavic Studies*
JGO   –   *Jahrbücher für Geschichte Osteuropas*
OSP   –   *Oxford Slavonic Papers*, old series
RR   –   *Russian Review*
SEER   –   *Slavonic and East European Review*
SR   –   *Slavic Review*

HISTORIES OF RUSSIA AND ADJACENT LANDS

Michael Hrushevsky, *A History of Ukraine*, ed. O.J. Frederiksen, Preface by George Vernadsky (New Haven, 1941).

David R. Jones (ed.), *The Military-Naval Encyclopedia of Russia and the Soviet Union*. Gulf Breeze FL: Academic International Press, 1976-. Planned to number about 50 volumes, this work contains comprehensive and detailed information; a key reference work.

Philip Longworth, *The Cossacks* (N.Y., 1969).

Richard Pipes, *Russia Under the Old Regime* (London, 1974); a solid, provocative book.

Nicholas V. Riasanovsky, *A History of Russia* (N.Y., 1969); the standard text in English, being accurate, well written, balanced, cognizant of Soviet interpretations.

Russkii Biograficheskii Slovar', published with gaps in 25-vols. (M.-St.P./P., 1896-1918); invaluable for articles on the Romanovs and contemporary Russian statesmen.

Tibor Szamuely, *The Russian Tradition*, ed. with introduction by Robert Conquest (N.Y., 1975); provocative interpretations, masterful scholarship.

Robert Wallace, *The Rise of Russia* (N.Y., 1967); a popular work outstanding for lavish illustrations and fresh observations on the Russian past.

Harry B. Weber (ed.), *The Modern Encyclopedia of Russian and Soviet Literatures (Including Emigre and Non-Soviet Literatures)*. Gulf Breeze FL: Academic International Press, 1977-. Approximately 50 volumes projected. The best reference work on the topic in any language.

Joseph L. Wieczynski (ed.), *The Modern Encyclopedia of Russian and Soviet History*, projected for 50 or more volumes (Gulf Breeze FL: Academic International Press, 1976-); an absolutely indispensable reference work.

E.M. Zhukov (ed.), *Sovetskaia Istoricheskaia Entsiklopediia*, 16-vols. (M., 1961-1976); a most comprehensive, thorough reference work. Invaluable to scholars.

STUDIES OF SEVENTEENTH CENTURY RUSSIA (CONTEMPORARY AND HISTORICAL)

Baron, Samuel H., editor and translator, *The Travels of Olearius in Seventeenth-Century Russia* (Stanford, 1967). Extremely valuable for Alexis and his reign; well translated and edited, though Olearius' frequently obscure dating often goes unclarified.

Collins, Samuel, *The Present State of Russia* (London, 1671). Collins was Alexis' physician and friend, hence this memoir contains unique information on the tsar and his court; but a new and critical edition is badly needed.

Cross, Anthony (ed.), *Russia under Western Eyes, 1517-1825* (N.Y., 1971). Contains much valuable material on Alexis' time; heavily weighted in favor of English observers.

Ellersieck, Heinz E., *Russia under Aleksei Mikhailovich and Feodor Alekseevich: The Scandinavian Sources* (unpublished doctoral dissertation, University of California at Los Angeles, 1955). In guiding the reader to Scandinavian archives, Ellersieck provides extensive information from those sources on Alexis' character and government, church policies and economic development, the role of foreigners. The best pages deal with Muscovite foreign policy and war, unique information and novel interpretations being freely offered. This work should receive careful attention from specialists, but it has, unfortunately, been little appreciated.

Gordon, Patrick: *Passages from the Diary of General Patrick Gordon of Auchleuchries in the Years 1635-1699* (London, 1859; reprinted, 1968); see also A. Briker, *Patrik Gordon i ego dnevnik* (St. P., 1878).

Kallash, V.V. (ed.), *Tri veka. Rossiia ot smuty do nashego vremeni: istoricheskii sbornik,* vol. 1 (M., 1912). A rich treasury of colorful material otherwise not easily available; also contains useful scholarly essays.

Keep, J.L.H., "The Regime of Filaret, 1619-1633," SEER, 38 (1960), 334-360. An excellent political study.

Kliuchevskii, V.O., *Kurs russkoi istorii,* vol. 3; reprinted in his *Sochineniia,* vol. 3 (M., 1957) and available in English translation as *A Course in Russian History: The Seventeenth Century,* trans. Natalie Duddington, Introduction by Alfred J. Rieber (Chicago, 1968). Ever brilliant, insightful and informative, and particularly valuable for Alexis and his reign.

Konovalov, S., "Patrick Gordon's Dispatches from Russia, 1667," OSP, 11 (1964), 8-16.

Lewitter, L.R., "Poland, the Ukraine and Russia in the 17th Century," reprinted in Riha.

Loewenson, Leo, "The Works of Robert Boyle and 'The Present State of Russia' by Samuel Collins (1671)," SEER, 33 (1954-5), 470-485.

Medovikov, Petr Efimovich, *Istoricheskoe znachenie tsarstvovaniia Alekseia Mikhailovicha* (M., 1854). Although dated, still of value to scholars.

New Cambridge Modern History: Vol. 4, ed. J.P. Cooper, *The Decline of Spain and the Thirty Years War,* 1609-48/59 (Cambridge, 1970), Vol. 5, ed. F.L. Carsten, *The Ascendancy of France,* 1648-88 (Cambridge, 1961). Valuable for seventeenth century Europe in general and Russia in particular.

Novosel'skii, A.A. and N.V. Ustiugov (eds.), *Ocherki istorii SSSR, period feodalizma,* XVII, v. (M, 1955). Despite ideological rigidity and some interpretative peculiarities, this is still possibly the best single study of Russia in the seventeenth century; lavishly illustrated.

234   SELECTED BIBLIOGRAPHY

Paul of Aleppo, *Puteshestvie Antiokhiiskago Patriarkha Makariia v Rossii v polovine XVII veka, opisanno ego synom arkhidiakonom Pavlom Aleppskim.* Trans. from the Arabic by G. Murkos. 5 vols. (M., 1896-1900). *The Travels of Macarius, Patriarch of Antioch.* Trans. from the Arabic by F.C. Belfour in 2-vols. (London, 1829-36). Murkos' edition is quite good. I have not examined the Belfour translation, but William Palmer advises that it be used in conjunction with his own second volume of *The Patriach and the Tsar,* where the "manifest errors of the translator, caused by ignorance of the Greek ritual and ecclesiastical customs, have been in many places corrected." Paul's extensive and accurate memoirs are invaluable for both church and state affairs in Alexis' time.

Platonov, S.F., *Sochineniia,* vol. 2: *Stat'i po russkoi istorii* (1883-1912) (St.P., 2nd ed., 1912). Contains a fine, brief study of Alexis' upbringing and character, as well as useful studies of Muscovite government in the period.

Pogodin, M.P., *Zhizn' i trudy.* Ed. N.P. Barsukov in 22-vols. (St. P., 1888-1910). Extremely important.

Shchapov, A.P., *Sochineniia* in 3 volumes with a fourth supplementary volume (St. P., 1906-1908, Irkutsk, 1937; reprinted, 1971). Many valuable articles.

Solov'ev, S.M., *Istoriia rossii s drevneishikh vremen,* vols. IX-XIV (M., reprinted 1961-62) in books five-seven). Still the most detailed account of the period by a single author, and a sturdy classic indeed. The entire twenty-nine volumes is being translated into English and published by Academic International Press.

Uroff, Benjamin P., Grigorii Karpovich Kotoshikhin, *On Russia in the Reign of Alexis Mikhailovich: An Annotated Translation* (unpublished Ph.D. dissertation, Columbia University, 1970). Uroff's work should be made generally available; otherwise consult *O Rossii v tsarstvovanie tsaria Aleksieia Mikhailovicha* (St. P., 4th ed., 1906); brief selections of this uniquely valuable work are available in the Blinoff and Vernadsky anthologies listed below.

Vernadsky, George, *The Tsardom of Moscow,* 1547-1682. (New Haven, 1969). Unbalanced in coverage and occasionally inaccurate, but the finest English language treatment of the period.

ANTHOLOGIES

Blinoff, Marthe (ed.), *Life and Thought in Old Russia* (Pennsylvania State University Press, 1961).

Harcave, Sidney (ed.), *Readings in Russian History,* vol. 1: *From Ancient Times to the Abolition of Serfdom* (N.Y., 1962).

Laran, Michel and Jean Saussay (eds.), *La russie ancienne: IXe-XVIIe siècles.* Preface by F. Braudel (Paris, 1975).

Riha, Thomas (ed.), *Readings in Russian Civilization,* vol. 1: *Russia before Peter the Great,* 900-1700 (Chicago, 1969).

Vernadsky, George *et al.* (eds.), *A Source Book for Russian History from Early Times to 1917.* Vol. 1: *Early Times to the Late Seventeenth Century* (New Haven, 1972). For scholars this is the best anthology of its type in English, though the selections are disappointingly brief.

Zimin, A.A. *et al.* (eds.), *Khrestomatiia po istorii SSSR XVI-XVII vv.* (M., 1962). Extremely valuable.

STUDIES OF ALEXIS AND OTHER ROMANOVS

Bain, R. Nisbet, *The First Romanovs* (1613-1725) (London, 1905). Vigorous, well written, opinionated; still of considerable value.

Bashilov, Boris. *Tishaishii tsar' i ego vremia* (n.p., n.d.). Sketchy and brief, but does contain some interesting observations.

Berkh, V., *Tsarstvovanie tsaria Aleksieia Mikhailovicha* (St. P., 1831). For the specialist.

Bogoslavskii, M.M., *Petr I. Materialy dlia Biografii.* vol. 1 (L., 1940; reprinted, The Hague, 1969). Contains much information on Alexis' later years, his second marriage and its children, the power struggle which followed his death.

O'Brien, Carl Bickford, *Russia under Two Tsars*, 1682-1689 (Berkeley, 1952). A pioneering work of enduring significance; useful for this book for its account of the power struggle following Tsar Fedor's death.

Schuyler, Eugene, *Peter the Great, Emperor of Russia, A Study of Historical Biography.* Vol. 1 (N.Y., 1884). Detailed, accurate, unbiased, still of considerable merit.

Stashevskii, E.D., *Ocherki po istorii tsarstvovaniia Mikhaila Fedorovicha.* Part I (Kiev, 1913). A useful political study.

"Tsar Alexis and his Rules of Falconry," SEER, 3 (1924-25), 63-64. Interesting, but not well edited or annotated.

Ustrialov, N., *Istoriia tsarstvovaniia Petra Velikago.* Vol. 1 (St. P., 1858). Of similar value to Bogoslavskii (above).

Zabelin, Ivan, *Sochinenie.* Vol. 1: *Domashnii byt russkikh tsarei v XVI i XVII st.* (M., 3rd. ed., 1895). A detailed, rambling study of value to this book for its material on Alexis' childhood, his children, the public and private lives of the royal family, the Kremlin and its furnishings.

Zamyslovskii, E.E., *Tsar' Fedor Alekseevich* (St. P., 1871).

Zaozerskii, A.I., *Tsar' Aleksei Mikhailovich v svoem khoziaistve* (P., 1917). A revised edition of this title was published as *Tsarskaia votchina XVII v.* (M., 1937). Excellent treatment of Alexis' economic interests, his character as an entrepreneur, operations of his Privy Chancellery.

SOCIAL-ECONOMIC HISTORY, MILITARY AFFAIRS, CLASS STRUGGLE

Avrich, Paul, *Russian Rebels*, 1600-1800 (N.Y., 1972). Scholarly and well written, fine bibliography and useful footnotes; of value to this book for the Razin rebellion.

Bakhrushin, S.V., "Moskovskoe vosstanie 1648 g.," *Nauchnye trudy*, vol. 2 (M., 1954), 46-91. A splendid account which corrects errors in earlier scholarly studies.

Baron, Samuel H., "The Transition from Feudalism to Capitalism in Russia: A Major Soviet Historical Controversy," AHR, 77 (1972), 715-729. A useful guide to Soviet discussions of this subject.

– – –, "Vasilii Shorin: Seventeenth-Century Russian Merchant Extraordinary," CASS, 6 (1972), 503-548. Fine study of an important and elusive figure.

– – –, "The Weber Thesis and the Failure of Capitalist Development in 'Early Modern' Russia," JGO, 18 (1970), 321-336. Interesting and provocative.

— — —, "Who were the Gosti?" CSS, 7 (1973), 1-40. An excellent study which fails to consider that entrepreneurial instability elsewhere in Europe did not curtail capitalist development.

Blum, Jerome, *Lord and Peasant in Russia from the Ninth to the Nineteenth Century* (Princeton, 1961). Comprehensive, valuable.

Buganov, V.I., *Moskovskie vosstaniia kontsa* XVII *veka* (M., 1969). A painstaking and useful study of the musketeer uprising of 1689.

Chistov, K.V., *Russkie narodnye sotsial'no-utopicheskie legendy* XVII-XVIII *vv.* (M., 1967). Considers how pretenders and tales of "distant lands" functioned in social unrest; an original, thoroughly absorbing book.

Culpepper, Jack M., "Legislative Origins of Peasant Bondage in Muscovy," FoG, 14 (1969), 162-237. Detailed and useful.

Esper, Thomas, "Military Self-Sufficiency and Weapons Technology in Muscovite Russia," SR, 28 (1969), 185-208. A fine overview of an important subject.

Fisher, Alan, W., "Muscovy and the Black Sea Slave Trade," CASS, 6 (1972), 575-594. Sheds needed light on the diplomatic and military problems Alexis faced in this region.

Fuhrmann, Joseph T., *The Origins of Capitalism in Russia, Industry and Progress in the Sixteenth and Seventeenth Centuries* (Chicago, 1972). Argues (*contra* Baron and others) that capitalism made meaningful progress under Tsar Alexis, and that serfdom was the major barrier to still further development. Valuable footnotes and bibliography.

Hellie, Richard, *Enserfment and Military Change in Muscovy* (Chicago, 1971). Erudite, detailed, controversial.

— — — (ed. and trans.), *Readings for Introduction to Russian Civilization* (Syllabus Division, The College, The University of Chicago, 1970). Well-annotated selections from the Law Code of 1649, commercial charters and records, documents and decrees dealing with enserfment before and during Alexis' reign.

Kellebenz, Hermann, "Marchands en Russie aux XVIIe et XVIIIe siècles," *Cahiers du monde russe et soviétique* (Oct.-Dec. 1970-January-June 1971).

Konovalov, S., "Ludvig Fabritius's Account of the Razin Rebellion," OSP, 6 (1955), 72-101.

— — —, "Razin's Execution: Two Contemporary Documents," OSP, 12 (1965), 94-98.

Kurts, B.G., "Sostoianie Rossii v 1650-1655 gg. po doneseniiam Rodesa," *Chteniia v Imperatorskom Obshchestve istorii i drevnosti rossiiskikh pri Moskovskom Universitete.* Part 2 (1915), 1-268. Important for the events in Moscow during 1652.

Lewitter, L.R., "Ivan Tikhonovich Pososhkov (1652-1726) and 'The Spirit of Capitalism'," SEER, 51 (1973), 524-553. Valuable also for the reign of Tsar Alexis.

Loewenson, L., "The Moscow Rising of 1648," SEER, 27 (1948), 146-157. Quite good.

Miller, David, "The Nature of Urban Violence: 1648 in the Provincial Towns," unpublished paper delivered at the American Association for the Advancement of Slavic Studies meeting in Atlanta, Georgia, 1975. Argues that the 1648 uprisings were scarcely urban in nature and not the product of class struggle.

Pashkov, A.I., *et al., Istoriia russkoi ekonomicheskoi mysli,* Vol. 1: *Epokha feodalizma* IX-XVIII *vv.* (M., 1955). Useful for the views of Ordin-Nashchokin and for Alexis' economic policies.

Raeff, Marc, *Origins of the Russian Intelligentsia, The Eighteenth-Century Nobility* (N.Y., 1966). Important even for the seventeenth century.

Rexheuser, Rex, "Adelsbesitz und Heeresverfassung im Moskauer Staat des 17. Jahrhunderts," JGO, 21 (1973), 1-17. A valuable treatment of the possession of estates by the nobility and army composition in Alexis' time.

Vernadsky, George, "Serfdom in Russia," reprinted in Harcave. Still an excellent introduction to this much-debated subject.

POLITICAL, ADMINISTRATIVE, LEGAL STUDIES

Anderson, Thornton, *Russian Political Thought, An Introduction* (Ithaca, 1967). Useful for the Alexis-Nikon clash.

Crummey, Robert O., "Crown and Boiars under Fedor Ivanovich and Michael Romanov," CASS, 6 (1972), 549-574. An original, important essay which is at least suggestive for Alexis' reign too.

– – –, "The Reconstitution of the Boiar Aristocracy, 1613-1645," FoG, 18 (1973), 187-220. Also important for Alexis' reign.

Dewey, Horace W., "The Decline of the Muscovite *Namestnik,"* OSP, 12 (1965), 21-39.

– – –, "Immunities in Old Russia," SR, 23 (1964), 643-659.

– – –, "Judges and the Evidence in Muscovite Law," SEER, 36 (1957-58), 189-194.

– – – and A.M. Kleimola, "Promise and Perfidy in Old Russian Cross-Kissing," CASS, 3 (1968), 327-341.

– – –, "Trial by Combat in Muscovite Russia," OSP, 9 (1960), 21-31.

Druzhinin, M.N. *et al.* (eds.), *Absoliutizm v rossii* (XVII-XVIII *vv.*) (M., 1964). Contains several valuable studies.

Esper, Thomas, "Recent Soviet Views of Russian Absolutism," CASS, 6 (1972), 620-630. A useful guide to a most stimulating discussion among Soviet historians.

Keep, J.L.H., "Bandits and the Law in Muscovy," SEER, 35 (1956), 201-223. A fine study of local government and administration.

– – –, "The Decline of the Zemsky Sobor," reprinted in Harcave. Masterful.

– – –, "The Muscovite Elite and the Approach to Pluralism," SEER, 48 (1970), 201-231.

Kleimola, A.M., "The Duty to Denounce in Muscovite Russia," SR, 31 (1972), 759-779. Very useful.

Medlin, W.K., *Moscow and East Rome: A Political Study of the Relation of Church and State in Muscovite Russia* (N.Y., 1952). A profound, important study.

O'Brien, C. Bickford, "Early Correspondence of a Muscovite Diplomat (1642-1645): Some Bibliographical Notes on A.L. Ordin-Nashchokin," CASS, 6 606-619.

Sakharov, A.M., *Obrazovanie i razvitie Rossiiskogo gosudarstva v XIV-XVII vv.* (M., 1969). Stresses autonomy of political and non-economic factors in shaping the nature of the Russian state.

Torke, Hans J., "Continuity and Change in the Relations Between Bureaucracy and Society in Russia, 1613-1861," CASS, 5 (1971), 457-476, with subsequent discussion in 6 (1972), 1-12.

– – –, *Die Staatsbedingte Gesellschaft im Moskauer Reich: Zar und Zemlja in der Altrussischen Herrschaftsverfassung, 1613-1689* (Leiden, 1974).
Tikhomirov, M.N. and P.P. Epifanov (eds.), *Sobornoe ulozhenie 1649 goda* (M., 1961).
Veselovskii, S.B., *D'iaki i pod'iachie v XV-XVII vv.* (M., 1975). An important work, despite occasional inaccuracies and a general feeling that the book fails to realize the full potential of its subject.

DIPLOMATIC HISTORY

Hunczak, Taras (ed.), *Russian Imperialism from Ivan the Great to the Revolution* (New Brunswick, 1974). Interesting essays.
Konovalov, S., "England and Russia: Three Embassies, 1662-5," OSP, 10 60-104.
– – –, "England and Russia: Two Missions, 1666-1668," OSP, 13 (1965), 47-71.
Lantzeff, George V., and Richard A. Pierce, *Eastward to Empire, Exploration and Conquest on the Russian Open Frontier, to 1750* (Montreal, 1973).
O'Brien, Carl Bickford, *Muscovy and the Ukraine: From the Pereiaslavl Agreement to the Truce of Andrusovo* (Berkeley, 1963). A solid and pioneering study.
Porshnev, Boris Fedorovich, *Frantsiia, Angliiskaia revoliutsiia i evropeiskaia politika v seredine XVII v.* (M., 1970). An original, provocative, difficult book.
Vernadsky, George, *Bohdan, Hetman of the Ukraine* (New Haven, 1941).
– – –, *Political and Diplomatic History of Russia* (Boston, 1936). Quite valuable.
Wieczynski, Joseph L., *The Russian Frontier, The Impact of Borderlands upon the Course of Early Russian History* (Charlottesville, 1976). Examines the role of the frontier and of expansion in Russian history; an important book.

CULTURE, THOUGHT, RUSSIA AND THE WEST

Anderson, M.S., "English Views of Russia in the 17th Century," SEER, 33 (1954), 140-160.
Baron, Samuel H., "The Origins of Seventeenth-Century Moscow's Nemeckaja Sloboda," CSS, 5 (1970), 1-17.
Billington, James H., *The Icon and the Axe. An Interpretative History of Russian Culture* (N.Y., 1967). A brilliant, imaginative book notable for both arresting generalizations and interesting factual details.
Cherniavsky, Michael, *Tsar and People: Studies in Russian Myths* (N.Y., 1969). Brilliant and insightful, very important for understanding the ideology which supported tsardom.
Gardiner, S.C., "Translation Technique in 17th-Century Russia," SEER, 42 (1963-64), 110-135.
Likhachev, D.S., *Kul'tura russkogo naroda X-XVII vv.* (M.-L., 1961).
Malnick, Bertha, "The Origin and Early History of the Theatre in Russia," SEER, 19 (1939-40), 203-227. Very important for this book.
Mazon, A., and F. Cocron (eds.), *La Comedie d'Artaxerxes présentée en 1672 au Tsar Alexis par Gregorii le Pasteur* (Paris, 1954).

Medlin, William K. and Christos G. Patrinelis, *Renaissance Influences and Religious Reforms in Russia: Western and Post-Byzantine Impacts on Culture and Education (16th-17th Centuries)* (Geneva, 1971). An absorbing study of the subject.

O'Brien, C. Bickford, "Russia and Eastern Europe: The Views of A.L. Ordin-Nashchokin," JGO, 17 (1969), 369-379. Of great importance for this book.

Platonov, S.F., *Moscow and the West.* Trans. and ed. Joseph L. Wieczynski. Introduction by Serge A. Zenkovsky (Hattiesburg, Academic International Press, 1972).

Riazanovskii, V.A., *Obzor russkoi kul'tury. Istoricheskii ocherk.* Two parts and three fasicles (N.Y., 1947-48). A good introduction to the subject.

Treadgold, Donald W., *The West in Russia and China: Religious and Secular Thought in Modern Times.* Vol. 1: *Russia, 1472-1917* (Cambridge, 1973). A solid, monumental study.

Voyce, Arthur, *Moscow and the Roots of Russian Culture* (Norman, 1964). A brief survey with much valuable information.

Vucinich, Alexander, *Science in Russian Culture. A History to 1860* (Stanford, 1963).

Zenkovsky, Serge A., *Medieval Russia's Epics, Chronicles, and Tales* (N.Y., 2nd ed., 1974). A large and invaluable collection.

CHURCH HISTORY

Andreev, V.V., *Raskol i ego znachenie v narodnoi russkoi istorii* (n.p., 1870; reprinted, Osnabrück, 1965).

Andreyev, Nikolay, "Filofey and His Epistle to Ivan Vasil'yevich," SEER, 38 (1959-60), 1-31. Important for the origins of the Third Rome doctrine.

– – –, "Nikon and Avvakum on Icon Painting," *Revue des Etudes Slaves,* 38 (1961), 37-44. Excellent.

Avvakum, *The Life of Archpriest Avvakum by Himself.* Zenkovsky's *Medieval Russia's Epics* (above) contains most of the English translation by Jane Harrison and Hope Mirrlees. Of several fine Soviet editions, see N.K. Gudzii (ed.), *Zhitie protopopa Avvakuma im samim napisannoe i drugie ego sochineniia* (M., 1960).

Avvakum, "Selected Texts from the *Book of Discourses,"* SEER, 8 (1929-30), 249-258.

Borozdin, A.K., *Protopop Avvakum. Ocherk iz istorii umstvennoi zhizni russkago obshchestva v* XVII *veke* (St.P., 1898).

Cherniavsky, Michael, "The Old Believers and the New Religion," SR, 25 (1966), 1-39.

Crummey, Robert O., *The Old Believers and the World of Antichrist: The Vyg Community and the Russian State,* 1694-1855 (Madison, 1970). Excellent in every way.

Dewey, Horace W., *"The Life of Lady Morozova* as Literature," ISS, 4 (1967), 74-87. A valuable study.

Graham, Hugh F., "Peter Mogila–Metropolitan of Kiev," RR, 14 (1955), 345-356.

Kapterev, N.F., *Patriarkh Nikon i Tsar' Aleksei Mikhailovich,* Vol. 1 (M., 1909).

Morozova. See her *Life* in N.I. Subbotin (ed.), *Materialy dlia istorii raskola za pervoe vremia ego sushchestvovaniia.* Vol. 8 (M., 1887), 137-203; excerpts are in A. Stender-Petersen, *Anthology of Old Russian Literature* (N.Y., 1954), pp. 387-404. Also see N. Tikhonravov, "Boiarinia Morozova," *Russkii vestnik*, no. 9, 59 (1865).

Palmer, William, *The Patriarch and the Tsar* in six volumes (London, 1871-76). An exhaustive, rambling collection of documents and annotated materials dealing with Alexis and Nikon. This is an invaluable collection for the study of both church and state in seventeenth-century Russia, and I have made extensive use of it. Palmer reveals himself as a brilliant, careful—if opinionated—scholar; his work should no longer be ignored by Russian historians.

Pascal, Pierre, *Avvakum et les debuts du Raskol* (Paris, Hague, 2nd ed., 1963). A masterful study of enduring value.

Spinka, Matthew, "Patriarch Nikon and the Subjection of the Russian Church to the State," reprinted in Harcave. A good introduction to a difficult subject.

Zenkovsky, Serge A., "The Old Believer Avvakum, His Writings," ISS, 1 (1956), 1-52. Very interesting and useful.

— — —, "The Russian Church Schism—Its Background and Repercussions," RR, 16 (1957), 37-58; see also 17 (1958), 157. Reprinted in Riha.

— — —, *Russkoe staroobriadchestvo. Dukhovnye dvizheniia semnadtsatogo veka* (Munich, 1970). Extremely important.

Zenkovsky, V.V., "The Spirit of Russian Orthodoxy," RR, 22 (1963), 38-55. A stimulating interpretative essay.

A NOTE ON ILLUSTRATIONS

The following illustrations are from V.V. Kallash (ed.), *Tri veka*, I (Moscow, 1912): page 2 of this book (facing page 32 of Kallash), page 3 (page 129), page 26 (facing page 162), page 34 (page 91), page 42 (page 173), page 78 (page 193), page 86 (page 91), page 92 (page 103). From A.A. Novosel'skii and N.V. Ustiugov (eds.), *Ocherki istorii SSSR, period feodalizma, xvii v.* (Moscow, 1955), we have taken the illustrations on page 9 (page 363 of *Ocherki*), page 58 (page 680), page 136 (page 355), page 148 (page 261), page 182 (page 283), page 184 (page 299), page 194 (page 379), page 198 (page 237), page 220 (page 644), page 224 (page 329). The illustration on page 6 is from Samuel H. Baron (ed. and trans.), *The Travels of Olearius in Seventeenth-Century Russia* (Stanford, California, 1967). The illustration on page 142 is from Samuel Hazzard Cross, *Mediaeval Russian Churches* (Cambridge, Massachusetts, The Mediaeval Academy of America, 1949), plate 67. The illustration on page 175 is often featured in books devoted to Russian art. See Camilla Gray, *The Great Experiment: Russian Art, 1863-1922* (New York, Harry N. Abrams, Inc., 1962) and V. Nikol'skii, *Surikov* (Moscow, 1925).

INDEX AND GLOSSARY

Saundra Gentile and Gayla L. McCarty did valuable work in helping to prepare
this index.

ACADEMIC INTERNATIONAL PRESS

THE RUSSIAN SERIES

1 S.F. Platonov *History of Russia* Out of print
2 *The Nicky-Sunny Letters, Correspondence of Nicholas and Alexandra, 1914-1917*
3 Ken Shen Weigh *Russo-Chinese Diplomacy, 1689-1924* Out of print
4 Gaston Cahen *Relations of Russia with China . . . 1689-1730* Out of print
5 M.N. Pokrovsky *Brief History of Russia* 2 Volumes
6 M.N. Pokrovsky *History of Russia from Earliest Times . . .* Out of print
7 Robert J. Kerner *Bohemia in the Eighteenth Century*
8 *Memoirs of Prince Adam Czartoryski and His Correspondence with Alexander I* 2v
9 S.F. Platonov *Moscow and the West*
10 S.F. Platonov *Boris Godunov*
11 Boris Nikolajewsky *Aseff the Spy*
12 Francis Dvornik *Les Legendes de Constantin et de Methode vues de Byzance*
13 Francis Dvornik *Les Slaves, Byzance et Rome au XIᵉ Siecle*
14 A. Leroy-Beaulieu *Un Homme d'Etat Russe (Nicolas Miliutine) . . .*
15 Nicholas Berdyaev *Leontiev* (In English)
16 V.O. Kliuchevskii *Istoriia soslovii v Rossii*
17 *Tehran Yalta Potsdam. The Soviet Protocols*
18 *The Chronicle of Novgorod*
19 Paul N. Miliukov *Outlines of Russian Culture* Vol. III (3 vols.)
20 P.A. Zaionchkovskii *The Abolition of Serfdom in Russia*
21 V.V. Vinogradov *Russkii iazyk. Grammaticheskoe uchenie o slove*
22 P.A. Zaionchkovsky *The Russian Autocracy under Alexander III*
23 A.E. Presniakov *Emperor Nicholas I of Russia. The Apogee of Autocracy*
24 V.I. Semevskii *Krestianskii vopros v Rossii v XVIII i pervoi polovine XIX veka*
25 S.S. Oldenburg *Last Tsar! Nicholas II, His Reign and His Russia* 4 volumes
26 Carl von Clausewitz *The Campaign of 1812 in Russia*
27 M.K. Liubavskii *Obrazovanie osnovnoi gosudarstvennoi territorii velikorusskoi
        narodnosti. Zaselenie i obedinenie tsentra*
28 S.F. Platonov *Ivan the Terrible* Out of print
29 Paul N. Miliukov *Iz istorii russkoi intelligentsii. Sbornik statei i etiudov*
30 A.E. Presniakov *The Tsardom of Muscovy*
31 M. Gorky, J. Stalin et al., *History of the Civil War in Russia* (Revolution) 2 vols.
32 R.G. Skrynnikov *Ivan the Terrible*
33 P.A. Zaionchkovsky *The Russian Autocracy in Crisis, 1878-1882*
34 Joseph T. Fuhrmann *Tsar Alexis. His Reign and His Russia*
35 R.G. Skrynnikov *Boris Godunov*
43 Nicholas Zernov *Three Russian Prophets: Khomiakov, Dostoevsky, Soloviev*
44 Paul N. Miliukov *The Russian Revolution* 3 vols.
45 Anton I. Denikin *The White Army*
55 M.V. Rodzianko *The Reign of Rasputin—An Empire's Collapse. Memoirs*
56 *The Memoirs of Alexander Iswolsky*

THE CENTRAL AND EAST EUROPEAN SERIES

1 Louis Eisenmann *Le Compromis Austro-Hongrois de 1867*
3 Francis Dvornik *The Making of Central and Eastern Europe* 2nd edition
4 Feodor F. Zigel *Lectures on Slavonic Law*
10 Doros Alastos *Venizelos—Patriot, Statesman, Revolutionary*
20 Paul Teleki *The Evolution of Hungary and its Place in European History*

FORUM ASIATICA

1 M.I. Sladkovsky *China and Japan—Past and Present*

THE ACADEMIC INTERNATIONAL REFERENCE SERIES

The Modern Encyclopedia of Russian and Soviet History 50 vols.
The Modern Encyclopedia of Russian and Soviet Literatures 50 vols.
Soviet Armed Forces Review Annual
USSR Facts & Figures Annual
Military-Naval Encyclopedia of Russia and the Soviet Union 50 vols.
China Facts & Figures Annual

SPECIAL WORKS

S.M. Soloviev *History of Russia* 50 vols.